HUMAN INSTRUCTION MANUAL
PART 1 - The 5 Laws

Written by:

DONALD ALLEN WILLIAMS

Human Instruction Manual
Part 1 – The 5 Laws
By Donald Allen Williams
Copyright 2016 ©
All Rights Reserved

Title ID: 6149102
ISBN-13: 978-0692673539

Printed by CreateSpace, An Amazon.com Company
Available at Amazon.com, CreateSpace.com, and other
retail outlets

SIGNATURE

HUMAN INSTRUCTION MANUAL
CONTENTS OF PART 1 – The 5 Laws

5 CORE CONCEPTS (CC):
Utilize these pivotal concepts in human understanding and personal success.

Making the effort to make a conscious decision puts you in control of your own life. *If you do not like the outcome you can always change your mind.* The choices that you make completely impact your life. Unless you begin to grasp the awesome power of choice you will be at the mercy or your own indecision.

Your perception is the direction or viewpoint you use to observe reality. Your choice to perceive, think and act is what you apply at every moment of consciousness. Each of us delineates our world between an outer and inner world. It is the contrast of these two worlds that confuses true perception and choice. It is the understanding of both worlds that clarifies our ability to control them.

Awareness is a practice of observing your own and others' thoughts and actions through the lens of intuitive references. Your awareness devotes the full use of your senses and mindful thought to realize all aspects of yourself and the world. When fully engaged in this practice, you become awake to your full potential. Living without awareness is like living life asleep, never knowing all you can become.

HUMAN INSTRUCTION MANUAL
CONTENTS OF PART 2 – The Creation Process

5 CORE CONCEPTS (CC):
Utilize these pivotal concepts in human understanding and personal success.

CC # 4 – PURPOSE ....
Purpose is the greater goal of the "True Self". A legitimate purpose can reveal itself through worthwhile intentions. Those intentions will always be reflected by your actions. In order to determine a purpose, it is important to first establish a deep understanding within yourself. To seek a purposeful direction requires self-honesty and reflection.

CREATION PROCESS:

CC # 5 – APPLICATION ....
Your approach is the way in which you apply the knowledge you gain through your perception and your chosen awareness. It is propelled by clarity of purpose. The way a topic is approached often determines its outcome and is an important action to mindfully take. This this why application of approach is so important to your success in life.

STAY AWAKE ....
Staying awake is the means by which you maintain your awareness, even when it is most difficult. This becomes very challenging, as almost everyone you know will make falling out of awareness (asleep) seem appealing. Staying awake is taking steps to maintain your awareness and is your main self-responsibility throughout your life's journey.

88 Thoughts to Consider ....

The LOGO
"**H**uman **I**nstruction **M**anual = H.I.M."

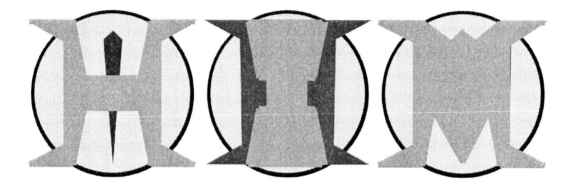

The LOGO was inspired by the use of the following "Super Hero" like logs of: Batman, Superman, Flash, He-Man, and the "Greatest American Hero" the television show. Taking shapes colors and meanings from those characters.

The circle means energy and unity. The circle represents a complete cycle in time. The yellow circle is also the sun and source of human energy. The black "Spike" represents a human with the legs together with arm at the side, the yoga pose "Corpse". The black "Spike" also resembles the male's sperm's successful fertilization of the circle or female egg which is the creation of human life. The combination of the black "Spike" and the yellow circle also create a reptilian's eye.

Humans have a reptile brain that is responsible for the destructive "Service to Self" perception of the world that largely prevents the real control human intrinsically seek. Lastly the red color of the "H" halves represents magnets which are typically seen painted red because otherwise the iron metal in them would rust. The combination of sun energy and electromagnetic energy runs the energy flow of the human body. Either humans are magnetically attracting or magnetically repelling what they want from their life experiences while alive. Likewise humans are either their own hero or seeking a hero to fill the void of one.

Once humans grasp the understanding that they themselves are the superhero that they are seeking to save themselves. By taking control of their thoughts, emotions, and body the human can become, do, or have what every the human wants. Discover the clarity required to develop the self-esteem needed to defeat the shadow self that has been in your way and holding you back. The time has come to become the hero of your own life now. Go from "Zero –to– Hero"!

Foreword

"Move forward towards your future with excitement and anticipation!"

"This is Donald Allen Williams saying "I am outstanding because I feel healthy, I feel happy, and I feel excellent! Eventually you will too" Before long you will too because you are ready, willing, and will follow the instructions given that were created for your benefit. The Human Instruction Manual has been written for you to understand yourself and the world you live in. Please enjoy the experience this material has to offer. The instructions are designed to benefit you my new friend.

I believe you are going to follow the instructions because you want success in your health, wealth, and relationships. Knowing you will follow through. I make this prediction regarding your results. Something amazing and wonderful is going to happen to you. As long as you are ready and willing to take instruction. If you do take to following the instructions and are ready your life will react in a beneficial manner to the content provided. No matter what your personal journey in life holds know this truth. The contents contained herein will provide you with the knowledge necessary to control your mind and conquer your fears so that you can do, become and have your heart's desire.

The Human Instruction Manual is designed to bridge the gap in understanding the "Woo Woo" or your intangible connection through senses and the "Science" or tangible connection through the senses."

The author and contributors to this book express their sincere appreciation that you have decided to use it as a tool in your investigation into the area of personal management. This book has been written with the intention of helping you to improve the quality of your life. By discovering simple and intuitive concepts that are natural and a part of all humans, you may come to understand yourself and others in a profoundly different way. These concepts are basic and pure in nature yet are commonly overlooked. The "Chief-Aim" is to guide you to understand these concepts so that you become able to navigate through your life with awareness, confidence and purpose.

Neither this book nor the concepts within it will directly solve any or all of your problems. As with any of the problems or issues that affect you, **only you have the power to bring about change for the better in your own life**. The information simply reveals to you a doorway before you that has always existed. It will be up to you to develop the courage and discipline to step through it.

The concepts and tools within this book will show you the way to find your own inner power, which you can use to propel you along your path. However, understand that only you can take action to gain the wisdom necessary to determine your own direction in life. Only you can produce the proper thoughts, decisions and actions necessary to carry you along your path. Apply the concepts and tools in this book to become who you truly intend to be.

There has been care to carefully limit the amount of examples surrounding the concepts presented in this book. The intention is to stimulate you to think and emotionally feel deeply about all possible applications of each concept, rather than limit you to only those provided. This approach will also allow you to consider the way the concepts can be applied directly to your own life.

Please understand that there are no experts in any subject matter. No one is talking at you or down to you. No one is your superior or boss. Other humans who read this book are most definitely no wiser than anyone who chooses to read this book. Every human is merely a student of life. The information presented comes from personal experience and direct evidence of facts as they are understood. The information is applicable to any human, young or old, short or tall, skinny or fat, strong or weak, educated or illiterate, intelligent or not, male or female, and can be applied to your own life in ways that will bring great benefit to you. Passing and sharing this way of thinking and emotional feeling with you has the potential to improve your situation, if you choose to allow it. Enjoy the journey to your new life now!

SPECIAL NOTICE # 1
– Signs –

As you read these signs are given periodically to help you the reader absorb the information

"Take a break here" and   "pause"   to   "relax"   and   "reflect"

SPECIAL NOTICE # 2
– Color Pictures –

In order to keep costs down on printing and make the book affordable black and white printing is most effective. There are several color pictures that lose their full impact due to this decision. All pictures in this book are located at **www.geton2it.com/h-i-m-pictures/** the online home of the Human Instruction Manual (H.I.M) and the best place to contact Donald Allen Williams.

Get ON 2 IT!

Pre-Instruction

This book was created with the intention to express important concepts simply, concisely and with as much clarity as possible. It is designed to stimulate introspective thought within the reader. Here are a few tips to consider when reading the Human Instruction Manual.

✓ Take breaks often to reflect on each concept or idea.

✓ Try to continuously connect the concepts presented with the intuitive concepts within yourself.

✓ Be prepared to re-read sections and the entire work more than once.

✓ Any time you see a question, stop and try to honestly answer it. Ideally, write the answer somewhere (perhaps in the margins of the book). This will help you to achieve a deeper understanding of yourself through the self-reflecting thought process. That process is important for you to change your mindset to the new paradigm expressed in the book.

1. Read the entire book cover to cover. Ask yourself -What did you learn from the information? Pick one item to practice. What action will you take to implement and practice the item in my own life?

2. Take notes. If a personal owned book, underscore that which you find important. Take note especially for anything you wish to memorize. Mark a "?" question mark for anything you do not understand or that you question? If there is room, make short notes in the margin of the pages. Write on a note pad anything that inspires ideas or potential solutions to any problem that flashes to your mind.

3. Complete each chapter before you stop. Make the time to get the big picture to grasp and understand the information contained as well as pay attention to your emotional reaction.

4. After you completed your first reading start from the beginning and do it again. The second times purpose of studying is to understand and comprehend the information given in each paragraph or section. What action or actions did you take after your first read?

5. Take additional notes: Memorize any useful self-motivators that inspire you to action. Again, underscore additional words and phrases that are important to you. Use a dictionary to look up words you do not know or understand. Always check its synonyms.

6. Do a third reading or listening to merely go over the material you underscored as well as memorize additional self-motivators that appeal to you.

7. Sometime later re-read the book again because you will change and the information that you pickup will be different relative to your new changes. Keep looking for the gems of wisdom you are seeking and you will find them.

Repeat this extremely simple process over and over. Each time you will discover more and more about yourself. For best optimization do this process regularly.

Read the entire manual all the way through as fast as you can the first time. This gives you a broad overview of all the important information contained. Reread the book. Reread this material again, again, and again. Every time you reread the book you will learn something more because you will start to get the bigger picture. *There is so much information that you will continue to learn as you reread.* As you learn more the greater your personal belief will become in yourself. You will understand the foundation of the factual knowledge and the purposes for the quantum laws. You will become more aware of all the opinions and theories that are non-beneficial to your life. Everyday read at least a page of this or other related factual knowledge to keep learning. Change up your learning methods from reading, to watching, and to listening.

Remember you do not learn by teaching you learn by doing and applying it. The first time you apply the facts and understand the information you will hit new sweet spots and find what not so sweet spots are for you. Apply and fine tune the things that are working and adjust to what is not working. The purpose of this factual information is so you learn what to apply and why. The point is to make factual information known so you can it apply to your life

Engage the information given. Study and think to comprehend it! This means dedicate thinking and planning time. Apply the information into your own life and plan to use it. That is taking action and doing something useful with what you learned. Take out a notebook. Date it. Write at the top what you want most in life. Make a clear statement that sums it up. Underneath write what you want to achieve from your study. Keep these in your mind as you continue. Practice keeping a permanent notebook record. This allows you to check your progress and to notice the number of accomplishments you have achieved.

When you read Concentrate! Read as if the author were a close personal friend and was writing to you and you alone. The author of this book cares deeply for you and only wants the best for you in your life. Know what you are looking for. When you read you must write your own conclusion based on direct use and application. Ideas come from unexpected places so keep a note pad nearby to take down creative ideas, a flash of inspiration, or an answer to a problem. Write it down immediately. Ask yourself "What does this mean to me or for me?" Be alert for useful information you can apply directly to your life immediately. Now is your personal opportunity to eagerly read and apply this form of study to know and master its contents. The book is written for you so gain from it. If you do something new you will discover many wonderful things will happen to you and for you. You will know through this experience the ways to make things happen for you.

Introduction

You are the most important living person as far as you and your life are concerned. This is not ego but this is the centric experience all life uses to ensure its own survival. Your particular direction in time and space has lead you to the following factual information. You have been under influence internally and externally by self-suggestions. When used beneficially these self-suggestions can become self-inspiration and self-motivation. Control of your self-suggestion leads to benefits and potential hidden within you.

HUMAN – relates to men or males, women or females, people, groups, communities, clubs, teams, and businesses of or relating to the characteristics of the "Human Being". Especially a person as distinguished from any earth animal or non-earthly entity.

You are a human in form but you are not your body. You are the operator and driver of the body given to you. You are a mind with a body. The body was designed for your use, use the vehicle wisely. *The human body is the host for your spiritual essence to have the human experience.* This is the simple non-complicated fact you must understand if you are to experience the full potential your life has to offer you.

Find yourself desiring to take action. Mental, emotional, and physical actions make up the experience of your entire human experience. Action can and will bring into reality your desires, dreams and wants. These actions help you achieve your objectives and outcomes. As long as none of them do not violate the universal laws of nature or take away the rights of other humans in the process or pursuing those desires, dreams, and wants will happen.

You are implored and it is suggested that you remain and keep an open mind (thoughts and heart). Observe! Listen! And Discern Feeling! Fully engage your senses and allow them to aid you to learn and fully experience.

1) **To be able to see does not mean your attention is given to what you see, but to observe is the active process or application of using your sight to see.**

2) **To be able to hear does not mean your attention is given to a sound, but to listen is the active process or application of using your hearing to hear.**

3) **To be able to feel does not mean your attention is given to sensations internal and externally, but to perceive by discerning the experience of emotion or sensation is the active process or application of feelings.**

Those who are ready, open, and willing do actively observe, listen and discern their feelings to maximize the learn potential of this factual information will get the most from it. These are all desirable mental, emotional, and physical, actions to be applied daily in your life. Seek out what is applicable to you. Only then can you make amazing things happen in your life.

Factual information is more than just information. Information can be factual as in facts or non-factual as in opinions and theories. A lot of information feels real but it is often not factual or real.

Avoid polarizing belief conflictions that confuse your ability to accurately observe, listen and discern feelings. A different language will need be used. Instead of good or positive and bad or negative a different use of language is used. A factual concept that is based on the benefits to you or for others is used. Thus beneficial is anything that brings benefit or an advantage gained from something or for somethings. Non-beneficial means simply not providing benefit or taking benefit away from something or for something.

All of the factual information contained is valuable and will get you to achieve results. Your results count! Try to continually evaluate the worth of the factual information you are provided. Evaluate it based on your reactions. Specifically the beneficial desirable actions that you would have not taken in the future had you not learned from this factual information.

The factual information contained provides instruction for its use and application in your life. Instead of your current pre-programmed reactions you will be guided to take actions that lead to optimal beneficial outcomes for you. After the beneficial habits are formed, their new reactions will override your previous reactions, giving you control of your internal and external function to achieve. Please begin to evaluate the way you are stimulated mentally, emotionally, and physically into taking actions in desirable directions.

Humans will and do experience problems, challenges, and situations that are new. *Those who know what they want will be able, with practice, to recognize that which they believe will aid or help them.* Your beliefs may help or hold you back. You do not know and will not know that what you do not know yet. *All experiences allow for a learning experience leading to growth.*

There are three levels of thinking that will aid you.

LEVEL:

1) ***You are aware of what you know.*** This is what you think you know and your belief systems (BS) seems to support this understanding.

   Example: You know what is required to tie your shoes.

2) ***You are aware of what you know but also recognize there are things that you do not know.*** This is when you seek information or guidance from someone you think knows something you do not know yet. This someone has been proven by some means, your belief system supports your understanding, and to know a certain unique knowledge.

   Example: You know you do not know what it is required to replace a flat tire on your bicycle. So you go to a bicycle repair shop or similar place to get the flat fixed.

3) ***You do not know what you do not know.*** This means you remain open and willing to let humans, events, and circumstances teach you a new or different way to experience, perceive, or relate to your belief systems.

   Example: You are willing and open to have a mentor teach you the ways to optimize your ability to learn, understand yourself, and apply factual knowledge in uniquely different and new ways.

You always have two distinctly unique and supremely powerful tools available for your use. Your power of "Will" and your power "To Do". Your "Will" is your mental control and use of thought. Your "To Do" is your physical control to take action. Both powers are linked and driven by your ability to channel your emotional intentions into energy for power usage.
Both the power of "Will" and "To Do" can and will change the course of your life.

Can or cannot are choices. Learn to take charge of your power to make choice. It is okay to make choices and to change your mind. *It is beneficial to develop the ability to make decisive choices.* With more practice and factual knowledge you will have the confidence to use the power of choice.

Allow yourself to be captured in awe and thrill. Use curiosity and wonderment to open you up and recognize having this awe and thrill. The awe and thrill of factually knowing that every human has one thing in common. So amazingly awesome and powerful that only the supreme creator could have created it. It is the human brain and its connecting nervous system!

Human institutions of learning do not teach humans the ways in which to fully utilize and use the human brain to its maximum functions. Especially to and for the humans best benefits. Yet the mechanical and electronic computer was designed and patterned to replicate the powerful functions of the human brain.

The human mind is divided into two functions. The sub-conscious mind has powers that the conscious mind can tap into and use. Specifically the powers that pertain to the mind-to-emotion and the emotions-to mind interfaces that include passions, instincts, tendencies, moods, formation and elimination of habits. Emotions spark thoughts and thought spark emotions. *Emotions are your energy links from spiritual to internal, and external nervous systems.* The links are combined into an automatic feedback system.

The power of "Will" is the human brain under your own control. To understand the powers of your mind examine what it means to obtain an "Understanding" first. Think and break down the word "Under-standing". Where you are "standing" is at the base of your feet. The base or basics are the simple elements of factual knowledge or the strength to build upon. The "under" refers to the underneath of the base or basics. All beneficial learning builds from underneath your current knowledge base. *Factual knowledge lifts you up to the next level because you have a greater understanding and stronger base to building underneath you.*

The concept to aim high is a mischaracterized definition of understanding. Setting an achievement of lofty goals is only rewarding in the learning process of understanding by what it took to get there. Once achieved, because of misdirection, often the achievement fades and must be surpassed. This is not to say that seeking improvement is not a worthy endeavor. It simply means that the real value comes from the experience learned, thus understanding. *The real aim is to learn what it takes to achieve your aim.*

Why have goals then. The word "Goal" is derived from the sports metaphor of a series of actions leading to earning a point or points. But a game is just a game and so are the points of the "Goals" achieved in a game. For once a game is over the meaning of the game is done. All "Goals" or "Points" achieved in the current game are meaningless to the next game. This is the trap of the desire to set and achieve endless "Goals". You will never be satisfied.

The real objective is to have desires, dreams, and wants that inspire and motivate you into action. Take this simple question and ponder it. "Do you know what you want?" Most humans blindly follow what they have been told or lead to want but do not have a legitimately uniquely defining want of their own choosing. Surely everyone wants to be healthy, valuable, and in relationships with others to share those wants for and with. What makes you inspired and motivated to want those enough to take the actions necessary to achieve their attainment? *"Why do you want what you want? That is the main question.*

You are not limited in your wants as long as they are non-conflicting to the universal laws of nature or take away the rights of other humans. Those two deciding factors work for you or against you depending on your ability to respect them. Do not take this personal. It is the way the program you experience, called your life, was designed. The reality in which we all live is designed to function based on those set of simple basic programs. No one has a choice about the program that is the truth and fact of it.

Your compensation for the downside of the program is quite impressive. *For whatever the human mind can conceive and bring itself to believe, the human mind can achieve.* For those humans who learn the art of creation which is controlled by the art of self-inspiration and self-motivation as a function of human power of "Will" and power "To Do". Thoughts must be manifested in to action. *Thought become things.* This is the resultant of a practiced mindset. *The choice or determination to cultivate a beneficial mental attitude is up to you.*

No matter what it is you do. Define your purpose for doing it. There must be a reason. A very clear and concise reason for an outcome. Otherwise you actions will be unfocused and unguided. Above all know your main objective. This is your chief aim. Because when you consciously become aware of what you want. You will begin to recognize what will aid you in achieving it. Knowing what you are looking for increases believability.

Many humans struggle with the aim high concept because they do not believe that they can achieve the high aim. The root challenge is the believability. Unless humans can bring themselves to believe the end outcome the ability to achieve it is not created from within. Start smaller then and build up your believability. *Set realistic milestones you can believe in. Achieve the milestone and increase your belief to focus on a larger milestone.*

The reason of having a chief high aim is to have a focal point to direct your energy towards. The purpose must inspire and motivate you into action. Know your distant, intermediate, and short term milestones. *Aim high simply means never sell yourself on the idea of settling for less.* Aim to achieve more and you will succeed more. *This builds momentum and momentum will continue to build as long as you do not settle or sell yourself short.*

Every single human alive has problems of some sort. Because of this you are no exception. Some humans have more than others but all humans have problems. Stop being hard on yourself by thinking you are the only human with problems. ***All humans have problems! Embrace the fact and move on.*** This is part of growing and accepting change. Subconsciously or consciously you want to eliminate any problems you encounter. These problems are going to be personal, family, or business related.

Actively make and have thinking time. During your thinking time use your conscious mind to determine specific potential outcomes to bring about and create a solution for the problems in your life. Seeking solutions are beneficial. During this process write down the outcome that would possibly or likely bring about that which you desire. The reality of such thoughts influences your belief. The outcome needs to be made with a beneficial focus. Eliminate the focus on the "Negative" or the "Lacking Of". ***Develop an optimistic mental attitude.***

Develop the courage to say "No" and "Yes". Make those words serve you. Humans often give into the fear of "Opposites". When you want to or need to say "No" do so and stop saying "Yes" when that is not what you want. When you want or need to say "Yes" do so and stop saying "No" to something that you do want. *Believe and develop the courage of self "Truth" by saying "No" and "Yes".* The courage will strengthen you. Also your believability to directly affect outcomes with a simple word is powerful. Thus your believability will rise and you will be able to achieve more because of the increase. "Yes" this really works! "No" more settling!

The use of "No" and "Yes" difficulty is an example of a blessing or benefit in disguise. *By developing the courage and changing your habits to use "No" and "Yes" honestly with yourself you grow.* Many things will change in your life because of the decision to be truthful to your own desires, dreams, and wants. Often adversity brings with it the seeds of equal or greater benefits. To take on the new habits of studying, thinking, making planning time is important. These habits only stick with a regular routine. Doing so may be an adversity for you. That friend is why you need to want to do it. For the equivalent or greater seeds will bear many more fruits for you. To accomplish this requires learning the art of self-motivation. Use the powers of "Will" and "To Do".

A beneficial or optimistic mental attitude is the answer to your disappointments. All disappointments, difficulties, and problems are exactly the same. Because all are necessary to be overcame to achieve your future, intermediate, and present milestones. *For as you achieve and step closer to your major defined purpose many other successes will occur.* As long as there is no conflict with your major defined purpose any additional desires, dreams, and wants will be fulfilled. Think of the way your purpose can make the world a better place. In what ways can it make it better now and for future generations to come? Conflict comes from immediate gratification and self-serving motivations. Remember it is a program and do not take it personal.

Share with others what you have learned as you grow. Let them make the decision to follow your evidence as an example of what is possible. Develop an abundant attitude. *Share your blessings and refrain from hording them.* For they contain only limited value if other humans cannot learn of them. As long as you give humans the opportunity to decide you have done your part. The rest is up to them to make the decision for their own benefits.

You must pay your dues. Failure is part of the experience. There is a cost or price for achievement or success. What are you willing to give? Every achiever must pay these dues to succeed. The price or cost is simple. Study, think and make time to plan as a regular habit. The cost and price is your time, energy, and resources. ***There is always an exchange of energy required to make anything.*** *You feed your body food for energy. Feed your mind and emotions regularly and your creative output makes things happen. The time given allows all of those seeds to take root and to grow.*

If you apply the same factual information to your personal life or business dealing the results remain the same. Applying what you learn into your own life means all of your life. *Become the example of what is possible and lead others with that example.*

In business for example. Management often has problems maintaining or increasing sales. If the employees were helped and trained with this information their lives and quality of life would increase. Sales representatives, officers and general staff can achieve their personal milestones and problems. When the work force from the top down and from the bottom up have their personal problems taken care of their ability to focus while at work increases. The work force will automatically help their company achieve milestones in all areas. Success breeds more success and achievement breads more achievement.

Imagine you owned a company. If you took what you learn here and applied it to your life and business dealings. If you shared it and spoke favorable to it. If you incentivized your business to learn and use the factual information also think of all the success and achievements you will be responsible for bringing into this world. The point is this factual information works for anyone who is ready and willing to learn from it and apply it.

As times change businesses must change also. At one time if you built the best humans would come to you. If you build "It" "They" will come is different now. Today this is not true. It is necessary to merchandise, market, promote and sell. *Excellent service is a must for success. That is the service of going above and beyond because you can and you do it well.*

When you do your best to serve others beneficially without accepting compensation or recognition it comes back easily several thousand times if not ten thousand times fold. You serve others well because you want the same in return. You planted seeds. Those seeds pay off in the long run. When you see a nut what do you see? Do you see food? Do you see a tree? Do you see a house built from the tree? Do you see fire wood? Do you see a forest of trees? Your seeds are like that nut. You plant it and use it wisely and anything is possible.

When you combine a definitely clear major purpose in life to pursue with an optimistic beneficial mental attitude is it the starting point of all constructive, meaningful, and worthwhile achievement. ***The golden needle that weaves it all together is service.*** In a given environment, circumstance, or situation the beneficial mental attitude sees the greater service for one's self and others at the same time. Optimism works the same way. *Seeking the triple win is the best option.*

You win, they win, and everyone else prospers and wins because both win either directly or indirectly. *With the triple win everyone's quality of life rises.* The optimistic beneficial mental attitude consistently increases one's believability for the attainment of your major purpose in life. For that reason alone is enough to want to develop it and continue developing it.

Language contains the possibility for strong verbal suggestions. Learn to utilize that possibility to increase your potential mentally, emotionally, and physically. Suggestions work like keys to open the subconscious mind. The program and your powers come from your five senses. There also is an internal dialogue from the subconscious to the conscious. This is also called self-talk. Verbal self-suggestion uses self-talk to rewire and reprogram the subconscious.

Rewire and reprogramming is done by memorizing and repeating a word, a phrase, sentence, or saying. This requires repeating it so frequently that it is imprinted indelibly long term into your subconscious. The consequences of the repeating lead your conscious mind to operate on a new program. The new program is ready to be activated at "Will" now. The "To Do" power kicks in immediately and takes action on the new program.

Influence is also suggestion. Influence can be internal or external. External influence suggestion comes from the environment you live in. Self-suggestion is purposefully controlled from the internal environment of your mind and emotions. Self-suggestion becomes automatic when it is repeated so much that the human no long needs to consciously think about it anymore. Automatic suggestion is the end result. The suggestion acts independent of thought and is run by the unconscious mind.

The subconscious mind is a giant that never sleeps. It keeps you alive and running all of your life. The conscious mind is powerless while asleep but dreams in potentials you can have in your awaken state. *When the conscious mind is awake its potential power is unlimited.* Many humans think that they are awake but in reality they have not woken up to their potentials yet. *When both work in balance and in harmony super powers are ignited.*

Self-motivator: Memorize one at a time. Write it out 50 times. Verbally repeat it with enthusiasm 50 times a day, space it out during the morning, afternoon and evening. Do this practice for 2 weeks. At which point the motivator should be memorized completely on random recall. Then go to the next one and repeat the process.

INTROSPECTION

It is necessary to inspect so you get what you expect to desire to change your personality from non-beneficial to beneficial. Write down your long term major definite purpose in life. Review it daily to see what progress you are making. Your ability to recognize, relate, and assimilate with a beneficial optimistic mental attitude has the power that will open any door, meet any challenge, and overcome any obstacle. These actions will help you achieve beneficial health, wealth, and relationships.

As you continue use this formula and process to become introspective.
Double RR Double AA Formula: (R^2A^2)

Recognize:
Identify the principle, idea, or technique and observe if it works for someone

Relate:
A means to connect or join together, to establish a relationship. Start with the most important person, as far as you are concerned, YOU! Relate the principals to yourself. Ask yourself *"What will this do for me?"*

Assimilate:
This means to make similar or alike, to incorporate, to absorb, and to become a part of. Observe what ways can you use the principle given to achieve your desires. In what way can you absorb the principles into my behavior? So that they become part of you. What way can you develop a success habit or success reflex? Then do this immediately, so the best option will be taken.

Action:
Means to denote use, follow through, doing. When are you going to use it? When are you going to start? Then follow through doing it now!

Each ingredient of the formula is important and has special meaning. But when combined they form a formula for your success. These can and will aid you to achieve success. Practice this formula, begin to develop and start you success reflex – a trigger phrase that will immediately direct your mind when you recognize a success principle.

Basic Information

HOW DO YOU FEEL?
This is the single most important question you will ever ask yourself. Your life is about feeling. Whether you are aware of that fact does not change anything. What an excellent question! Questions are an important part of curiosity. Let us examine the parts of this question. First is the reflex response that humans have for the question. Most humans will say "Good", "Bad", or something close to that response. Most humans do not ask for any clarification of the question. Humans have been taught and trained by other humans not to ask too many questions. Second there are emotional feelings and physical sensations that provide feelings. What kind of feeling? To clarify "How do you feel emotionally"? By being more specific from the previous general question adds a level of complexity now. Asking more questions can help answer a specific question.

Let us continue this examination with more curiosity. Humans know where physical feelings or sensations come. Physical sensation is created by electrical connection via a complex network of nerves that are woven through the entire human body and permeate all the organs and systems contained in the human body. Where do you feel emotional feelings from in the human body? Most humans will point to the location of the heart. This answer is correct and incorrect. If a human were to break their neck and sever their spinal cord the human still has emotional feelings and can feel them. The heart is an involuntary organ that works as long it is beating. Emotional feeling does come from the heart but it comes from the energy created from the heart. As long as the human is a live the human will have emotional feelings. That adds mystery to the question "How do you feel emotionally?

So know you know that emotional feelings come from the energy of the heart. When did energy have its own sense of feeling inside the human body? A human can consciously remember by recalling to the first time the emotional feelings occurred. Maybe unconsciously those emotional feelings started even further back in time. There is no way to know unless there is memory. All of this requires a lot of thinking. When is the time? It that most likely happened at birth or sometime shortly afterwards. That brings any human to another set of stumper questions "Who are you"? Or "Why are you"? Or "Why are you who you are?

"How do you feel emotionally"? There may not be a known answer to that question. Not one that a human can fully comprehend. In fact all of the above questions are very fascinating and can be quite challenging. In the life of a human there are a lot of unanswered questions. The "HUMAN INSTRUCTION MANUAL" will aid you to answer these questions and many more questions that you have always had. More importantly it will explain the way humans operate and function in ways that are completely logical and clear. Be prepared to discover clarity! Be prepared to develop self-esteem that you never knew existed within you. Learn to defeat your shadows and fears because you created them. Decide to empower you thoughts and emotions to do, become and have everything you can dream. The power is in you to completely control your life.

UNDERSTANDING

Pay attention when you say "I Get It". The need to be "Right" and to be not "Wrong" is a trap that has been entrained into human consciousness. The human ability to remain open to learn new information goes down to zero because you think the "Answer" is all of it. The belief that you "Know It" also makes your willingness to accept change drop down to zero. The style of education humans are given makes them very unable to learn the rest of their lives. This is very important when you think you know it all you actually stop being able to learn. However it is important to grasp the basics of a subject.

The concept of grasping information is important but no one ever gets it perfectly. When learning a concept it is important to grasp the basics because you cannot go around being confused your whole life. Being confused is not what is being suggested here at all. Learn to become humble and say "I Get It – So Far" and remain open to learning. There is always so much more to learn because there is so much more in this world that you do not know. It is beneficial to grasp knowledge but wisdom comes from knowing that you can never fully "Get It" all. Ask yourself "Do you grasp what you are being taught and do you think you can use the information?" That is a start. Ask more questions now.

Understanding comes from the bottom down and builds a stronger base. Learning based on the word "Understanding" alone does not build up. To grasp what you have learned requires an inspection from underneath or below. The more you learn the more you have to reconsider and inspect what you thought you already knew. When a building is going to have a new level added above, the level below must be inspected to make sure the new weight can be held by the floor or base of the first. Factual knowledge builds underneath and shores up the base information. The more you learn the stronger your base becomes because you are making it stronger. When you have a balance of complete willingness to learn and a complete willingness for change something magical happens. You learn to surrender to the greater knowledge that you do not know when it becomes available to you. Learn to think and use language like these phrases:

"I get it so far and I know there is so much more to learn"
"There is so much more that I do not know"
"I believe that I am grasping this information"
"There is no way that I fully get it all because there is much to learn"
"I am grasping what is being taught"
"I think I can use this information"
"I am gaining understanding"
"Wow what more is there to learn?"
"I do not know what I do not know"

"HOW"

Humans are taught the obvious and are tricked into spending all of their time and energy in never ending pursuits of the obvious. A common statement that paralyzes humans and stops them before they start is "I do not know "HOW I am going to…" It is obvious because no one else knows "HOW" either. The "HOW" is irrelevant. Humans do not have to know "HOW" because "HOW" is the after effect of learned knowledge. Unless there is past experience of course you are not going to know "HOW".

Society emphasizes that it is important to know the "HOW" because society wants humans to focus on the obvious "no one has the answer to your particular HOW". In this focus on "HOW" humans will always believe that they are never capable of achieving what they want. This belief has tricked the human race globally and successfully keeps humans in a state of never achieving "much". Be it on purpose, by design or blind ignorance it matters not. It does appear that the elite classes give the illusion of some success to the remaining humans to remain elite and everybody else remains virtually salves. An indirect slavery where there is no uprising. Humans are kept to busy worrying that they are not good enough to form large groups of humans that can stop the indirect slavery. For if collectively humans recognized that they have power and that they can rise to the levels that they wish the elite would have a problem. They would no longer be the elite. That would create competition and significantly reduce the elite's power to control. The "HOW" is used to eliminate competition because the real question is "WHY".

LEARNING
When doing anything for the first time humans become conscious of something new. Prior to learning something new the human was unconscious that the new something even existed. By consistent practice the new something becomes a new habit or pattern. This is when unconscious competence takes place. Unconscious competence happens when doing something new becomes automatic. There is no need to think about it anymore because the habit becomes automatic. Did you just notice that you learned the process in which the human mind learns? Re-read this paragraph until you grasp this process in full because this is the way you function and operate.

FACTUAL KNOWLEDGE
Most of what humans think they know as fact is not the true facts. The majority of real true facts are lost amongst the opinions and the theories. What you have learned and have been taught is true from a certain point of view. Yes, a certain point of view of the truth. Usually the point of view comes from someone who thinks the facts are the true facts. A lot of humans just do not know any better than what they were told by someone else. Can you discern the real facts?

TRUTH
You are going to discover that many of the truths that humans cling to depend greatly on the human point of view. This is also called perception. Your truth as you believe it is dependent on your point of view. One of the greatest secrets is that the human race has been programmed to run, avoid, and turn their back on the truth. This keeps humans enslaving themselves and their self-appointed elite rulers just have to sit back and relax. This is why the majority of the world has never known this factual information. The way magic works on planet earth is very different from what you think you know and this is information with the complete truth. Focus on the fundamentals and mastering basic information. Always go back to the basics for the real truth.

Avoid the so called guru experts there truth is usually self-serving and limited. The bases for truth comes from outside human society. False opinions and theories make the truth difficult to accept. First truth is ridiculed and feared. Secondly the truth is violently opposed. Thirdly it is accepted as Truth. This occurs because humans want to defend lies because the truth almost always requires humans to start taking responsibility for their own lives.

GURU EXPERTS

There is a disadvantage many humans have been taught to believe "unless you can actually see it and experience it, do not believe it". Wonder where that comes from? The content and information of this manual is not coming from some "Guru" or some short lived "Juice Factory" motivational or inspirational speech given from a rah-rah stage of hype with all the jumping up and down, music, and dancing. You know a "Juice Factory" where you have to come back to be "Juiced-Up" again. The "Juice Factory" owners freely say "I am giving you one problem in exchange for another" and they always keep you wanting more. As if you are not enough without them. In nature every creature does not question if they are enough like humans do. Nature is sustainable and maintainable. Humans are part of nature also. So humans are more than enough. Stop seeking the easy way and seek the facts instead.

HIS-STORY

History is written by the winner, hence "His-Story" is told. Throughout "His-Story", be it sometime in the past or now, the greed for control of necessities has created monopolies which are controlled be the winners. Also throughout history the monarchs and ruling elite classes have always inter-married. This has led to many well known cases of inter-breading health illnesses. The reasons gleamed from such actions relates to the claim or the "Right to Rule" specifically. The rulers always believe that they are genetically better and smarter due to their DNA. This superiority by DNA is their birth right because they were genetically programmed to rule. Interestingly enough the claim to rule always comes from the rulers themselves. After all not much has changed over time and the ruling classes still want to have the working classes do all of the work. As a result the working class has always been held down to a much lower energy vibration frequency. Any form of slavery will lower energy vibration frequency. Whether slavery is overtly open with chains and whips or covertly hidden with misleading information it has the same effect. Slavery has never ended, the methods to enslave change to confuse the perception.

DNA

Whether the elite know it or not the DNA argument is correct but DNA is not exclusive to rulers. The genetic model of the human animal is the same for all animals because everything living and not living is made up of elements. The elements are made of atoms that are giving off energy vibration frequencies. This concept is a factual biological quantifiable scientifically proven and documented reality of science. This is no fantasy based on mysticism. DNA is a crystalline structure that emits a unique energy vibration frequency. This is not related to spirituality. You do not have to believe on faith either. The fact is true to this day. There is something about the individual power each human has over their body and mind to use energy vibration frequencies that the "Rulers" want to keep secret. Evidence shows the elite class is desperate to keep this a secret because if you knew the simple facts the use for all rulers to exist would disappear.

SCIENCE FACTS – CHEMISTRY 101

Throughout "His-Story" human science has created technological instrumentation that can see smaller and smaller particles. Human science is extremely arrogant in what it proclaims are facts. Human arrogance thinks it has found or discovered something and calls it a fact only to soon rediscover some time later what was once called a fact was actually a limited opinion based on the previous times scientific limitations.

Everything on earth is made of atoms. At the time atoms were discovered they were called the smallest particles. Sometime later atoms were discovered not to be the smallest particle after all. Current instrumentation now knows that atoms are made up of electrons, protons, and neutrons. These electrons (-) circulate around a nucleus that contains protons (+) and neutrons (neutral non-charged) particles. The smallest of these three is the electron (-). All electrons (-) are held in orbit around the nucleus based on an electromagnetic charge which is a form of energy vibration frequency stabilization. The total charge of the nucleus proton charge (+) is held in balance with the electron charge (+).

Given "His-Story" obviously there must be something smaller that we cannot see yet beyond the smallest known particle the electron (-). It is now known that the electron (-) itself is made of holes and is not solid. The smaller the size the particle is the higher the vibration frequency; the larger the particle size the lower the vibration frequency becomes. The prevailing current human scientific evidence indicates that when taken to a small enough degree nothing is actually solid. Everything is a form of energy that is vibrating at a unique frequency. By comparing matter energy vibration frequencies to the properties of water, matter is like ice when solid, matter is like water when liquid, and matter is like a vapor when a gas.

SCIENCE FACTS – PHYSICS 101

Although modern human science uses "Wave Science" it does not completely understand "HOW" a wave is transmitted (from Earth based transmitters as a beam) to a satellite (a relay which acts as a receiver-transmitter) to an antenna (receiver). Science cannot comprehend "HOW" it works but it obviously does. Science knows it works by emitting a signal frequency which is sent by a transmitter and the frequency can be picked up by a receiver but the "HOW" exactly still remains elusive. The same challenge is applied to cellular and wireless frequency devices. Do you really care "HOW" those instruments work while inside elevators inside buildings or underneath the ground in tunnels? Cellular towers transmit for miles while satellites transmit for hundreds of miles. Signal frequencies permeate virtually everything it passes through organic materials like wood and life forms, plus inorganic materials like rock, brick and mortar buildings made of glass and steel.

All that is known is that the energy vibration of the frequency does not travel in one focused beam. The frequency wave goes in all directions like a bubble. A user can virtually go anywhere and pick up a signal as long as they are in range of the signal. This means that the energy vibration frequency is permeating all space. No matter where you walk as long as you are in the range the signal is being picked up. Therefore the signal is not a line or beam but an energy field. Energy vibration frequencies that are small enough will permeate throughout a whole room.

This is a concept that is a challenge for a lot of people to comprehend because remember there is a disadvantage many humans have been taught to believe "unless you can actually see it and experience it, do not believe it". But that is what energy vibration frequency is, it is believable now; you cannot see it because it is smaller than what is seen in the physics of physical matter. This takes the energy vibration frequency to the particle size or the quantum level and the study of the quantum level is known and commonly called quantum physics. Just because you cannot see it with your eyes does not mean that it is not physical. The energy vibration frequencies are like an invisible gas that goes through everything and it is part of the physical universe. By comparison to the science of a hundred years long ago it is almost magical. That which was once considered science fiction is completely real now. So believe it or not we just cannot see it without physical eyes.

In summary understand that energy vibration frequencies exist and that everything on the entire planet is made up of energy that is vibrating at a uniquely specific frequency. That means every single thing is the same at the smallest levels and everything is made from the same materials called atoms. The only thing that makes something different is the mixture, combination, and ratios of the various elements that are made from atoms. Humans are also made up of these same elements that contain atoms. All atoms are made up of three types of particles: electrons (-), protons (+) and neutrons (neutral). All matter is energy that vibrates with a frequency.

ENERGY

All energy vibrates. The vibration is measurable as a wave. The wave vibration is an information carrier. Frequency is the method that the information is encoded. Energy flow in physical matter requires three elements: Negative (-) Positive (+) and Neutral (•). Energy is discharged from the negative and transferred to the positive. Neutral (•) acts as the pause or ground. The neutral (•) ground in matter is the neutron. The neutron keeps matter visible and solid. Energy vibration frequencies that are quantum are without a neutral (•) so the energy passes through matter unaffected. Energy not used is potential energy. Potential energy is beneficial if there is a capability and capacity to discharge the energy with flow. Energy can build up and become non-beneficial due to no discharge and this energy state is correctable. This stored energy that is non-beneficial flows back into itself to manage the lack of natural energy flow. The fun fact is the hydrogen atom does not have any neutral (•) neutrons and is the lightest element of matter.

UNIVERSE

The universe is a term that will be used often to describe unseen forces of energy. The universe is everywhere and comprises everything including all materials seen and all the energies of the quantum field that are unseen. The majority of the universe is shapeless and formless. There are multiple dimensions that are layered with each other all separated by energy vibration frequencies.

Many names have been given to the universe. The names do not matter and only confuse the fact. Focus on the facts. There is a creative force that is above all things. Consider this force the prime energy vibration frequency that is the highest in possibility. This source frequency is the spiritual God force. The unimaginable intelligence mind of source created the universe with energy vibration frequencies. The highest energy is extremely logical and simplistic. Consider the enormous size and complexity. The energy of the quantum field is organized by a set of quantum laws that act as set of programs that run constantly controlling the universe.

Understand the universe is the spiritual God force. Eliminate the entrainment of human societal control from your life. Refrain from the humanization of the spiritual God force. The spiritual God force is everywhere and is everything. Humans are completely responsible for their own life and destiny. If a human has a problem with a company or a business the human goes to the man or woman in charge. Religion has confused the point with a savior middle man. Talk to and make all of your requests directly to the universe. As you will soon discover the quantum laws clarify all ambiguities and concerns you may have about such topics, concepts, and beliefs.

DEATH

Humans fear the unknown. Death is considered unknown and feared. Unfortunately there are a lot of confusing opinions and theories that add to the fear of death. There are human institutions that exist to argue and wage war over these so called facts. As is the case in most instances humans only have part of the facts and that is why it appears so confusing. Death is simply a new birth process to a different place much like your birth into this existence.

SOUL

The soul is an electromagnetic plasma ball about the size of a baseball when captured by human instrumentation. Humans photograph them and call them orbs. The soul weighs approximately 20 to 25 grams and is based on the Hydrogen atom. Hydrogen atoms do not have any neutrons to ground the plasma to the physical body. Hydrogen atoms are also eclectically neutral. Life memory is stored inside the soul and is unique to each individual human.

SPIIRIT WORLD

Once in the spirit world the soul is adjusted to its new birth. There is oneness with all spirit. Souls tend to the growth of other souls. The energy vibration frequency of the spirit world is much higher than the frequency of the physical world. From a soul's point of view examining a human life on the physical world appears very slow because of the frequency difference. One of the challenges souls experience while being a guide is the necessity for patience because communication with humans must be slowed down dramatically.

Many souls become guides and aids to souls reentering the physical world. Souls wait and enjoy their time in the spirit world. Eventually the soul is tasked or requests to reenter the physical world. A complete life plan is created and previewed before departure back to the physical world. Human life is a form of education or a type of school. There are specific life paths and alternate paths created based on the ability to learn this new life time's lessons. This is why the future is known to the spirit word because the planning process and preview is part of the grand purpose. Each life time has markers or signposts that are designed to guide the human along its designed path. This path is not always followed. Between lessons and the journey between them humans can choose whatever decisions they wish and request anything that they want. All is provided to humans in accordance to their assigned and agreed to life path and the quantum laws that are designed to assist the life experience. All requests from humans are answered according to that human's best interests.

LIFE

When the soul leaves the spirit world to reenter the physical world a new birth process is set into motion. The life and parents are pre-chosen according to the details of the life plan. When the new human host's baby body reaches a particular electromagnetic resonance with the soul's electromagnetic field the soul's energy plasma ball enters the body and forms a unified energy resonance. The soul's plasma ball energy field then triggers the body's systems to boot up sparking a new human life. The soul's electromagnetic field is centered and anchored to the human heart. The energy field then slowly increases in size as the human body grows until the energy field is several inches around the human body.

AURA

This field is called many things. One of the more common names is called the aura. The soul's energy field is the human mind. Thoughts, emotional feelings, and memory of those thoughts and emotions as well as all experiences are stored in the mind. Reincarnation also has some very specific requirements. The DNA of a human body must resonate with the soul spirit energy. Although not all features are preserved from live to life the four sense structures (being the mouth, nose, ear, and eye structure shapes) that are distinctive features that make up the face generally do not change much at all. This is because DNA is a frequency field that holds past body memory. The human body carries the memory of past lives in present time in DNA. This make DNA a living experience recording device of sorts.

LIFE PURPOSE

Upon entering the new human host's body the soul's previous memories of the spirit world and all past knowledge of previous lives is removed. This information is stored but is not normally accessible during the new human life time. Sometimes this memory upload is not completely successful. Some remnant memories remain intact. In some cases this is part of the life plan for specific reasons. In most cases a second upload takes place sometime prior to puberty when the universe creation program is installed. Once the creation program is uploaded the puberty process begins. Rare instances have been recorded of clear memories from past lives.

The memory wipe is very important to human life experience. There are several reasons why the wipe is done. The primary reason is to ensure all choices and decisions made during a life time are completely genuine. Human life is a kind of education after all and there is no cheating allowed in school. Sincerely genuine choice and freedom of "Will" is completely allowed. This also ensures that everyone enters their new life with a clean slate. The next reason is that past life memory would affect the current new life and a human's ability to stay on task during this new life time. The last reason is that past life knowledge maybe used for self-serving reasons and that goes against the quantum laws. The quantum law help humans actively seek personal growth through the universe, passively surrender to the universe, reconcile and find the truth and purpose universe has for you, and lastly the accumulated knowledge of the human experience.

Each human life has three main purposes. There is a specific purpose designed and agreed to during the life plan creation process. This is called the life purpose. The life purpose is a primary set of reasons and learning objectives. Spirit guides are present in each human's life to aid and help the accomplishment of this purpose and its numerous objectives.

The second purpose is for the universe's purposes. Each human is part of a grand purpose and larger picture. The quantum laws utilize humans in service to the greater plan. The time that is provided and given between learning lessons and pivotal life events for every human in their life plan is used to serve the universe's purposes. Each human is part of the balance, rebalance, unbalance, and shifting that must take place to ensure all life paths are kept on track. Since freedom of "Will" is allowed and preserved the quantum laws are in place to aid and help universe maintain order to the complexity of the universe's purpose while maintaining the individual purposes of every human at the same time.

Some humans can become disconnected from their life plan and purpose because this occurs other humans are used by universe to realign those humans back on a path putting them back in line with their life plan. As a human life unfolds the original life plan and the actual life path do not always line up. This is why guides, aids, and helpers from spirit are required. This is to assist universe with making sure the original life plan is maintained overall. For this reason any time reference from spirit may not be clear or match up either. The experience of time is a frequency that is alterable to shifts in current life paths with the original life plan. The universe does as it does to ensure the best opportunities are provided for each human's best interests in completing their specified life plan. Time is often used and required to make these changes while still meeting the additional requests of each human while alive. The simplicity and logic of the quantum laws aids, helps, and assists the universe in this process as well.

The last purpose is to take advantage of the time in between life path requirements. This is the purpose of the moment. The objective is to enjoy the human experience while adding beneficial Karma to the soul. The best way to achieve this is to serve others and focus on healing past Karma. Using the purpose of the moment allows each human the ability to achieve more out of a life time than the original purpose of the life plan. This is the main reason why freedom of "Will" must be allowed and preserved. The purpose of the moment is critical for excelling beyond or picking up the slack if a human became disconnected and off the original plan's path. The three purposes are enter-linked yet separate. This is why every human has the power to make and shape their own destiny and why although the future is already written it can be changed for your benefit or non-benefit. The power of choice is always up to you. The power of choice is the purpose of the moment.

NEAR DEATH EXPERIENCE
For instances that are planned and unplanned an expedited system is used to get souls back on their path. If a soul has risen due to an early death or has been ejected from the body in a particular manner such that the soul's ability to return to the body must be assisted then intervention is required. Many times the soul is greeted by loved ones on the other side, given instructions that are usually not fully remembered, and sent back to the human body in the physical world. In very rare situations a soul may cross over into another dimension until it can be located and reestablished in the body. There are some souls that have developed the ability to leave the human body and astral travel at will.

IGNORANCE
Human are "Naked"! "Naked" does not mean bare without clothing. "Naked" refers to a level of ignorance to a greater knowledge. Such as thoughts are deeds and deeds are thoughts. In this manner thoughts become things. The same way that everything is made up of energy. The energy vibration frequencies of thoughts transmitted by the human mind can change physical matter. There is knowledge that humans just do not know or understand, yet. As humans learn more the ignorance does not go away because there is always something more humans do not know. Humans are not that smart to know quite a lot still. When humans teach each other what they know and express it as fact this compounds the ignorance. This is because often what is called a fact is actually an opinion or a theory and is not a fact at all. Hence humans suffer from generations of compounded ignorance that is socially taught and reinforced as facts. Just because humans believe or do not believe something to be true does not change the way that things work, have worked, and will always work.

DIS-EASE
Medical science uses the word disease to name virtually everything that is related to illness or sickness. The word disease actually means "Dis-Ease" or "Not-at-Ease". Homeopathy is a form science that treats "Dis-Ease" by minute doses of natural substances that in a healthy person

would produce symptoms of "Dis-Ease". Homoeopathic remedies contain nothing but a carrier solution. The carrier solution carries a frequency.

When examined by the "Naked" eye there is nothing that can be seen that distinguishes one homeopathic remedy from another. The difference is the energy vibration frequency contained in each remedy. Homeopathy procedures state that if a human has certain symptoms the remedy to make those symptoms disappear is the same frequency. The remedy to make those symptoms go away carries the same frequency. The human body in effect is telling the human operator a frequency is causing "Dis-Ease". The "Dis-Ease" is eliminated once an outside frequency matches the frequency. The human body is telling the human owner the cure to the "Dis-Ease". Hence like cures like or frequency cures frequency. Frequency neutralize each other and this cures the current "Dis-Ease". The most amazing part about homeopathy remedies is the more diluted the carrier solution is the stronger the solution becomes. This is because higher frequencies are more potent the higher they become. Homeopathy is energy healing. The ability for living organisms to be healed and fueled by energy vibration frequencies is therefore possible and provable. Food and water are forms of energy. This is also why humans can heal themselves and can heal other humans as well.

NATURE
Nature which includes the fauna or animals, creatures, insects, and the flora or the plants, trees, shrubs, and everything else in the environmental regions and habitats across the globe functions largely on instinct. Instinct is considered an innate, typically fixed pattern of behavior in response to certain stimuli. These responses are instinctively triggered largely by the changes of the seasons amongst a wide range of stimuli that vary between species to species. Whether you know about the triggers or the reasons they exist does not matter. These things happen anyway. Nature's fauna and flora will still respond that same way regardless of what humans think about it. Human opinion and theory does not change the facts of instinct nor does it change the facts that humans are still a kind of animal. Examining nature provides enormous insight into human challenges because nature does not fight its natural instincts to make new ones that do not work.

Since humans are just a special form of animal, humans must also have instinctive responses that are fixed patterns of behavior. Some of these are natural in development where as others are unnaturally created by human society living. Unnatural habits and patterns become settled or regular and these tendencies or practices are especially difficult ones to give up at times. These habits are learned and taught by other humans, social environments, and personal choices. These patterns and habits in humans form instinctive mind memories that are triggered in response to certain stimuli just as in nature. The brain is the body's computer processor and these patterns and habits act as fixed programs that keep being reused for efficiency purposes. The brain's memory holds these programs unless they are not used or unless the program is changed or updated.

HUMAN BODY

The human body is extremely sophisticated and there are numerous books that elaborate and discuss the inner workings of the human body. These books are either biology or medical in their focus. In general the human body is described as having 12 body systems. Most of these books agree that there are 12 systems but the breakdown of a few of them overlap or are categorized differently. There are 9 of the 12 that are not in dispute: Integument (skin), Skeletal (bone), Muscular (muscle), Nervous (nerves), Circulatory (heart), Lymphatic (immune), Digestive (stomach), Respiratory (lungs), and Unitary (kidney). There are 2 systems that are either separated or placed together being the Reproductive (Male / Female) and the Endocrine (hormone – Male / Female). This makes either 11 systems or 13 systems. For the majority of these books the Endocrine system is one and each of the Reproductive is counted separately one male and one female. This is where the resolution of 12 systems comes from traditionally from human science. The 13th system is considered the whole body.

Wait something does not add up here. If all of these systems are added together that means each body has male and female body systems in them. Obviously that is not the case. Consider that science is missing or confused about one of the systems and is leaving a system out altogether. That may explain the mystery and inconsistency. It might also provide a greater insight into some questions that are never answered. Let us examine this from a logical point of view. What does DNA tell us? There are 23 chromosomes pairs not 24 pairs. Why is that? Well if there are two parents then why are there not 12 chromosomes from each parent? If you take the 23 and divide it by 2 the result is 11.5. What does that mean? The half means that the human will either be male or female. That leaves 11 systems remaining. In the 12 system model each male and female reproductive system is considered separate and in the 11 or 13 model system this is accounted for with 11 systems two of which are either male or female being counted twice (9 + 0.5 +0.5 +0.5 +0.5 = 11). This still counts male and female systems in the same body. The 0.5 chromosome already accounts for this where does the 11 remaining chromosomes come from?

What if science is missing something that science does not want to take into account? Let us go back to the beginning and take the 9 undisputed systems off the board. That leaves us with either 2 (hormone / reproductive) or 4 systems (hormone male / hormone female /male reproductive / female reproductive) remaining. Logically a human is either a male or a female so one of the systems is split and whether male or female both have hormones. This means 9 systems plus 1 hormone system and 1 reproductive system (9+1+1 = 11). That gives us 11 again but still accounts for reproduction in it. What if there are 11 systems and there is a 12th system that has not been accounted for yet by modern science? What if there is a system that runs all other systems? Science says that the brain runs the body but that is part of the system already accounted for being the Nervous system.

What if the missing system is that of the "MIND"? That explains a lot! Now there are 12 systems that add up correctly. There are 11 that are always present in each human and one system is split into 2 which produces either a male human or a female human. This gives us the 11 complete chromosomes and the half chromosome for the gender or 11.5 chromosomes. This means that each parent provides the information required to make a complete human body. The 12th system is the "MIND" and there are 2 parts to the "MIND". Every human personality is unique by expressing 2 distinctive elements those of thought and those of emotion. These elements are not considered physical yet every single human has them and their presence is accounted for as a system that is provable with factual evidence.

In humans, each cell normally contains 23 pairs of chromosomes, for a total of 46. Twenty-two of these pairs are called auto-some, each looks the same in both males and females. The 23rd pair, the sex chromosome, differs between males and females. So every cell in the human body carries the information for the "MIND". Is that not interesting to you? There are 12 systems, 11 systems that are physically evident and seen by science and 1 system that is seen by science only in the chromosomes but not as a separate known system of the body. The "MIND" is the overlooked system.

MIND

The mind is made up of thought and emotion and is an energy vibration frequency field. Emotional feelings are an internal response to a thought. Thought is an internal response to an emotional feeling. Thoughts and emotional feelings alternate because thoughts create emotional feelings and emotional feelings create thought. This alternating effect takes place constantly. The alternating currents of energy vibration frequency between thoughts and emotional feelings create an energy pulse that is dependent and independently a "Cause and Effect" system. This is the same "Cause and Effect" that physics uses in scientific examinations of physical motion. Note that feelings are an expression of an emotion and both are the same and both are energy vibration frequency signals. The human brain processes energy vibration frequencies the energy then processed information for thought. Memory is not contained in the brain but is contained as energy throughout the entire human body in each and every cell. The memory is collective, collected, stored, and unified into an electromagnetic field known as the soul and is present in the aura field.

Emotional feelings work the same as thought except the heart is the processing unit for emotions. The energy pulse that the heart produces is sending an energy vibration frequency wave throughout the entire body. This is why tactile feelings, emotional feelings, and thoughts appear at once during the same time period, moment or experience. The brain and the heart connect the electrical system of the body and their altering energy animates the human body with life. The soul is located in the area of the heart. This is why consciousness can stop and the brain can be dormant yet the heart still beats. The heart must beat and is an involuntary organ that works independent to the rest of the body. The human heart soul connection is the life force. Once the heart stops the entire body dies because of this important and intricate connection.

ELECTROMAGNETIC FIELD

The human body is powered by an energy filed known as the electromagnetic field and is also known as the soul or mind. The human body is a hologram construct of energy vibration frequencies that emit light. Another common name given to the soul or the electromagnetic field is the light body. The light body is organized into 7 separate yet connected subfields. Why 7 fields? Recall above that there are 11 physical systems to the physical body that have chromosomes in pairs or 11 x 2 = 22. Each chromosome is in a pair because one carries thought energy vibration frequencies the other carries emotional feeling energy vibration frequencies. The 12th system is called the mind which is present and represented in every cell of the body. The 12th system has 7 parts non-physical and 5 parts physical. The inputs that are physical are the 5 senses which provide feedback and information to the mind. The inputs that are non-physical are the 7 fields that make up the mind electromagnetically.

In mathematics there is a golden ratio that signifies and denotes the circumference of a circle or sphere to its diameter from its center. This ratio is 22/7 and is also called "PI"! The 7 subfields are required to be in resonance with the human body to be able to contain the energy plasma ball known as the soul and known as the mind. The electromagnetic energy field is projected from within the body as a complete sphere with the heart as its center. These 7 separate energy fields contain information energy vibration frequencies. Each of the 7 contains the vibration for the known visual light spectrum: Red, Orange, Yellow, Green, Blue, Indigo, and Violet. The fourth or green sphere also emits pink light. The fourth sphere is centered at the heart which beats energy throughout the human body. Food energy comes from 2 sources in nature one being fauna or animals (the pink flesh) and two being flora or plants (the green chloroform). There is a reason for everything in nature!

5 SENSES

The human body also has 5 senses. Four of those are only in the head. These four senses of taste, smell, sound, and sight provide information but do not feel. That is to say that the information from those senses does not occur by feeling but contain elements within thcm that can feel sensation. Each of these four senses provide a feedback system that takes in special kinds of information that is not seen as physical but is still real. Taste provides a signal that tells the body of the contents of the food or liquid being consumed. Taste buds on the tongue are picking up energy vibration frequencies from the food or liquid and sending that information to the brain to be processed. Smell provides a signal as well. The sent in the air is picked up by the sense receptors in the nose from the energy vibration frequencies of the sent in the air and the information to the brain for processing. Sound provides a signal to the brain to be process by passing the energy vibration frequencies in the air and elsewhere to the ear drum. Lastly the complexity of the eye takes in light energy vibration frequencies that are transmitted to the brain to process as a picture that works like a television screen in reverse. The ability to feel sensation nearly covers the entire human body. The ability to feel sensation provides tactile energy vibration frequencies to the human brain for processing.

Collectively all the 5 senses act on an energetic level bridging the soul energy and the physical energy making a collectively focused sense called the 6th sense. The 6th sense is always present but because human society and human institutions repress its function most humans are not aware of its presence and influence. Like a muscle the 6th sense can be strengthen and utilized. Since this is not practiced from birth onward because it has been repressed and feared many humans just to not believe it is even real because there is not an automatic response. The same occurs with the human muscle because if the strength is not kept up the muscle weakens and atrophies or diminishes.

All sensory information is a form of communication. This communication acts as a feedback and guidance system for the body. The human body receives sensory communication all day. Mostly these messages are interpreted from the outer world as information and communications from humans and other external sources. So the question is not whether you are communicating. The real question is whether you are aware of everything that is communicated. Spirit communication to your soul is ongoing whether you are aware of it or not does not matter. Spirit communicates with humans through our five senses.

"CLAIRS"

A human that uses any or all of the 5 senses for spirit communication is called Clairsentient. Clairsentient humans are sentient as all humans are but these individuals also perceive the energy vibration frequencies that are much higher and come from the spirit world. Instead of senses the term "Clairs" is used to distinguish them. Commonly there are 4 major "Clairs" with the sense of smell included in with another "Clair".

Clairsentience is the most common and means clear feeling and mixes the ability to feel tactile sensation and emotions. Experiences associated include but are not limited to: Unexpected emotions that come from nowhere. Gut feeling or physical reactions that take place around people, places, and things all of these having unique circumstances about them. Physical feelings that appear disconnected from the physical world. Making a gut decision or having a sensation as if someone touched you also occurs. Due to the nature of the sense of sent being rather limited it is also included as part of Clairsentience. So smelling the essence of smell with no physical origin is connected and occurs. Common examples include flowers, perfumes, or smoke.

Clairvoyance means clear sight and utilizes the sense of sight. Common experiences include but are not limited to: Things humans see mentally or with physical eyes. Vivid dreams or dream like experiences that occur while awake or asleep. Seeing flashing or sparkling lights, these lights and flashes are plasma energy balls or souls. These energy plasma balls can be detected and seen in photography are commonly called orbs. In some instances objects are seen to move with no explanation. Seeing other things like number sequences, names, places, and things like objects is included. Seeing spirits move or from the corner of the eye. Also the ability to see the human body's "MIND" electromagnetic field, also known as the aura, accompanies this ability. The human body's eye and the "Mind's" eye are linked in the place that is commonly referred to as the mind's eye or the 3rd eye.

Clairaudience means clear hearing and utilizes the sense of hearing. Although this is not as common these experiences include but are not limited to: Hearing music, voices, or sounds that do not have a known origination. Some humans hear their own name upon waking or during specific events. Overhearing an additional meaning inside or part of regular conversation that answers a question or hearing a specific song on the radio is also part of this kind of communication. Celestial type of music that is heard from nowhere, hearing high pitched sounds in one ear, and even hearing an audible voice in the human mind can occur.

The remaining "Clair" is very unique and special. It involves the essences of knowledge that serves. Clair-cognizance means clear knowing and utilizes the sense of taste. Did you ever hear someone speak of the taste or essence of an experience? Taste serves to provide humans with a quality about something or a knowing about it. Common experiences of such knowing that serves includes but is not limited to: Knowing something without knowing where it came from is the taste of an experience. Discovering something new that was always present is receiving an "aha" revelation is the ability to taste that part of an experience for the first time. Just as taste serves to inspire humans to eat this "Clair" inspires knowledge and action. Being able to do something or fix something new for the first time, having wise words or phrases that emanate and come through as if from someone else, and becoming inspired to create or make something new are often associated with this ability.

CONSCIOUSNESS

There are two forms of consciousness. First is the conscious mind that represents thoughts relating to logic, reasoning, recent memories, personality, and individual identity ("WILL") and emotional feelings that relate to a cause or an effect. Second is the majority, the unconscious mind holds two functions. First function is to keep the human body functioning, operating, and alive. That means all involuntary systems required for the body to function. The operations of the body are preserved, balanced, and interlinked together. The second is to contain and manage past emotions and memories from present and pervious lives in an inactive state. Memories are referenced, organized, and related to symbols. Memory recall requires and uses this symbolic language for response triggers. This is also the programming center for habits and patterns for long term use. It functions as a fully integrated whole and needs no separate parts. The mind is very protective of the unconscious and consequently takes everything personally to defend its integrity. Highly efficient and organized this part of the conscious mind uses the least amount of effort and takes the path of least resistance. All spiritual intuition passes through the unconscious to login those communications. Most important of all, the unconscious mind does not process "NEGATIVES". To the unconscious mind everything is just a form of information to be stored. Humans created the concept of "NEGATIVES" to control other humans by way of unreal fears.

CONTROL

The concept of control is completely relative to the individual human. Competence or the grasp of understanding is the center focus of control. Incompetence is not being aware of an aspect of understanding. Once awareness or consciousness becomes the control focus then what was once unconscious moves from incompetence to competence. All mental controls of the mind work on "Cause and Effect". Meaning the same thought, emotional feelings, and actions activated will cause the same effect. This also means that every consciously intentional thought, emotion, and action is a uniquely magical event for the mind to experience. Plus this means that every thought, emotion, and action done without conscious intent or unconsciously is still a cause of all that happens. These facts apply to the external universe and to the internal universe of the human by the way of the mind or soul. All cause and effect whether conscious or unconscious means all thought, emotional feelings, and actions are taken with responsibility and is responsible for all that happens. The only way for a human to gain maximum control of the internal and external universe is to assume and take complete, total, and full responsibility for being the cause to every effect experienced. In other words control requires self-responsibility of thought, emotional feeling, and actions to get the results you want. Becoming the cause takes responsibility and generates results. Becoming the effect places humans on the defensive creating justification and reasons that are external in nature. Becoming the effect places the human into the victim position thus the human gives excuses and feels powerless. Control can only happen when you consciously take responsibility and apply what you have learned.

EMIT, TRANSMIT and RECEIVE

There are five ways humans sense everything feelings (textures), taste (bitter, sweet, sour), hearing (sound), smell (the scent of objects) and sight (colors, shapes, and sizes). Everything appears to be so different yet they are the made of the same materials. "HOW" can this be? Oh, yes, the obvious "HOW". Because there are nearly an unlimited number, almost an infinite number, of potential combinations of atoms and there are the same number of energy vibration frequencies to match. The change may be very slight even but that difference creates a different energy vibration frequency. This makes everything humans experience with their senses different. The unique expression comes from the mixture, combinations, and ratios of the energy vibration frequencies. Think of atoms as nature's ingredient list and the unique expressions are nature's recipes.

These are concepts humans have to grasp and understand in order to be maximize responsibility. Everything on the planet is made up of atoms which is a proven scientific fact. The smaller contents of atoms are simply all energy vibration frequencies. All of the energy vibration frequencies differ and vary from one another differently. Recall there is a disadvantage many humans have been taught to believe "unless you can actually see it and experience it, do not believe it". Everything that is seen and not seen is made up of energy vibrating frequencies. So everything is a type of energy vibrating unique frequency.

The organic human body is much more complex than any machine, instrument or computer humans make from inorganic materials. The human body is the most sophisticated relay system which has twelve interlocking systems with the brain being the computer processor. The emotional center of the human body is the heart which powers the relay system. The human mind comprises the energy field of the unique human spirit that is held within the human body and emanates just outside of the human body. There are many names given to this energy field throughout the world but it is the same energy field. The human body is a relay system meaning that is just like a satellite in space and it is a receiver, emitter, and transmitter. The human body certainly emits, transmits and is a receiver of energy vibration frequencies. This is the powerful super-secret gift that the human spirit, the human heart, and the human brain enables each human above all other creatures in nature. The fact is that each human has this super power available for their own use is extraordinary.

Now you know the human mind emits, transmits, and a receiver of energy vibration frequencies. But let us take this one step further now. You also have the power and ability to create any frequency that you want with your mind and transmit it because of this super-secret gift. Like the ability to walk and run this ability takes practice until it is mastered. Once you know what you are doing and why you will have the ability to fine tune and dial in with your mind the energy vibration frequency that you choose and transmit it.

Humans also have the ability to transmit energy vibration frequencies subtly with little power or can blast with huge amounts of power. This range is possible because the mind works like a transmitter. With practice humans can control the power level and learn to increase the power to be very intense. The mind is similar to but more advanced than a satellite, a radio antenna, a cellular tower, or wireless transmitters. The greatest difference is the human mind energy vibration frequency levels are much higher. Inorganic technology can only send energy vibration frequencies in a straight line with a limited distance, where the further the transmission is from the source the weaker the signal becomes. When the human mind transmits, the transmission goes out in all directions in a sphere and even passes through the earth. Human mind transmission is instantaneous. Meaning the human mind transmissions go all over the globe. The human mind's energy vibration frequency is sent out with the same power; no matter what the distance is it holds the exact same power and does not get weaker with distance.

The amazing part is this is no longer an opinion or a theory it is scientifically proven real. The human minds ability to send energy vibration frequencies is completely real. Even more amazing is it always works unlike technology. It always works! For some humans the ability to accept this fact is challenging because their willingness to learn and to accept change is focused on the "HOW" again. When examined this is no more impressive or complicated than explaining "HOW" a cellular phone works, a wireless device works, and CD or DVD works. Do you question "HOW" these technological items work or do you just take for granted that they work never learning or caring "HOW" they work? Heck even magnets use an energy field that cannot be visibly seen. Obviously, just because you may not believe it does not happen does not mean that it is not happening. The human mind works the same way yet you may have difficulty believing it. The human mind is much more powerful though because the energy vibration frequencies permeate everything and nothing can block it. Let us be ultra-clear here when the human mind sends out a transmissions nothing can block them.

Remember the human mind is can emit, transmit, and receive. This means human mind energy vibration frequencies are being picked up by other human minds all of the time. This human mind energy vibration frequency also affects physical matter. Scientific experiments prove that matter gives off vibration and can hold unique frequencies. Everything has a unique and different vibration. Those vibrations are constant and they always stay unless something affects it. When matter is affected the atoms do not change much in vibration but the frequencies change. If matter is hit by any electromagnetic wave its frequency changes. Electromagnetic waves are forms of radiation and include radio waves, microwaves, infrared, visible light, ultraviolet, x-rays, and gamma rays.

It has now been determined that the atoms stay the same but the frequency of those atoms can become different. The atoms energy vibrations frequencies may change very slightly by an outside source. When multiple materials were tested their vibrations remained constant. The same materials were tested again after a human subject would emit a specific energy vibration frequency based on an emotion. These materials would not change physically in a way the human eyes can detect but in testing the frequency of the item changed.

The most interesting of these tests was done with water in order to visually see the frequency changes. This time instead of checking the frequency the water was frozen. The frozen water was spliced thinly so crystallization of water could be seen. Water crystallization patterns will always remained constant. After water was affected by the human mind energy vibration frequency based on emotion changes were seen. What was also fascinating was that each emotion affected the crystallization of water differently. This is massive physical scientific evidence that proves the human mind transmits energy vibration frequencies and the frequencies affect physical matter.

SCIENCE FACTS – QUANTUM PHYSICS 101

What does this mean? In effect it has been proven that everything is energy that vibrates and that vibration held nearly constant can change in frequency if a powerful enough source can affect it directly with another frequency. Everything is energy vibrating a unique frequency. The energy is the same but it is all vibrating at a different frequency. The human mind is so powerful that it can transmit energy vibrations frequencies that affect physical material.

This is what science calls the study of quantum physics. This is a science and it is no more magical or mystical than modern day technology. When you turn on a television set that is getting a signal from an antenna or a satellite dish energy vibration frequencies are in use. When you turn on your cellular phone and make a phone call or receive a phone call energy vibration frequencies are in use. When you connect to the internet with a wireless frequency (Wi-Fi) device it works using energy vibration frequencies. Your mind is an emitter, transmitter, and receiver of energy vibration frequencies and it is similar to but more powerful and higher in power than a radio frequency.

Choice

"Always remember you have the power to decide."

There is an amazing power within every single person whom ever lived, is currently living and will ever live. That power is choice. The way you choose to make every single decision and take every action directly affects outcomes and shapes your world. Deciding not to make a choice is still a choice. *You can never escape the role of choice and the awesome power it gives you to influence your life.*

The world owes you nothing but you owe everything to yourself! The attitude that the world owes you some hero like adulation makes you no hero. This is such a common mistake. Eventually reality will set in but the habit formed will under mind you. Because as this false hood takes hold the inability to achieve from it creates the victim mentality. Humans blame nearly everyone, everything, and any idea possible except themselves. Those same humans seek relief from this pain and suffering by indulging in substances and entertainment. This dulls it but will never remove it. These immature behaviors will cause you pain and suffering in your job, home, savings, friends, and your family.

Do you want to wonder around aimlessly seeking the answers? Or do you want to find them and learn them from someone who knows the facts? Can you remember the younger part of you that believed anything is possible? Recall the way you felt then because you changed your thinking and have suffered because of it. You lost touch with the mental, emotional and physical attitude that unlocks the process that is part of nature and never fails. This is why you have failed in the past. *The answers are often very simplistic. If you can accept this you will have a new life.*

Do you want a new life? It is suggested that you start to take proper ownership of this life and that will transform you into the new life you are seeking. The human being you are is clearly the greatest miracle and gift you will ever possess. You are someone important, worthy of aid in learning the truth, and you can still accomplish great things with your life. Providing that you are willing to pay the price: invest time by canceling all other appointments or interests, invest resources in yourself to make your monies worth it to you, and be willing to change all unbeneficial habits with an optimistic attitude. *You must be willing to do what is necessary to do the work to overcome those habits that have been taking your maximum potential away from you.*

What will touch you about this knowledge is the truth of the facts. Do not be hard on yourself because you were never told these facts. You can never go wrong when you learn the quantum laws in nature and go with them. For those who go against them are doomed to suffer until you learn them. These laws are not complicated. *There is no con or super quick easy way to success. This is because you must undue the part of you that does not serve you. Just like a child goes through growing pains to become an adult physically. You will likely feel those growing pains as you grow in mental and emotional maturity.* No goals can be achieved by being preached to but by observing and listening to the real life examples of true experience. Those stories allow one to relate another struggles to your own. Follow these experiences and you will be successful in achievement of your goals also. There is nothing written here that has not been learned and applied with success as its outcome. These examples let you know that if another human being can accomplish their goals, dreams, and desires so can you. Just look at what others have achieved in one life time. The process when learned will allow you to do the same if not more.

Have you observed, watched, and felt that there is much knowledge written or spoken by humans who have not really achieved much success in total health, wealth, and relationships. No matter what you choose to measure this content against you will find it a complete rarity in its completeness and comprehensiveness. Appreciate that you are being given wisdom that comes from experience and that this factual information works but more than that it never fails.

You must be warned that as you proceed to learn this information you are very likely to be carried away with its amazing valuable power. Do not miss the hundreds of direct and indirect skills, tools, and methods intertwined within the obvious; because the human that chooses to perceive with observation and wonderment will get all of the extra gems. Gems to become empowered with and to reach their maximum potential. So before you proceed past this general introduction it is suggested that you take some notes with a blue inked pen and some loose leaf paper. Make a dot with the ink to mark you place or the time stamp if you are listening and write down the way this information can be applied to your life as it currently is now in your personal or business life. Be creative and write down any and all ideas that occur to you. Then and only then after taking notes, continue keeping in mind that completing this in its entirety is what will transform your life. Focus on that completion and commit to that end.

As you complete the learning of content daily take time to pause for a while and reread your notes completely. Think about them as you go about your day in and day out routines to observe your current habits and the possibilities of new ones. Ask yourself continually what you have just been learning. Make this a new habit a daily one and continue this process. Your happiness and success will become more possible to achieve as you apply what you have learned and continue to re-read or re-listen to the material as much as possible. *Everything worth having is worth your self-investment first and that is not work because it will bring many joys into your life.* This all comes from the voice and evidence of experience.

Some of what you will experience may be confusing at first. That is okay because you are about to learn many new things that go directly against deeply held habits and belief systems (A.K.A "BS") that do not work with or compliment natural laws. However you will be blessed with thousands of amazingly wonderful beneficial experiences for rewards as you make those changes. These rewards will come in ways greater than you ever dreamed possible. If you are willing and ready, let this information take you by the hand and lead you to a new life where the world you always lived in never existed previously.

BEGIN WITH THE BASICS FIRST

Right now in this very moment through out every part of the world there are always those who wonder what they can do to get closer to their own personal gleaming life's dream. There is self-improvement and self-development. Before your aim is any of those you must have a solid foundation to improve or develop from. *That foundation is in learning and mastering all forms of the basics.*

Few will go deep and find the secrets from the depths of their hearts to find this great achievement. As most will just continue to aimlessly wonder, dream, and wish for answers never knowing what to watch or look for, hear or listen to, and to feel or have the ability to discern the real truths of life. One day something may happen to awaken them with a shock and realization that they are in nearly the same spot or worse off compared to the time they first started but did nothing about those dreams. That was when they were younger but now those wondrous dreams are lost and all they ever do is wonder about where all that time went and why it all went sour.

All humans want something that is not currently in their own possession now. This takes form in one of three areas ultimately being health, wealth and relationships. Here is a common list: money, position, and prestige, known for unique achievement, the opportunity to aid others, real love, an amazing marriage, a rewarding career, children, and a place to call home. Every single human yearns for their own kind of fulfillment, their definition of success, to be happy, experience joy, to be healthy, and become wealthy. These are personal searches to find the riches of life. All of them are normal and nearly universal as desires and dreams. Everyone holds a different value to each of them but in some ways they are all wanted by other humans.

Those inner urges inspire and motivate humans for some more and others less but none the less they are always there driving humanity forward and upward. These urges lead to motion, to momentum, and culminate into taking some form of action. There is no exception in because this applies to the highest and lowest of creatures. *Everyone has the same opportunity as other humans.* This has no bearing in high or low places, educated or uneducated. If you were born with a human body, this all applies to **_YOU_**!

Call it success or failure, a blessing or curse, the world created in duality is perfectly designed to provide endless opportunity and to bring beneficial dreams and desires into reality. There will always be those who have fallen down into the ruts of life and fail to pick themselves up. Many have no valuable examples to learn from. There is a reason why one human succeeds and another one fails. There is an answer and you will find your answer if you are willing and ready to seek it.

There really is a magic formula, a prescription, a perfect recipe, a set of rules, a number of principles, a group of systems, and the all laws of nature that act as your personal treasure maps to your desires, dreams, and wishes. When followed in the proper sequence the process yields benefits to life for those that seek them. The difficult part that most humans face is twofold. The way nature works is often so simple, logical, and obvious that they are not even seen because you have been taught by many humans unknowingly that life is complicated and difficult. Nothing can be further from the truth. That is the second challenge. For some reason humans are so stuck in their muck that they say they want the truth but when examined most humans run the opposite direction to the truth. There are many reasons for this muck.

If you are willing to be totally honest with yourself and accept the truth of the way nature works you too will find the treasures that you seek. During the search something amazingly wonderful happens. You will acquire factual knowledge for yourself. The knowledge will give you empowering experiences to build success upon. This set of events will inspire and motivate you. Then and only then will you begin to recognize for yourself the necessary ingredients that have always existed within your own power and command.

Humans give up large incomes all the time to give their talents and skills over to a higher power. They always become successful in a different way. Humans around them or whom they aid or assist always feel a warm sense of appreciation and caring. These aids never live below their previous condition because their valuable service always rewards them with success. You may realize that not all humans in the line of service thrive. There are reasons why some do and most do not. Those that are a success use their own personal drive to make the fullest of all that they have been given and freely use those gifts each and every day of their life by choice. This is a generous, self-sacrificing desire that is not held down or held back. Remember this is power received because a choice was made.

Moving from inspiration and motivation to action requires ambition and initiative. These questions must be asked. Why does one develop ambition if there is currently no ambition? Why does one develop initiative if there is currently no initiative? Why does anyone motivate themselves or anyone else into action? These are questions that are often asked but instead of "why" the questions always begin with "how". Humans from all walks of life are fixated by the "how".

Make a choice to develop a desire, dream, or a want. Learn to make a decision and stick with it. What causes a desire to grow from a seed? That is "why" anyone begins anything. **Does the seed care about "how" to grow or does it just grow?** Interesting question? These answers will become extremely self-evident once you learn to read, listen and feel for the message that is applicable to you. Not anyone else but you. Remember there is a type of magic that resonates from desire. The reverse of that is also very true. The magic in anything lies within the skill of the magician. All skills require three necessary ingredients as does any human endeavor that reaches a level of success.

These three things continually came up again and again. They always prove to never fail. Also these three things were learned and proved every single time. Continually testing the use of these three ingredients in both success and failure made it very clear that mastery requires all three together. The real value that gleamed was always the way to inspire and motivate one's self after a failure. The truth is that when you share with others the benefits and beauty of your experiences their value continue to multiply and grow. What is shared with you is a wealth of knowledge that has been found to be factual and true from experience.

If you are willing to continue on this journey on you own personal treasure hunt you too will be able to discover the systems in place that never fail to remain constant. You will truly learn to bring all worthwhile desires, dreams, and wants to their fullest reality. ***The most valuable of treasures have been hidden so that those to seek to hold envy, hate, or greed will not find them.*** This is the way that these treasures have been kept form all of human kind. The hiding place is so obvious that it is never seen my by most. The true and abundant riches of life are created with perpetual replenishment. *The hiding place can be found by every single living human.*

As you are reading, listening, and feeling into this deep humble truth. Take this knowledge as if it were discussed by your own personal closest best friend in a special conversation with you. In confidence with you and only you alone. Unless you make it your personal desire to understand the magic trick, it will undermine your belief in the quest for this rare valuable treasure. This information is dedicated and created for you friend. This information comprises the true riches that you have been seeking friend. The hiding place is always in plain sight you just have to know what you are observing and know what is really happening. This removes the veil of mystery to reveal the simple facts.

Have you ever had an experience that seemed to just stand out form a long time ago? Do you connect with it as a learning experience in which you tested a limit or a perceived limit? Do you hold that memory with fear or have you moved beyond it looking back at yourself? Do you as an adult look upon the experience differently now? Give yourself true credit because it is more than likely that you succeeded but not in a way that you thought the success would take place. If you analyze your actions today compared to those experiences of the past do you notice a pattern at all.

Motivation and inspiration come from desires based on some basic need. Often the value of an object or experience will not show its truest value to you until long after a perceived failure. At times it feels like everything will be lost but upon reflection what was lost compared to the learning value is worthless by comparison. A major challenge that makes you stronger or better prepared for future events is always worth it as long as that lesson is learned.

Such inspiration and motivation develops the internal generation for beneficial actions to be taken. After even small success do you continue to push on? Even if you know there is a chance for embarrassment or failure? Do you try and try again with persistence? After several attempts you will always learn one of two things. Things that work or things that do not work?
It is always as simple as those two things. Change something and try and try again. As long as at least one person has accomplished what you are attempting and has achieved some measure of success there is an example to inspire and motivate you. This "understanding" is learned exclusively in this manner. Notice that the "how" is more an after effect of the "why".

Humans learn what works and what does not through persistence. What to say and what not to say. When to listen and when not to listen. When to use recognizable feelings and to become aware of new feelings. *All anyone needs to do is to repeat, mimic, or model from a worthy personal experience or valid outside example and the desire will eventually be achieved.* This is the required action knowledge that will make you the example for others to look up to. Be honest with yourself that is the acknowledgement you are really seeking anyway. To know that you hold proof of evidence which makes you a worthy example for other humans in some way. That younger you also used the same methods you just never knew that before now.

The three part process that leads to success:
1 – Self Inspiration and Motivation will lead to taking Beneficial Action.
2 – Real "Understanding" comes from a decisive "Why" to begin with.
3 – Learn all Activity Knowledge by Practice or with a Mentor's Direction

No matter the age children are naturally happy. A child does not concern itself with poverty or riches. The same can be said for all the creatures in nature. *As long as there is a place to sleep, something to eat, and enough room to have imaginary play every child is happy. The basics are where real happiness comes from.* Everything else just distracts form that simplicity. If you grew up with a caring adult asking for you to share your experiences you develop a voice for your identity. Imagine the power that voice has when as an adult you have conversations about all of your beneficial and non-beneficial experiences with someone who really cares. The human just wants to listen and not push anything on you. Notice again that these are very basic but extremely powerful activities. There is a single motivation and inspiration behind them. The doing of listening creates the unique "how" because of the "why". This would be an example of keeping good company. The company listened but never interjected anything to influence you to be anyone but yourself. The activity knowledge of experiencing the value of having been heard is the example to learn to listen to others.

Keeping non-beneficial company creates allowed influence into your life. Take the example of smoking. There is nothing beneficial about smoking. Yet the human that introduces smoking to another is doing so to build a better feeling inside of themselves for doing it. After all if other friends join you doing something non-beneficial justification for the activity develops. Pay attention that the same basics are present. There is a single motivation and inspiration to have others join in to justify doing something unhealthy. When done long enough smoking becomes a habit. Notice the way the desire to smoking was started. The root of the habit is the "why" of wanting to feel accepted by oneself and by others. The activity knowledge of smoking becomes the new habit of smoking.

The examples of listening to another or introducing smoking are both choices. Notice the way both work on making you feel important. You relate that feeling to those humans. This is why the human that was listened to felt comfort and appreciation. The human who started to smoke felt the same exact experience of comfort and appreciation because of buying into the smoking activity. Notice the importance of taking action and the reaction that follows compliments and mirrors the results. These simple activities create patterns and those patterns generate habits when done long enough. Habits always come from persistent practice of an activity. The pattern when done long enough is mastering the activity knowledge of the activity. The simple and basic parts of the process are always the same.

BENEFIT

Tell the truth or tell a lie. It is a choice! Decide the value of the long term outcome of every action first. When you tell the truth out of the motivation and inspiration to take responsibility of something happening that is called a beneficial action. *The action is beneficial because everyone wins with the truth because the facts are given.* Tell a lie out of the inspiration and motivation to escape responsibility or hide something and the only perceived winner is the one who lies. This is non-beneficial because the receiver lost the ability to have true facts. The one who was lied to then passes the lie to others and the false facts effect everyone involved. *False facts that are told to others creates compounded ignorance.*

Those that devote their entire life to becoming the example of what is possible pass the example on to others. In this way the real facts tell the truth about what works because there is evidence to give that proves it. Those humans who desire to achieve the same outcomes want to emulate the facts for themselves because there is a similar value system. When the example is false no one gains any value in the end. These examples either create the environment for success or for the removal of success.

The challenge is becoming ready to discern the facts from all the fiction. The three part process makes you ready to discern facts because it never fails to work. Generate the personal initiative to learn the facts, utilize your talents to suit your aims with facts, and develop the sensitivity to recognize valuable skill sets related to those facts. All of these will create the environment for proficiency that is necessary for mastery of any subject. ***Mastery is not a duplication. Mastery comes from knowing and applying the facts to one's own unique desires, dreams, and wants.***

Every decision that a child makes begins patterns of thought. That will later create a tremendous impact on later life. When an adult makes a decision it is either beneficial or non-beneficial depending on their past experiences in coming to decisions. Just like the seed that grows into a tree. The small things that create benefit will always lead to bigger and better benefits. The small things that create non-benefit will always lead to bigger things that are non-beneficial. These facts apply directly to making decisions. Beneficial decisions must be followed up by taking action. Without action a beneficial decision becomes meaningless. For desire alone can die for the lack to achieve its fulfillment. Often a time frame is required to act quickly before the opportunity passes. This is why you must always act immediately on a beneficial decision.

ENVIRONMENT

One of the most important lessons for humans to have in order to significantly desire beneficial change can be difficult to take. It normally forces itself on you when you need to become aware of it if you have not done so already. You are the subject of your environment. So by all means necessary select the environment that will best develop towards your desire, dream, and want objective. This often requires much change and possible upheaval to notice the great benefits of the new environment over the previous one. *Sometimes an unexpected change of environment will propel you faster than you could ever imagine beforehand.*

The best influence and environment that you can have is one that you create. This is why it is so important to choice wisely when getting married. ***A husband or wife is the greatest influence to creating the optimal environment.*** For a husband and wife team that works to create the best environment for the other will increase their shared success. This is why it is said that behind every great man is a woman and behind every great woman is a man. *Environment is as much physical as is the company that you keep.* Always choose your friends and associates wisely. For the most part humans that you keep company with will always have the same environment with them unless they decide to change. Never wager or bet that a human will change because that time may not come relative to your own needs and growth.

Always seek individuals of intelligence and character. That combination of traits will be a gold mine of wealth to you and your pursuits in life. When you make a decision to search you will find what you are looking for. The quantity may be large or small and it may take some time or patience. The result will be full of quality and well worth any wait. *Spending time with one to five such individuals regularly will change your environment and outlook on life with swift speed. Anyone who has a beneficial influence on you is valuable to you.* Likewise you are always an example to other humans and are valuable to them. Creating optimal environments and being in them maximizes your ability to practice and master all forms of health, wealth, and relationships.

ADVERSITY

Adversity is the opportunity for change in disguise. For every adversity carries with it the seed of an equivalent or greater benefit. Take a moment and pay attention. What do you do when everything goes wrong? What do you do when you feel like there is no place to turn to? What do you do when you are faced with a serious problem? It is okay to be desperate if it spawns a desire to change within you. Sometimes humans invest all that they have and they must or feel they must get there return back on whatever the initial investment began with. The human feels that they tried their best but have not made a sale. The best option is to seek guidance and be open to change. *For when the answer arrives it may not be familiar to you. Why should it be familiar to you? If it were familiar to you, you would have already known and done that. For that is the reason why so many things happen in life unexpectedly because you would not see, hear, or feel what you needed to otherwise.*

The desire for change and for guided wisdom creates a sincere driving force that the world cannot miss, even if it wanted to. All apparent obstacles remove themselves as if by magic. *The practice of trial and error helps develop inspirational dissatisfaction or constructive discontent.* This causes a human to desire to take action. This is the way of learning "understanding" derived from the root "why" of self-created inspiration and motivation that creates action. The "understanding" aids one in making their own personal success system that is tailored to their own desires, dreams, and wants. *The upward climb is rapid once these principles are embraced openly.*

VALUE

Nearly any human endeavor can be resolved into a formula. Notice what you are doing when you are successful and the environmental dynamics involved. Most humans who able to know the facts still fail long term because they do not apply the greater principles or laws. *The personalized success formula takes the facts and principles and uses them in harmony with each other. This is the way to make a system that never fails.*

Everyone has value to offer others. For some the value appears greater for others it may appear lesser but *every single human has a significant and meaningful value.* Study and know your own value. Study and know the value of the product or service your value represents. Has it ever occurred to you not to think for yourself? That is okay most humans just do not know any better because they are already afraid in the first place. This is an example of being a product of habit. *A habit is only beneficial if it severs you to meet your self-supporting ends.* Often you will learn an important lesson if you remain open to learning.

Do not ask a human for their time! Do not waste your time either. There is a way to make your time work for you instead. Consider creating a system that sells twice as much in half the time. Anyone can develop a formula that will deliver maximum results to suit their needs or desires. It always comes down to making a choice. From the moment you decide to create something new and consciously think about the outcome the principles will be there to aid you. Success and failure can be reduced to a formula. Like a math formula the answer is there if you know what to do to achieve it. Start with basics and apply your success to avoid failure. That means you must learn to think for yourself.

No matter who you are it is wise and desirable to learn the techniques of salesmanship because you are either sharing a sale or pushing one. It is really that simple. To sell is just a method of persuasion to purchase your product, service, or idea. In a way you are selling the value to make a value proposition. With that in mind nearly everyone has had to be a salesman at some time in their life. No matter if you are a salesman or not the information is of the same value to you because the principles never fail to be valuable to one's success. The objective is to reduce your efforts into a process or formula that is reproducible. Doing so makes your efforts effective and an efficient use of your time.

If you are ready to change and willing to let go or give up what it is you are holding on to so you can learn. You will choose to write down the principles that you learn from your own successful experiences and your failures in whatever activity you hold interest in. You must desire to be interested in the activity or your energies will not be invested in a beneficial outcome.

You may have a different challenge. Some humans have difficulties extracting the basic principles of success from what you read, hear or feel through your experience. Even though you are currently reading, listening, and feeling a new experience at this moment this content comes from practice. You will soon discover that unless you start to think for yourself your ability to utilize and apply any principle will be minimal at best.

Overcome your fear to think for yourself so that you are no longer timid or shy. Many humans start out being afraid and timid because they had no example to teach them otherwise. There is a natural reaction response to having new experiences and in new environments a human will see, hear or feel some degree of fear. Naturally this response is a protection system embedded into you for survival and is part of your awareness ability.

Humans experience fears to a lessor of greater degree relative to each other within the same experience. Again this is a natural defense to protect humans from harm. When you make the decision to choose and become aware of your environments and experiences the fear part diminishes. Fear is only an automatic system set up to shock you into an extreme state of awareness in the event that you have not learned to become self-aware independently.

When self-awareness is practiced clarity can enter the pictures in your mind. For the odds and likely hood of the event taking place related to the fear imagined is confronted as being unlikely to harm you at all. Amazing things happen when fears are faced because the real beauty of the experience can be seen for what it really is instead of what was once imagined.

For an example many humans hold fear towards lightning and thunder. The instinctive reaction of fear makes them want to run and hide. However once the fear is faced the beauty of the storm with all its lighting can be observed with the same amount of safety. *Humans have fear of the unknown and see a door as a barrier because they do not know what lies on the other side of the door.* This is why a common metaphor is used when discussing and describing new opportunities in terms of a "new door appearing". For the human must get over the fear of the new opportunity to open the door to experience it.

For success is only achieved by those who try. There is nothing to lose at all by trying, for at least an answer is known. Whereas there is a greater possibility of loss by not trying at all. The desire to gain must be greater than the fear of loss in order to start overcoming the fear to try. Fear keeps humans paralyzed and is the exact opposite response for action required and necessary for success. The "do it now" thought process will never fail for that reason. Think of it as rushing quickly from one closed door to the next. Take note that rushing is not pushing but it is having an enthusiastic desire to take the next action or to act immediately. Never rush in out of haste but only in expediency to take the next action.

Whenever you begin to hesitate or procrastinate out of fear use the self-starter "do it now" to immediately create action. For there will never be the perfect time if you wait. Now is always the best time to take action. Okay so you can go from door to door now and enter without fear. What is next? The next fear comes from engagement. Starting to talk to a complete stranger can be a daunting experience.

Talking to talk and talking to engage are two different things. The voice must be controlled. Speak clearly and pleasingly loud enough to be heard. Rapidly say what is needed and only what is needed. Also known as being brief or having brevity. Appropriately use you hesitation as a pause for places of punctuation. As if you were writing while you speak. Remember to keep a smile in your voice to engage meaningful conversation. The smile is coming from the rush of energy you will begin to develop in taking the action to speak.

Never talk like a robot in a monotone fashion. Learn to modulate the inflection of the tone or pitch of your voice to stress or convey meaning. Doing this with awareness creates the arcing effect much like one musical key to another. This naturally gives your voice a pleasant harmonic authority. Humans will listen and pay attention to you because of it. In this manner all the energy that once went into making butterflies in your stomach will be used to make a song like the birds. Notice the way that all fear is not from a place of reason but can be changed when subject to taking action. Often thoughts of fear do not resolve themselves but taking action will provide resolution.

Consider starting a conversation with "I believe this will interest you also" or something similar instead of "May I take a moment of your time?" This statement cuts out the ability to respond with a "yes" or "no" and generates a curiosity of interest to find out more. Think about it, your response will likely be "What is it?" If it is for you it will probably be the same for others as well. The introduction is the hook to grab attention and curiosity so humans will listen.

There is wisdom from knowing when to stop. Trying to sell everyone you call or talk to may just eat up your time. Another experience happens too when you talk to wear another down you also wear yourself out in the process. There is no value to anyone once energy is low. The point is to increase efficiency of your use of time. So to trying to sell everyone you call on or talk to is not the most effective method. Yet so many will burn themselves out attempting to follow such instruction blindly.

Consider changing your definition of a sale into a value exchange. You are offering a value. You must know and believe in the value. If you believe and know the value the receiver will receive if they hold the same value. Would you ever give a gold ring to a child to play with, likely no. That is the same mind set to use with all value propositions. If your value and their value does not match up stop. Remember to think for yourself and to question instructions. Set a time limit and if the action takes longer than the time's limit evaluate the value in continuing the action. Value is about making the prospective receiver of the value happy to have obtained the value. The receiver must leave the experience feeling happy about the exchange.

Even though you have a gut feeling that the value will be respected outside of the given time frame stop. Do this and amazing things will happen. Your success in any value exchange will increase tremendously. Some humans are wired to argue or have experienced others who have argued with them. Never argue because no one really wins. When you leave in a given time that you set for yourself in a pleasant and happy manner you control the engagement and the way an experiences closes. A counter response will often take place, as long as you leave your contact information and you get their contact information. The counter response you will generate will be "you cannot leaving me". Those who needed to wake up and take action themselves will get it when you can walk away. This accomplishes providing a challenge to action without an argument.

Leaving in a given time frame with a smile does wonders for you in other ways. It keeps your attitude in a beneficial mind set to continue on because you are in complete control. Step back and examine it. You start with a smile and you close with a smile. You start the engagement and end it. Humans want control. In such a manner you get control. It is not possible to beneficially control others but you can do so for yourself.

The point is the value exchange requires energy. You will fall short of doing your best work if you are fatigued, tired, and worn out. This simple method or formula of using time will never fail to keep your energy up and increase effectiveness. There is no wisdom to be found in having killed your energy. The nervous system is recharged when the body rests. So you did not make a sale in a given time but you did rest up for the next one. The use of time is a key ingredient in success for any activity. Your time is your investment to spend so spend it wisely. For your use of time is under your control.

Fear of engagement can be the fear eye contact. This works both ways. Humans fear eye contact because the eye never lies. If you lie to yourself you fear that others will see the lie in you. So humans fear you will see their own self lies. Looking into another's eyes can be threatening for this reason. Some give an immediate response of "no" out fear of the unknown. Others may try to make themselves feel powerful by interrupting. No one likes to experience these things and that is where some fear comes from. If you keep to a time limit those actions cut out those responses.

A simple effective technique can be used for eye contact fear. Get the prospective receiver to concentrate on their senses. Steer their eye's attention on what it is you have to offer and their hearing fixated to your voice. When in a face to face always point to the object or the presentation as you speak and look at it with your own eyes. During a phone call direct their attention to a memory they can relate to from personal experience. Both methods keep the eyes on the subject and not the presenter. This technique guides others to look where you lead them to look.

Obviously this works best in person. The person to person connection is always the best option. Because if out of the corner of your eye you notice a head shake "no" or a nod "yes" you know where to go next. If you get a "no" pay no attention because the initial "no" is actually an "I do not know". Humans need time to take new information in and digest it. Often this time will be within your time frame and the perceived "no" will become a "yes".

That is when you close the door. The door is the sale. Where you ever instructed to close the door behind you. A sale is no different. Just as you open the door in front of you and must close the door behind you. So too you must open and close the sale. Many humans leave the sale open just like not closing the door behind you and walk away. That is rude. Best to end with a smile at a given time and close the door behind yourself.

If you are a good sport you play to the rules of the game. If you do you violate the standards of the game that is called cheating. The same is true in life. Set your own rules and follow them otherwise you cheat yourself of your own success. You also play games to win. If you play just to play you are no fun to play with. Value exchange is the same as playing to win. It can be a lot of fun when you win. The formula makes you an expert winner because it never fails.

The expert is self-taught by trial and error. Giving the complete effort of try, try, and try more. Learning what is beneficial and what is not beneficial. This is the rule that must be followed in life. This is true in becoming an expert in anything. The formula makes for beneficial reproducible habits. This is why many who master becoming an expert at one thing can often become a master of many.

Work under these methods becomes fun and joyous. The job no long is work because it becomes fun. Fun because it is no longer random or haphazard. Fun because there is value increase in discovering and becoming curious. The process of discovery leads to new truths. Humans react to triggers such as a certain word, a series words, or gestures. Words for example when used in certain phrases will set off a certain reaction in humans naturally. These reactions mean that the prospective receiver of value will purchase the value in a shorter time frame or will just waste your valuable time.

Who does not want to say the best thing in the best way to get a specific reaction? Of course you do. That can only happen with practice. Practice is the only work you will ever do that is completely worth the investment but only if you learn from those experiences. The upside is everything has a beginning and an ending. Thankfully the work of practice will not go on forever.

Humans that want to buy a value proposition must be asked. So ask your prospects to buy your value proposition. It is that simple just ask! Give humans enough time to say "yes". Always make it easy for them to decide to say "yes". They must have a want to decide and a desire to own the value you are offering. Also you want your value to be so valued so much so that saying "no" becomes a difficult and painful decision.

Be specific with an intricate and redefined delicacy. Be deliberate with a subtle and clear message. This makes the engagement subtle, effective, and extremely pleasing to everyone involved. Now the conversation is a fun and memorable one.

If you are positive and express beneficial value with a statement and follow it up with an affirmative question you will nearly always receive a "yes" response. This makes the "yes" a natural reflex action because the prospective receiver wants to have the same beneficial value.

Some examples you too will say "yes" to also:

1 – It is a beautiful day. (Positive statement) Don't you agree? (Affirmative question) Yes it most certainly is. (Positive response)

2 – You want to practice now so you have the rest of the day to do with as you please. (Positive statement) Is that not true? (Affirmative question) Yes (positive response)

3 – It would be great to have such a beautiful object. (Positive statement) Don't you think it is beautiful? (Positive statement) Yes it is beautiful. (Positive response)

4 – May I get your information now to get you started? (Positive statement and question) You do want to start now don't you? (Affirmative question) Yes (positive response)

5 – So if you do not mind, I would like to help you also if I may. (Positive statement) May I help you? (Affirmative question) Yes you may. (Positive response)

You must have a desire to obtain the "understanding" by practicing the activity to become an expert with activity knowledge of that activity. The power comes from known brief repeatable actions that have known repeatable success. This process helps prepare anyone to develop beneficial habits. Consistent outstanding repeatable responses in the shortest time frame possible will always maximize your results. These is no quicker way to become successful.

Although it is never obvious at the time it happens events from your past prepare you for your future. Unless you train yourself with the habit of self-reflection you may never reap the full value you have already been given. If you choose to develop the habit of self-reflection you will discover the purpose in having past events. This practice is very powerful and simple to do.

Success is the same in every single human activity. Although the activity changes the same principles will always be in use. The choice is yours use them or be used by them. This is the greater discovery. What does your success mean to you? That answer will determine your inspiration and motivation to make a decision. All benefits of health, wealth, and relationships can be yours. First understand what is really going on in you and around you. Second apply what you learn. If you succeed or fail the remaining gem is the knowledge you obtain from it. This sounds simplistic and that is because it is simple. Master the basic simple truths in life with the factual evidence life provides you and everything else falls into place.

Clearly the system works so choose to work the system. As you increase your ability to perceive your awareness will increase. Your purpose grows and becomes more focused the more aware you become. Then all you need to do then is apply what you have learned and keep applying it.

Remember to seek and discover your inspiration and motivation. That is the all-important "why" that spawns you to take action. What inspires or motivates you or any other human to act is the root cause. The root cause is a desire, a dream, or a want.

Generate a willingness to learn. The "how" you seek is "understanding" and it can only be achieved by doing it yourself with practice. This "understanding" comprises of what it takes to consistently get results for you. In fact "understanding" when learned gives you the proper application that best suits the activity. The facts become knowledge and repeated use of them gives you beneficial habits that become experiences. This makes you the expert and the example for others to emulate.

There are millions of activities to do. The knowledge from practicing the activity gives you specific activity knowledge. Factual knowledge comprises of the knowledge, service, product, methods, techniques and skills that apply to you particular interest. Activity knowledge is the outcome of "why" and it teaches you the "understanding".

The truth is it takes less energy to be succeed than it does to fail. That statement is a complete contradiction to must of what you have been told or personally believe. However it is completely true. The use of energy is work. When any human engages in any activity energy is used. The activity of living alone uses energy. This fact cannot be denied.

Concentrate your energy on a given task by placing focus on it. Much like the archer who aims with concentration by focusing his or her vision on the prize target. So must you with your energies to be effective. If the archer loses focus the target is missed. When you needlessly allow yourself to lose focus your ability to succeed falls rapidly. Once again simple as this seems it is the only way to obtain activity knowledge relative to the activity you hold interest in.

If you are going to do something put your heart into it. You have to feel that desire, dream or want to focus on it. Give and give more to give it all you have to give. That is the kind of focus you must make a habit for yourself. All success come from the heart. Do this and then relax. For the archer must relax to let go and release the energy of the bow into the arrow.

Focus requires concentrated attention, effort, and then relaxing. This is because focus itself cannot be held indefinitely. Remember there is always a beginning and an end. The relaxing is the focuses end. When you sleep your body is focused on recharging and that process ends with relaxing in to becoming awake. Then when you are awake the body is focused into energy use. Eventually you fall asleep and the process repeats itself. The natural world and you work exactly the same. The time of relaxation may very but it is always there. Examine your breathing for example you are relaxed and then you breathe in, the when you are full you relax to empty. The process never fails and continually repeats.

Pay special attention to this. Science calls the process of sleep and breathing an involuntary function. That means that once your body learned the way to sleep and the way to breathe it made it a habit. That is the exact way your successful habits work for you beneficially. They become automatic for you. The same is true of unbeneficial habits that lead to failure. They have become automatic and your actions undermine your possible success. Once again it is that simple.

Start with a success. Start with a good night's sleep. Whatever your activity is it takes your energy so get good sleep. When you start to take on new activities you will need more energy. So when you start you can expect that you will be and feel tired more quickly. This passes as you gain strength. Strength just means that you are more efficient with your energy and can do more with the same amount of energy.

Next make concerted effort to begin each activity at a certain time. Pick which makes you most effective 5am, 6am, 7am, 8am, or 9am. Then stick to that time each and every day. This makes a beneficial habit form. Repeating this process will all of your activities and interests.

Practice conditioning your mind and your emotions. Simply concentrate and show thankfulness, gratefulness, and appreciation. Next make a request for guidance and help. Always expect that that request will be answered throughout your day's activities. If you pay attention it always will be evident to you. This process does not take much time so do not let anything disturb you while doing it. This is your rest before the next actions and you must make it a concentrated one.

Let the energy loose and become enthusiastic with its use throughout the rest of the day. As you practice you will begin to make every minute count more and more in your favor. That gives your energy momentum and momentum builds up your speed. In this your energy creates energy and more energy.

Pick a time to eat the same every day for breakfast and lunch. Stop and relax at lunch time. Eat a light lunch that that satisfies you, never eat until you are full. Give the food space to relax in your stomach as it digests. If you do not give food room to digest and you eat to you are full. The stomach will have no room to relax so it will relax your entire body to make the room. That makes you feel sleepy and that is not an effective use of your time. After you eat condition your mind and emotions again and then continue on with your day.

If your activity is tiresome then help your stomach digest effectively. Take an hour lunch. Eat for the first half hour and rest for the next half hour. Do nothing that requires the use of your energy. You will be energized and ready to go. After you relax always continue with the concentration practice.

Learn to rest when it is time to rest. When you put in your eight hours stop working. Relax and get your mind off the job of work. Let your mind and emotions rest from those actions. If you do not relax and give your mind and emotions time to relax then you will not be able to effectively sleep. You have trained your mind to always be active. Then when you awake your mind will still be tired this habit is far from beneficial. Learn to relax more.

Learn to concentrate your efforts on just one task at a time. That way you can learn all there is to know about that one activity. Naturally this happens because your focus gives you all the mental and emotional energy you require to do so. No energy is wasted on unneeded efforts or distractions.

The same experiences happens with speaking. You say what needs to be said and you learn while doing it. Focus on speaking and nothing else and your message will be communicated. It teaches you what to say, when to say what and the way to do it from the practice of doing. Seeking to be effective makes your desire to achieve brevity and clarity possible in your communications. This is like any science it comes from trial and error or trial and success. Unless you try you never know what works for you or not for you.

Believe that you can create a memorable system and an organized system plan that will make repeatability a possibility. This is no different than memorizing your part or role as an actor does. You are then putting in the required feeling, emotion and timing. This can be for talking or a silent activity. The thought given to useful feelings, emotions and timing will always serve you and lead you to success.

Start to notice that so much of what you think is random is practiced and polished. This is what it takes to become successful at anything. All successful humans must do so and you must to if you want your success as well. Practice makes the actions and words the same because you learn what actions and words serve you and serve others. This is the way to live the part you choose to take activity in. In short you must act the part that gets you the roles you want and success will follow your actions.

Fun is the creative part of choosing your part and the script you want to write for yourself. Then modify as needed to improve your part, your role, and find your purpose within the experience you are creating. Flexibility to conditions allows your process to grow in new ways. Somethings remain the same and can be standardized. Even common but different conditions can be standardized if they happen often enough.

What happens if you are interrupted? Do you tighten up or relax? Play with the idea of a joke, laughing, and smiling to relieve tensions. These will relax you and anyone else involved. Have this response and the jokes available to appropriately shift gears and get back on track smoothly.

The notion that work is hard comes from the challenging of battling oneself. It can be difficult to break habits and to make new ones that serve you better. If being flexible and open to change is something you naturally resist then you will find your work to be hard. Become open to change and the new habit of change will reduce the difficulty of work. This is why embracing change will give you so much growth because the competition will likely fail to change as quickly as you did. If you make a game to compete with yourself the change may happen at lighting speed.

All challenge is beneficial because it asks of you to learn to control your mind and emotions to serve you better. If you listen to that request and change accordingly the challenge becomes a reward. This is an example of why some humans appear lucky and others do not. If you can turn a challenge around it appears as if by luck but you know that the reward is clarity of action.

Many humans fear talking to the humans in charge or the owner. You will find that if you condition your mind to redefine the problem with inspiration and motivation the problem is no longer a problem. Persistence will condition the mind to keep you trying until a suitable method is discovered. Just like all persistence the new action will become a new habit and the fear that once was will diminish itself away if by magic.

You too will discover that when you do something the same way you get consistent results. The time to achieve mastery is never the same but the ingredient of time is always a part of the solution. Practice and time are directly related to one's success of any interest. Much like time continues to pass on, nothing ever stands still for long. If you stand still you stay the same or become worse off. Beware of this because the power to avoid this is always of your own choosing.

The external world and the internal world is always in a constant state of changing flux. This is because all movement creates imbalances that must be rebalanced to function properly. Time is the flux required to succeed or fail. Less time is required to succeed than it takes to fail. If you are challenged to understand this examine continuous success. Like telling the truth it is much easier to succeed when you do beneficial things rather than the unbeneficial.

Surely there are those that achieve through non-beneficial means but that success happens by accident or because of the conditions of the time. If a human steals and the conditions are such that no other humans stop the human stealing the human may get away with it. The natural stumbles on the beneficial system and momentarily succeeds. Only by repeating the original system again and again will that success continue. If no system is used and all principles are ignored there can be no formula created.

Create a system that suits your activity. You will achieve in hours or days what it used to take to do in months and years. Those who have failure fail to create a system based off their experiences. Many just get buy or kick the can out playing a game. Are you going to choose to make and refine your system? Any way you can save time you will make yourself successful. The short term will require more time up front to practice and to create a system. The long term will be the compounded success of those actions previously taken reaped many times fold. The choice is yours to make and yours alone. Your focus must be on one thing and its completion until you complete that item. Then and only then can the next task be started and focused on. Since most humans must work it is wisest to aim to accomplish as much as possible in the most effective manner possible. That can only be done with a system that never fails to produce.

Remember humans react out of fear. If you do what you are afraid to do you will learn more and experience more than by any other method. The more fear you can face the more confidence you will generate to achieve. That means if you are afraid to go somewhere than you must go there and face that fear. When you tuck tail and run out of fear you pass up all the valuable opportunities and never even know it.

The larger the fear the greater the need you must develop to conquer it. Beyond those doors of fear before you lies endless opportunities. Face the fear and open the door. This must be stressed due to the huge importance it has on your ability to increase your success. When you learn your fears are not valid they will become neutralized and disappear. Think of the desires, dreams, and wants you have passed up on out of fear to take action.

The best human quality is achieved through facing fears. This is the quality of heart. The quality is more than the physical heart. The quality called heart is the quality of being the courageous and compassionate warrior. The human with the quality of heart will aid another human by being the example as a mentor. Unless you go out into the world and face your fears you will be slow to learn such qualities. Would you run from success if you had it? Be aware that many are quick to give success up out of fear. That is the fear of doing something big and many also pass that opportunity up.

Take a moment and reflect on the number of times you let opportunity pass you by because of fear. Maybe there are other reasons to pass up opportunity. Such as not knowing the value of learning from a mentor. Experience will aid you in developing "understanding" but a mentor will fast pace you to acquiring a specific knowledge. The challenge is locating a worthy mentor that is willing to teach. Willingness to learn from a mentor will give you opportunities that you never knew existed.

There is information at your fingertips now. Information alone is not knowledge. Information may contain knowledge but it is often watered down compared to all the opinion and theory it is mixed with. Factual knowledge is rare. Being able to apply knowledge through practice of its application gives "understanding". This is related to the ability to take a failure and make success from it. Trial and error is the practice of learning what works and what does not. Failure can teaches us what does not work.

Knowing to do something is to have the knowledge of an activity. Application of "understanding" is doing something the beneficial way because of practice. Practice creates skill and effectiveness of that skill. Efficiency means that there is effective use of time with effort. Efficiency focuses on minimal use of energy and resources.

Solving a problem does not require knowing all the answers in advance. This can be done when you are clear about what the problem is for yourself or what it means to others. Defining the problem clarifies the outcome you want to reach. Start with determining what you want to have occur in stages. Determine the long term, the intermediate, and short term requirements.

When you are unable to know the long term outcome you desire then any intermediate or short term outcomes will be more challenging to solve. The problem is solved backwards not forwards in time. This is the exactly the opposite of what most humans have been taught.

Knowing long term outcomes helps in determining the best options for intermediate and short actions that will lead to the long term outcome. This is called long term planning. This gives humans the power to pick general or somewhat abstract actions based on "understanding".

Short term outcomes are beneficial to long term outcomes because they help speed up the process. Having mental, emotional and physical health will aid you in the long term no matter what your desired long rage outcomes. Other intermediate outcomes to strive for are a clear set of personal morals, to gain resources, to be of beneficial character, to be your best in your current role in society and at home. All of the above add value to you and give you value to share with others whom value those values as you do.

The next step comes from the next immediate step to take action on. These are simple. What you want to accomplish today, tomorrow, this week, next week, this month, and next month. You do not need to know the answers in advance. Begin to determine what the next step is, it is that simple. Because focusing on all the steps in the future just bog you down and drain your focus. Wanting everything now actually stagnates your future success. Focus on the next step. Knowing your long term outcome becomes the inspiration and motivation to keep you going when things get rough in the short term.

Learn to write down short term outcomes. This way as you complete them you can check them off. This gives you a sense of completion and acknowledges short term success related to the intermediate and long term outcome you wish to reach. These bring you closer to your immediate desires in an effective way. This only requires one thing of you. You must want to take action now for the later to occur.

There are many who have all the knowledge and know what to do but fail to succeed. Knowing what to do and knowing the way to do it does not require action to actually doing it. With no action nothing can happen. Thought is action and doing is action. No action is not applying thought to doing action. For to physically have action of meaning requires focused thought that takes physical action. This is what is meant by having an inspiration or motivation to action.

This is why thinking is the single most important action to any activity. This is a habit that can be learned. When developed the control of your own will to take action becomes yours to command. Practice of beneficial thought is a skill worth developing. The skill of beneficial thinking will take you farther and faster than any other skill. Your mind is yours and yours alone, so take command of it and reap the endless benefits of doing so. Choose to make this choice and you will never regret it.

A wise decision is to make decisions and choices in line with your own skills and abilities so the actions taken will be more fruitful. You have to honestly know what you can and cannot do well. Everyone has unique talents and skills. So know yours and use them to your advantage.

A wise decision is to choose an excellent mate that compliments your mental, emotional, and physical health. One that is in line, focused, and supportive of your desires, dreams, and wants in life. A choice of such a relationship is not based on who you are or who he or she is but is based on what both are inspired, motivated, and desire to become because of the beneficial influence of the other. Who you are and what you are is because of self and exterior influence. Best to choose someone that uplifts you just by being themselves. This decision is not based on what you or the other has made of themselves. It is based on what that influence does to make you better because of who they are as they are being themselves.

If you want anything you have to go after it. Go after it means to pursue your interests at all times. This does not mean go after it by chasing after something. For when you chase after anything it simply runs away from you. When you purse you are focused on your achievement with the quality of heart required to be successful.

Have you ever pursed something just to have someone or a group tell you that you would fail? This can often be friends or family. Humans enjoy pushing what they chased on others and failed at because they chased. For the few that may believe such things that do not interfere with your opportunities are rare. You will discover that humans have been taught to sever themselves. If your pursuits serve others as well as yourself then everyone wins. Humans respect a winner and want to join a winner.

Inspiration and motivation is required to establish any kind of business. Without inspiration or motivation there can be no vision to create a winning business model. Reason alone and appealing to reason to motivate and inspire can work but reason alone does not work. Emotions are the key to your success. The inner feeling triggers your instincts and your established habits to have go power to persist when others give up. This inner power propels you into action and is in your complete control.

If you know your value and your value's worth you will build confidence. Confidence is knowing that you have something to offer in value. Confidence teaches a human what is knowingly possible. Necessity is the external force that aids humans into action if action is not a beneficial habit. Utilizing confidence will propel your success exceedingly high compared to the humans who do not build, learn and cultivate confidence.

Confidence will take you far. You can accomplish great things with your confidence. Often you will discover if you purse your abilities to your utmost limit something happens. The realization of your example and your leadership on a topic or field of interest will make you reinvest your time. No matter the degree of efficiency you can achieve the ability to sustain and maintain a certain level of success may drain you and burn you out. This brings us back to the importance of rest to recharge.

Multiply your efforts by leading others you can mentor. Not lead but mentor. Leaders are important but leaders want to remain the leader and that is the down fall of many would be leaders. Mentors lead with example and by example. Mentors want others to achieve the same level of success that they have achieved. It is this giving service mindset of a mentor that makes others inspired and motivated into action. Follow a leader till the ends or your days or learn form a mentor and lead your life and others to lives filled with success.

Multiplying your efforts create the environment for amazing things to happen. A willingness for change and a willingness to learn new things gives you unknown knowledge and the consequent power that comes with it. Going to the next level after becoming an expert at the previous level puts such doors directly in front of you. Such opportunity is waiting for you when you are ready to grasp it. Discovering what you can do to serve others in a way that no one else is serving others will also give you success. This can be very simple if you take the time to plan the next step. An exceptional opportunity to learn provides the exceptional opportunity to earn.

Never make shortcuts. Learn this lesson first with communication. Always go to the direct source and find out for yourself. A leader takes charge and never lets another or their own thoughts question anyone but the source. Let direct communication be your friend and you will have the needed facts to make solid actions. The source can help you if you can listen and display a willingness to change and to learn accordingly. If you need help then go directly to a source that can help you because the source has the evidence as the example to be the example you require. When you seek help learn to listen and ask questions. Do more listening then talking.

The point is to continue to learn and to be open to learning. This is simple if you have developed the beneficial habit to do so. Start to cultivate the habit to embrace change. Change always comes with any growth process. Next cultivate a habit to learn and be willing to let go or give up anything that prevents you from learning valuable factual knowledge. Learn to value learning and success will happen. Learning new facts creates creativity in the mind. The power to succeed is related to your ability to be creative.

Disaster just like failure is an opportunity to change. There is a lot strength to be gained in seeking change. In fact if you want to become physically stronger you must change your habits. Changing from a non-beneficial to a beneficial habit requires building new strength. New strength to build the new habit and strength to overcome the old non-beneficial habit.

New strength creates enlightenment to non-beneficial habits, it builds courage to face your own fears, builds an appreciation for opportunities given, and gives humans the will to work. Learn to be thankful, grateful, and appreciative for all strength building opportunities. Asking for help is seeking guidance and guidance often requires developing new strength to meet the change of non-beneficial habits.

Even when you create a system that never fails for you and you are confident in your abilities, something can go wrong outside of your own control. There are numerous humans that have succeed and failed due to outside sources that directly impacted their lives. Learn to seize those opportunities to learn for yourself. Not to capitalize on it but to prevent suffering the same losses. Learn to have resource reserves when an emergency enters your life because they are always unexpected. This is the practice of expecting the unexpected and reasoning out the appropriate actions necessary giving your particular situation in life.

Anyone can acquire a great fortune of their own choosing if that human obligates themselves and is honest to paying off all debts. Successful humans learn the value of paying their dues. This can be a debt or a willingness to make the time to learn what is required to achieve a certain success in a given activity. Acquiring something new or more requires some type of payment. This goes back to a value proposition. There is always an exchange of some form, be it resources or time. The cost to acquire is a given requirement that cannot be ignored.

The ability to evaluate an individual human accurately is a valuable skill worth learning. The value of such a skill pays out dividends. Being able to determine another human's potential and to recognize their current ability to utilize their potential is a rare ability. Experience with humans helps you become aware of another's reactions. This enables you the ability with practice to interpret them correctly.

Awareness to your environment will aid you to create a system of techniques that will increase accuracy and repetitively. The more repeatable and accurate that your system is the more effective it will be and it will make you more effective and efficient. A beneficial practice is learning the ability to avoid making a human feel invaluable. In eastern countries this is called the practice of saving face. Remember everyone is valuable just establish that their value does not meet your current needs and let them go about their own way gracefully.

A quick lesson on human assessment in evaluation is in order. The purpose of this assessment is to make you effective in making a friend, building a team, building a business, and in your romantic pursuits. Step one normalize your criteria making your own standard to compare and contrast. Do not waste your time getting names or personal information on the first round of any selection process. Give those who make the second round the personalized touch and get to know them better. Remember the first round is to be real with yourself and honest with your personal feelings.

Step two evaluate their level of character, the beneficial nature of their attitude, establish their willingness to learn and change to take in new knowledge. First you must know your criteria and second the way your criteria matches the human in question to those chosen value characteristics. Step three if a human does not match your criteria be as respectful, courteous, and thoughtful as possible in fairness. Never demean their value but recognize their value has a place somewhere. Give humans a chance to save face and allow humans the ability to redeem their confidence. Many humans self-reject themselves and this makes this part of the process their own choice.

Step four get all the information you can on the ones you want and pursue getting them as long as it feels natural to you. Treat them the same as the other humans you eliminated except this time give actual demonstration of your value proposition after knowing their values match yours. If the values match than get the human or humans on board with your team.

Step five have compassion and empathy for everyone you meet. The tables can be turned and your character is the only commodity that you have complete control over. For humans who have never learned this control or have given lax to its growth and given it up need your example to remind them of its true value and worth.

If you fail you must be willing to get up and start from the bottom and work yourself up again. Humans who succeed are willing to do so with humble character. Their attitude is beneficial in nature and thus a beneficial example to others. Those who continue to fail tend to be the ones who did not chose the humble route. Trying to short cut the learning process leads to greater loss even more quickly. The non-beneficial attitude does exactly what it says it causes no benefit and thus no value to others.

Leaders know the art of inspiring and motivating humans into taking action. The mentor who leads is the example and not only tells but shows the evidence. The mentor example is a much more beneficial leader because the mentor teaches with evidence. Evidence gives meaning that the followers can internalize to self-generate inspiration and motivation into knowledgeable actions. Whereas the leader alone normally gets a blind reaction to action that is not internally sustainable and maintainable. The greater value in your system once you create it is your ability to mentor and teach it to others by being the example. It does not matter if you are duplicating your efforts to mentor someone for your own team or to aid a human or humans to benefit their own teams. The point is that your value is known and teachable to others.

As a mentor train others as you learned and go step by step aiding them to master each step to the best of their ability. Inspire and motivate action by supporting their insecurities and fears by recognizing the process is not a race. Stress that it is different for each human given their own unique background. Use your knowledge to lead them to seek their own potentials at their own rate of achievement.

Remember with any perceived disadvantage there is always a greater advantage and it usually requires willingness to learn and to change to obtain it but it is certainly there for those who are seeking to succeed from it. Write it down. Guide humans to think it through and to write down all creative ideas that relate to overcoming the disadvantage making it an advantage.

Life will test your knowledge to see if you have learned correctly. Tests are the best way to see if your system requires adjustment or not. Tests teach you to always seek more than you have been currently seeking. You will discover that a major objective is a guide but as you adjust and accomplish you must also increase the objective to the next desire. This is perfectly normal and natural for as you grow your needs and desires change over time. Embracing change earlier on in your life makes those adjustments another step in the process for your own systems success.

A single purpose if your chief aim. It is advised that you seek many things in order to learn. Success takes knowledge of many things that can only be learned by experience and practice alone. For the finer and most beautiful of desires, dreams, and wants bring the most joy in their accomplishment. The finer things are abstract in nature. The essence or flavor of your experiences is what the finer things truly move the humanity inside of you. Because it is abstract it is never really found or reached because such essence is elusive for a reason. These are the experiences of the moment that last a moment.

It is wise to seek a better way or system. Perfection is not realistic and has a shelf life because perfection is relative to one's opinion or theory. Perfection is a trap if you think it is possible. Doing your best and improving on your best is called personal growth. No matter what you think your perception of perfection is, it is only valuable to you as you view the possibility. However when you seek the essence of success you will become more successful. Because your gauge of success is relative to your own achievement and to other humans who have achieved similar achievements. This is why the value of a mentor as an example is so powerful an influence on your own personal success. You know what it possible so you can believe it and achieve it because it has been done before.

Striving for the essence in any pursuit requires a chief set of objectives that aid in guiding you to the next step when it appears at the optimal time for action. This gives singleness of purpose and high focus required for improved success in any area of interest. As stated before focus on the next step and you will get closer and close faster than any other way. *Short cuts do not help in growth. In nature that is called growth defect. For the weakness of the defect will certainly show itself eventually.*

LIFE PHILOSOPHY

The focus on the next step that takes you closer to the essence of the abstract you are seeking is a life philosophy. There is no difference in attainment of tangible or intangible the process is always the same. Finish one step and go on to the next. The essence that you seek and that you are is reflected in your own personal life philosophy. For whatever you believe will ultimately shape your reality.

The essence of your life philosophy is that the philosophy itself must be alive to change and grow with you as your experience what you like and do not like as you live. This amazing power is yours and has always been yours. If you are ready and choose to develop one that suits your chief aim in life. Do you have a chief aim in life? Do you have a life philosophy to live by when you are challenged? You know that you will be tested and challenged in life to grow and become stronger in your "understanding".

Life means taking actions and doing something. If your life philosophy is just a set of words it means very little to you. The life philosophy you develop for your self is reflected in your actions and your action when viewed by other humans is the example you are seeking to achieve ultimately along your personal path called your life.

The inside joke here is that your habits as they are now currently form your living philosophy. Your set of beliefs define your philosophy and if your beliefs hold you back so does your life philosophy. Your own personal belief system or "BS" is running your life and only you can change your own "BS". In essence you become exactly what you think about.

A living philosophy is only meaningful if applied with action in your life. Appling your life philosophy will always be most meaningful to you in times of need because at such times the life philosophy may be all you have to aid you in your growth through the experience. This is the greatest value of creating a personal life philosophy. When everything seems to be falling down around and failing you, your life philosophy must be there for you to see the challenges through knowing you will survive to thrive and prosper after the clouds have passed on.

A PERSONAL LIFE PHILOSOPHY TO LIVE BY...

1 – The creator of all life, all nature, and all of the known existence is a beneficial creator that seeks you to obtain your maximum potential. The creator intended for you to live, so live life. The power of intention and the request of intentions answered from creation is fulfilled based off the service that it gives all who receive it. Self-serving intentions are non-beneficial and service to others intentions are beneficial. Take care of your own basic needs to serve yourself and your own health so as to have the health to create intentions to serve others to aid them in their personal growth.

2 – The truth is always the truth and facts are facts use them both wisely. It does not matter if you have the total understanding of truth or the facts both remain constant. You may hold disbelief due to ignorance but not knowing what you do not know is one thing. Not knowing or wanting to know what you do not know still does not change a constant. Truth is truth and the facts are the facts. The truth and the facts will always serve you.

3 – Humans are the product of heredity, environment, the physical body, the total of the conscious and subconscious mind, life experience, your emotions, your potential reached or unreached, and of their own choices, perceptions, awareness, desired chief aim in purpose, and the ability to apply those gifts of abundance under their own command. Each human possess powers known and no yet known to them. The human has the power to affect, effect, use, control, and the ability find a balance with all of these. You are allowed to use these gifts abundantly as you see fit and your live experiences will reflect those choices. For some build bridges and other build walls.

4 – Humans were created with the ability to bring balance to unbalance. This means to direct your thoughts and emotions to use the body you were given for a force of benefit of the greater collective in the living experience. Humans are to find harmony with their own purpose in line with a destiny of their own choosing. Part of that choice is valuing to care for the mental, emotional, and physical body out of respect for its creation. All that makes up the human was created to have the experience called life.

5 – Spirituality is a living and dynamic experience which is personal in nature. The universe and its laws are simple and logical. The attraction to one's own spiritual growth and understanding is the essence of life. The existence of spirit is enduring and special. This is why you want to treat others as you want to be treated. Because all of spirit is connected in some way. The details are not as important as recognizing that there is a spirit connection that attracts into and out of your life what is best for you when you seek and ask of it to do so with complete gratitude, thankfulness, and appreciation. You are allowed to apply the gifts of spirit if you chose and are ready to do so.

Ask yourself what do you do or what have you done if you have a severe physical, mental, emotional, moral, spiritual, family, friend, social or business calamity strike your life? When there is chaos? What do you do when there is no place to turn or go to for aid? This is the time to test your own faith and belief in your own personal belief philosophy. This is why you took the time to create it and live it in the first place. So make it work for you when life becomes troublesome or chaotic for you.

A lot of humans say they have faith but it is only a dream with no real live connection. Real faith and belief is applied continuously no matter when your chips are down or up. Real faith in one's self and belief is applied the same for every experience because practice, trial, and error has proven itself to you. At these times this is why you had success and failures to have contrast and experience to aid your struggles.

Your faith will always be tested at the times of your greatest need. The amazing part is the system never fails to aid you and that is a comfort you can count on. When you have problems keep them to yourself, give yourself space to be alone, and examine the event with factual knowledge and reason from your experiences.

Your creator is a beneficial creator that wants the best for you. The best for you may not be what you think is best for you. What is fair is fair just like what is truth is truth and the facts are the facts. Are the facts different than you know them to be? Can you challenge the facts and prove the facts in a logical manner? Remember that with every perceived disadvantage there is a greater hidden advantage if you choose to seek it out. This is not easy and will take a lot of courage. All of your fear conquering when things were better by comparison comes in very handy to you at such times.

Can you keep a balanced head and take in the situation with perspective and awareness? Do you take stock and inventory of all you have to be grateful for, thankful for, and are willing to show appreciation for them during such challenging times? You must if you are to use a reasonable mind and focused emotional will to overcome the challenge when presented to you.

Things to show appreciation for include but are not limited to: a healthy mind, healthy emotional center within you, a healthy body, any family and children, friends, the opportunities you have been given in the past, the privilege of your own life and the simple joy of still being alive. These are all hugely beneficial things that you may lose track of at such troubling times. Focus and remember to center yourself on what you do have and have been given in the past. As the past is an example of what is possible. Accept that you know what you desire will happen in some way in the near future. All will take place in a due time.

This is when you request guidance, help, wisdom, and aid in your struggle. From experience you must have the developed belief that you will receive your new desire, dream and want just like all of your past successes. You must not waiver on your own belief in yourself and your request from the greater powers of creation. Be thankful immediately with complete expectation knowing the answers will arrive. Such actions generate inspiration and motivation for physical actions. Pause and reflect on all possible options available to you by being creative and knowing what has worked for you in the past.

In times of trouble your ability to have a beneficial mental attitude is your best ally. Think and make resolutions to yourself and be committed to seeing them through to your next step and remain focused. Take physical action with confidence and a sense of purpose. Ask questions, check all options, keep a level calm head, and take control of what you can as soon as you can. Keeping everything in perspective and remain reasonable.

Do not give up or stay down. Up lift yourself with a beneficial attitude. Only tell others of your challenges when you have done all you can do to remedy the situation first. Often you will be able to resolve matters with your own efforts alone like you have done many times before. Try and you may succeed. Remember the fear exercise to try to know for sure. This is another reason why you learned to practice such skills in the past. Try and try and try again to know for sure. Be persistent but remember never push or in a troubled situation you may push too far and make things worse off.

This is why you practice when you can so you are ready when it really counts. Your personal life philosophy is your own answer to troubled times. Take special note that the essence of your personal life philosophy is that it must be alive to be real. Alive within you and you must make it active to be able to receive the benefits of it. For it to live you must act on that philosophy daily so that the habit is formed to aid you when you need it most. Words mean nothing but actions give validity as the example of the living philosophy in action.

One of the greatest secrets of the magician is the same secret you are seeking. The treasure and key to all your success lies within you. If you seek them outside of yourself you will spend your entire life doing so only to completely fail in your pursuits. For within you is great power and creative achievement has not been tapped yet. If you believe it is outside of you then you have given into influence and in doing so have given your powerful birthright away foolishly.

No one or no-thing can take away your birthright. You were born with enormous potential to accomplish many beneficial things in your life. Are you currently and actively doing that? Why not? You cannot lose something that is intrinsically part of your own DNA. *The true riches and treasures you seek are hidden in the fabrics of your own heart.* You have a mind to control the energy created in your heart for your own use. The most basic rule is no matter what it is that you desire, dream, and want; you must always start with yourself making a choice. The amazing part is that wither you believe this or not it does not matter. For this is truth and it is a fact. Everything starts with you and happens to you because of you.

So everything starts with you. The next step is to be of service to your fellow humans and the environment in which you live. By doing so, you are living in gratitude, thankfulness, and showing appreciation for your gifts and treasures by sharing your abundance. However there are natural barriers in you called blocks. These blocks stop you from knowing and trusting yourself. These blocks must be and can only be overcome by you. No one can remove your blocks except you. This is the true meaning of self-responsibility. The up side is you can remove those blocks.

Breaking down blocks takes use of your mind and emotions. Start with the way you are currently thinking. Examine the systems or plans you are currently using. Are you even using a system or a plan? What is working and what is not working? Like a department store takes inventory of their merchandise so to must you take inventory of your current situation. Also examine your use of time and your regular habits that needlessly eat up your time.

Your mind has two parts the conscious and the subconscious. Both effect your experiences. Becoming aware of your conscious actions will enable you to discover your subconscious actions and motives. The subconscious mind reacts to protect you and your current habits. Remember this because you may self-sabotage your efforts due to the subconscious programs that run you on auto pilot.

PERSONAL INVENTORY

Until you have taken inventory and know what you are dealing with, success will be difficult to grasp. Start becoming aware of what you do on a daily habit level. Within a few days many things will show up. Continue this practice for a few weeks, a month, and a few months. The way you do one thing will subconsciously enter into all of your actions. This is another reason why embracing change is so important. Without change you will never unravel your current blocks.

Take time to think critically and learn to relax and observe, hear, and feel what is going on around you and inside of yourself. As you become aware you will discover that recognizing your current actions is extremely valuable to you. Notice the way you relate to yourself and are relating to other humans around you. Obtain a mentor and assimilate what the mentor teaches you. After a while you will skillfully learn to convert what works compared to what you are doing now that does not work. The process is simple so keep it simple. Simple changes will make tremendous shifts that directly improve your health, wealth, and relationships.

By doing such a self-examination and inventory means you are taking new actions. These new actions will teach you about yourself if you are open and ready to take advantage of the lessons you learn. Do not wait till later. You have put this off for too long already. Start doing this immediately. Step back and pick one thing you have learned and begin to apply it to your life. Pick one concept, process, principle, or ingredient and write it down. Next make a list of all the creative ways that you can specifically apply it to your life as it is now. Take the top one and start doing it. Practice doing it until it becomes a habit for you. Then pick another and repeat the process. Remember only focus on the next step. The three ingredients which are absolutely required for continuous change and success in any human pursuit never change.

The three part process that leads to success:
1 – Self Inspiration and Motivation will lead to taking Beneficial Action.
2 – Real "Understanding" comes from a decisive "Why" to begin with.
3 – Learn all Activity Knowledge by Practice or with a Mentor's Direction

Activity knowledge is factual knowledge and truth of the activity, service, product, method, techniques and skills that directly relate to your particular interests. Find a mentor to master what works faster. Gaining activity knowledge requires active thinking, planning, and study time with regularity. This means using your conscious mind to affect the amazing powers of your subconscious mind. "Understanding" is the particular techniques and skills that consistently get results for you when applied. The application of these particular techniques and skills takes practice in learning and using them. You will learn only by honest trial and error.

The proper application of factual knowledge and truth is what you must practice. By practice "understanding" becomes habit. Practice is the actual repetitive use of knowledge. For many often give up and quit way before practicing enough. Before enough practice has been done the habit has not be learned and formed. The desire for quick results is a trap that leads to long term failure. Learn that lesson and you will be willing to pay your dues and put the time in to practice, practice, and more practice. In practice you learn the correct method that brings you repeated results.

Everything thought must be put into action. Inspiration and motivation to action is an inside job. Your internal drive comes from within and you alone can light that fire. Other humans may "charge you up" but until you can generate inspiration and motivation at will on your own taking meaningful actions will not last. No one can tell you what motivates you into action. Only you know what inspires you and makes the fire in you burn bright. You must want and have the desire to make things happen inside of you.

Life is full of challenges to aid us in growth. The ability to take a disadvantage and find the hidden advantage takes practice. For there is an advantage to be had from every disadvantage. This is where a beneficial mental attitude develops strength and endurance. With every adversity or challenge there is a seed of an increased or equivalent benefit. It is your choice to find the seed and burry that lesson's knowledge inside of you so that the experience can grow in you providing you the fruits of such learning opportunities.

Memorize, comprehend, and apply any and all principles that will aid you in developing a beneficial mental attitude. A beneficial mental attitude is only a benefit to you if it can be done at will. Radom application of a beneficial mental attitude is just as non-beneficial as not having one. In this instance there is only one set of options. Be either all in and on, or not all in and off. The choice is yours and that has never changed.

Turn your self-talk or internal dialogue into beneficial self-suggestion. Success can only be achieved by those who try and do. Keep trying and do not stop trying until you have discovered what works for you particular set of interests. For there is nothing to lose by trying and always something to be gained. You gain knowledge of what works and what does not work.

Perception

"The way that you view your life and your world shapes you."

YOU

Everything in human reality is governed by the way a person perceives oneself, the situations that are experienced in day to day life and the way the outside world affects the inner world of that person. *The understanding of who you are, the way you function, and the way you operate directly affects your ability to make wise choices and observe the world with crystal clear perception of the moment.*

WHO ARE YOU?

Take a few moments to think, speak or write a short answer to this question, as if you were introducing yourself to someone for the first time. In what ways would the words that you chose to describe yourself reveal the way you define yourself? When you describe yourself to different audiences, do you sometimes leave out details you do not want others to know about you? Have you ever hesitated or felt uncomfortable when describing yourself to others whom you think may not share your interests or viewpoints? Do you emphasize some parts of your self-description more than others? <u>Why do you think you do such things?</u>

Oftentimes, our concern that another may not accept us will prompt us to alter our behavior. If you perceive that another human does not align to you own beliefs or views what do you do? Do you convince yourself to modify the way you present yourself? Humans do this as an attempt to influence the other human or humans to change their perception of us. However, when you spend time with humans that have similar interests or beliefs as our own, humans tend to freely share more details about themselves. With the promise of acceptance or alignment (*and without the fear of rejection*), human become eager to foster a connection. *It is the strength of our character (as reflected by our attitude) that determines the degree to which you allow the fear of rejection to influence the way you define yourself.*

The key to self-understanding is to know who you are deep within you. The core of what makes you happy, inspires you to want to accomplish great things and contribute to the world we all share is rooted in the way you define "you". Believe it or not, your own perception of "you" directly controls your life. What defines "you" is generated by <u>you</u> and how much comes from that which <u>others have placed upon you</u>? What connotations do you or others attach when you express such things as: Your name, age, job title, marital status, single, political or religious views, interests, friends or associations, and where you live?

Regardless of the way others view you or the way you perceive yourself to be, you can ultimately only be yourself (*"The True You"*). *You can try to present yourself as something else, but you can never completely be anything except your true, inner self.*

The true self is the thinking and emotional feeling entity behind the wheel of "YOU". It has the ultimate power to define and control you and your world. The "Perceived Self" is that which you believe yourself to be. It is that which you have defined. It is a reflection of the influences that you have allowed through the sum of your experiences.

Take a moment to think about the graphic below:

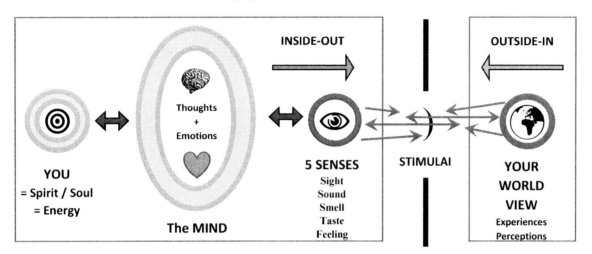

Humans define who they are by their experiences. Our experiences have been created from a constant and immense flow of stimuli that have been bombarding our senses since before we were born. Some stimuli are ignored, some are reflected back and some are filtered through our senses. *The stimuli that are picked up and passed through the senses become recorded and "interpreted" by the brain. From the collection of interpreted information, your brain creates a "reference library" which you use to define yourself and the world around you.*

In the natural world, animals process the stimuli from the world around them and react based on instinctual behavior. They do this for the purpose of their own survival. While some animals can develop behaviors based on simple, "learned" experiences and some can even form relationships with their own and other species, the way they process information is simple and functional, thus pure and in harmony with Nature.

Humans, on the other hand, have replaced much of their instinctive behavior with conscious decisions. We have the unique ability to develop complex concepts and ideas. We can truly "think" in a way unlike any other living thing on our planet. The decisions humans make can be driven by logic, learned behavior or relationships, or they can come from purely human factors like emotions or societal references. While animals in the natural world are forced to live at the edge of their senses, using instinct and learned behaviors to stay alive, we have the ability to use conscious thought. This allows us to make decisions that go beyond purely supporting our own survival.

Unfortunately, many of us forget that we have a "Conscious Self" or a "Mind" driving our brains and our bodies. Humans act as if their bodies represent their inner self. In fact humans merely operate the body, but humans are not their body. Some humans even "camp out" on the edge of their senses, absorbing all of the stimuli coming in and reacting to it, as if the outside world controls us, rather than the other way around.

Our senses and our bodies serve a very important purpose in our lives. They allow us to have a "human experience", so that we might better understand our world, operate effectively within it and contribute to its evolution. The best chance we have to maximize our human experience is to get the most mileage and performance from the bodies we have been given. To optimize our bodies' performance, we must maintain them in the same way we would a vehicle we plan to keep for many years.

In fact, the analogy of a human body to a vehicle can be applied on many levels. Consider your inner self as the pilot of your own body – fueling it, servicing it, maintaining it, reading its gauges for signs of trouble or fatigue. With this analogy in mind, look around you at your fellow humans and try to determine whose vehicle is truly road worthy for the long haul. What is the condition of the human body vehicle you are piloting? Are you the pilot, or do you let the vehicle drive you?

SHADOW SELF

Even though humans have only one "Self" inside, each human has the ability to project an image of themselves that differs from their "Inner Self" or "True Self". A human can create and develop this "Projected Self" as a reflection of the true self or a human can alter the projection to reflect something different. The "Shadow-Self" is perceived and projected by the human. In most cases the human has no knowledge that the human is even projecting anything let alone an "Un-True" perceived version of themselves. Humans can also choose to perceive themselves as either the "True Self or the "Projected Self". Those that view the outer world and its influences as the architect of the "Projected Self", choose to ignore that the "True Self" even exists this is what it means to have an OUTSIDE-IN world view. Whereas the human that are their "True Self" hold an INSIDE-OUT world view.

The "Perceived Self" is actually the "Shadow Self" because what you perceive to be that is not true casts a shadow over you. The "Shadow-Self" that you project outward is the shadow other humans meet. Unless you perceive that you are doing this the "Shadow-Self" over takes the inner light of the true you or the "True-Self". Do you know if you are being true to you or casting a perception you want others to see. So "Who are **YOU**?"

Which of these world mindsets are you living in?

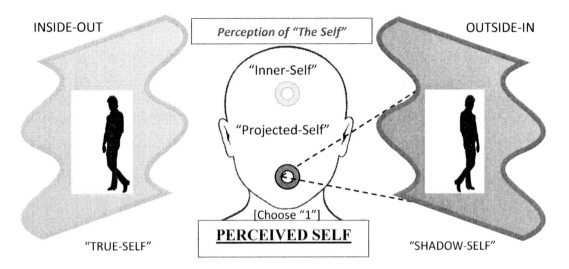

INSIDE-OUT

OUTSIDE-IN

Perception of "The Self"

"Inner-Self"

"Projected-Self"

[Choose "1"]

PERCEIVED SELF

"TRUE-SELF"

"SHADOW-SELF"

The outside world and humans you interact with provide you the impression of what you think you need to be. The outer world does not know the inner you nor does it care, yet humans bestow the power to depict their self-worth by this world mindset. *Only when you grasp and understand that acceptance comes from within can you liberate yourself, and in doing so, permit others to see your true purpose, your significance, and your real "True-Self".*

To ultimately take control of your own life, you must consciously choose to allow your "Projected-Self" to become your "True-Self" you must defeat the "Shadow-Self". By you doing so, the "True-Self" re-defines the "Projected-Self", instead of allowing the outside world to define their opinion of your "Shadow-Self". The challenge that is faced by most humans is the internal struggle with which you are and who you think you should be. This difficulty in overcoming this challenge leads us to see our own reflection through the eyes of others.

By acknowledging the two selves within you; by recognizing that you have the power to re-craft the "Projected-Self"; and by choosing to allow the "True-Self" to be the only light that shines from within you, you become the *"Conscious Self"* that shapes your own world and you eliminate the "Shadow-Self". So "Who are **YOU**, really?" Do you know who you are being yet? Are you being your "True-Self"? Are you projecting an image that others see that is your "Shadow-Self"? Do you live at the edge of your own senses or are you the consciously being the human that defines you and drives your own thoughts and emotional feelings?

PERCIEVED INFORMATION

Over a period of time, the information that comes in consistently becomes recorded as "truth" or "reality". This process is necessary for humans to move beyond the basics, to operate in your day-to-day lives and to advance toward working out more complex concepts.

For most humans, once the "truth" is established, it is rarely challenged as anything else. The process of establishing "truth" or "reality" can even be accelerated, so that we might move quickly to other topics. In your eagerness to process the next information coming in, you sometimes choose to accept something as being true without putting the information through a "thorough review". *Is the information a fact, an opinion, or someone's theory? That is the question to ask yourself about information.*

Society will utilize the mechanics of this process to reinforce societal norms. Some norms are established as a function of law to create and maintain stability. Other norms of society may exist to convince humans to be or do something they are not.

Sometimes there are elements within the society that will attempt to influence the whole society by convincing society to form unified references. These unified references act as if they were facts but in fact these are opinions or theories used to miss-direct, miss-inform, and to control a hidden truth. This is often done to bring unique advantage to those particular elements and indirectly eliminating the competition. These types of references are more effectively placed upon a society when the promoters of the messages are widely accepted by the majority of the recipients. This is the appearance of the "popular" or "celebrity" that knows nothing but is merely "acting" a part in the bigger "play". Humans for some reason take hold of this "entertainment" as reality and never know that they have been taken advantage of the whole time. Call this "political" magic or "sleight of hand" with make-up, cameras, and light.

While your perception of truth or reality takes form within you, in fact most everything just *is* ("is" being neutral). Even the idea of some things being "good" or "evil" are concepts that have been created by humans to bring meaning and societal control over individuals' actions. This is not to say that defining things in this way has not brought benefit to our societies. This point is simply to remind you that these concepts were created by humans for a purpose. Recognizing this can help you understand the way you and others are being influenced.

Now consider the words "can" and "cannot". Most people see "can" as a positive and "cannot" as a negative. In fact, both words are positive. When one says something "can" be done or someone "can" do something, they are affirming what they believe to be true. The same holds true when one says something "cannot" be done or someone "cannot" do something – simply affirming a perceived truth. Whether in fact something can or cannot be done or someone can or cannot do something is irrelevant. It is the positive affirmation that is driving the perception and therefore influencing the outcome. And by accepting that something cannot occur or be, the potential becomes a commitment. *"Cannot do"* can reflect the choice *"I do not want to do"*. The active person does not see "cannot". The active person only believes in "can".

When it comes to human experiences and the way we act upon the information given to us, our decisions in life can be viewed as either active or passive. When you consciously make your own decisions and act upon them, you are being active. When you wait for or expect someone else to make decisions or take actions for you, you are being passive. If you choose to be passive, regardless of the degree, you will never maximize your abilities. Only the active, conscious self can shape her/his own world as she/he intends.

PERCEPTION PROVIDES CONTROL
So the world around you (as you perceive it) is defined by you and is actually under your control! This is not to say that external individuals and groups will not continue their attempts to influence you. It does not mean that unfortunate events or difficult times will not come your way. But it means your ability to control the way you react to, prepare for, avoid or seek out all situations becomes solely within your own power.

It is vitally important to grasp this concept from the perspective of the conscious self, and the way it has the ultimate influence over an individual's actions and decisions and even one's own view of reality. It must be observed from the point of view of defining one's world from within (i.e., conscious thought), rather than allowing one's world to be influenced and defined from the outside. Once you gain this perception clearly and consistently, **hold onto it**, as it will become your key to becoming awake and aware.

REALIGNED POWER - EMPOWERMEN
Once you realize that you have the ultimate influence and control over your decisions and actions (and in turn, your ability to achieve whatever you want), you will need to practice using this "power" in your daily life. This is important to ensure the perception "sticks" and becomes part of your normal way of functioning. Part of this practice will be done by going into the "Observer Mode" (*explained later*).

After you have gained a fully realigned perspective, your life will change. This may sound overly profound or "too good to be true". However, recognize that a newly gained perception of one's world, by definition, means *that world* (one's own life) will change. This new perception will also bring about clarity with regards to the way your world works and the way the people in your world influence you. With your new perspective fully in place, do not be surprised when new things happen to you. You may start to notice "sign posts" or "markers" that lead you to new opportunities. Of course, you will need to recognize the markers and actively shape what you do with the information.

Your thoughts will guide you to where you need to go, but you must actually "think" to make anything happen. While many of us do not fully utilize our ability to actively think, our capacity for active thinking is boundless. Dreams, ideas and decisions (and what you become from them) are only limited by your imagination. You could say *"From our thoughts springs our being"*.

Consider the things in your life that will affect your perception of your world: Here are some examples

- People in your life (*including family and friends*)
- Society and the communicators of the societal norms
- The way you choose to accept incoming information
- Your decisions of the way you portray yourself to others

You should constantly consider who and what is influencing you and why. This will help you maintain your perception. Regardless of the intention of the influencer or the perceived benefit from the influence itself, being aware of it will allow you to control your reaction to it. Use this awareness of influence to make decisions that benefit you, not the influencer.

CYCLES

COLOR

Every complete cycle forms a closed loop. A completely geometrically balanced perfect closed loop is a circle. Cycle do not always look like circles but this drawing depicts the basics. Consider a rainbow which perfectly depicts the full visual light color spectrum. Remember that light is an energy vibration frequency. So everything that humans see is actually the energy vibration frequency emitted by an object.

The color black is the longest wave length and the lowest frequency. The color white is the shortest wave length and has the highest frequency. Both black and white are contrast colors of the same spectrum that provides contextual shape making up the gray scale. There are 7 colors that make up the rainbow. These same colors make up the 7 human energy fields.

PICTURE # 1 (Page 79)

A cycles actually go counter clockwise and begins going downward. The rainbow pictured is mirrored to provide a colorful explanation. In this illustration an energy particle is starting from the place of rest in balance or point "0" the particle wave moves towards imbalance or point "1". The energy particle moves towards lower equilibrium or point "2" then starts its journey upwards towards imbalance "3". Once half a cycle wave is complete the energy particle passes through a place of mid-balance or point "4" starting the second half of the cycle. The energy particle then moves towards imbalance or point "5" heading towards upper equilibrium or point "6". The energy particle then passes through imbalance or point "7" the final stage of the cycle until the energy particle comes back to the starting point of balance or point "0". The "0" point is the beginning and the end of every cycle.

Below the cycle loop is the graphical equivalent to the path explained above. The length from the beginning of the wave to the end before the cycle repeats is called the wavelength of the balance x-plane. The height of the wave is measured from the equilibrium to the balance x-plane. The wave height is the same above the balance x-plane as below and is called the amplitude. The wavelength is the **_INTENSITY_** (X-Plane) and the amplitude is the **_POWER_** (Y-Plane) of the wave. The number of times the cycle repeats is called the **_DURATION_** (Repetition) of the wave.

PICTURE # 2 (Page 80)

Illustrates the 7 Year Cycle and provide a visual representation for better understanding.

PICTURE # 3 (Page 81)

Illustrates the 7 Year Cycle over 3 cycles a period of 21 year.

PICTURE # 4 (Page 82)

Illustrates the 7 Year Cycle over 7 Cycles or 49 Years. The odd number of cycles of 7 provides for cycles to link with each other or overlap because every cycle wave has a down and an upside.

CYCLE LOOP

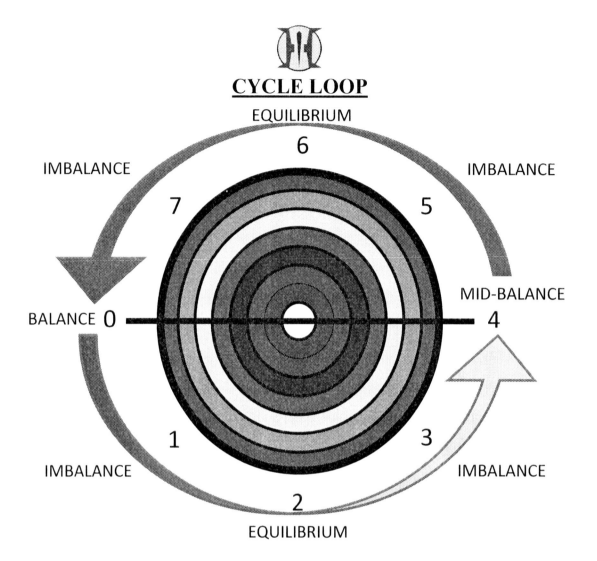

EQUILIBRIUM

6

IMBALANCE

IMBALANCE

7

5

BALANCE 0

MID-BALANCE 4

1

3

IMBALANCE

IMBALANCE

2

EQUILIBRIUM

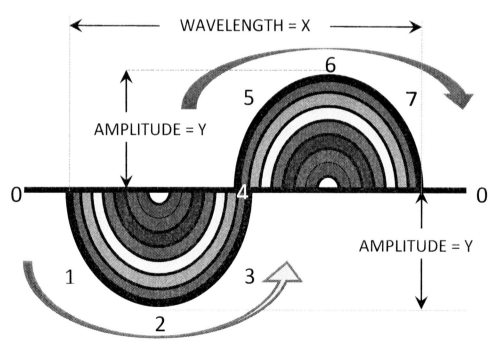

WAVELENGTH = X

6

5

7

AMPLITUDE = Y

0

4

0

1

3

2

AMPLITUDE = Y

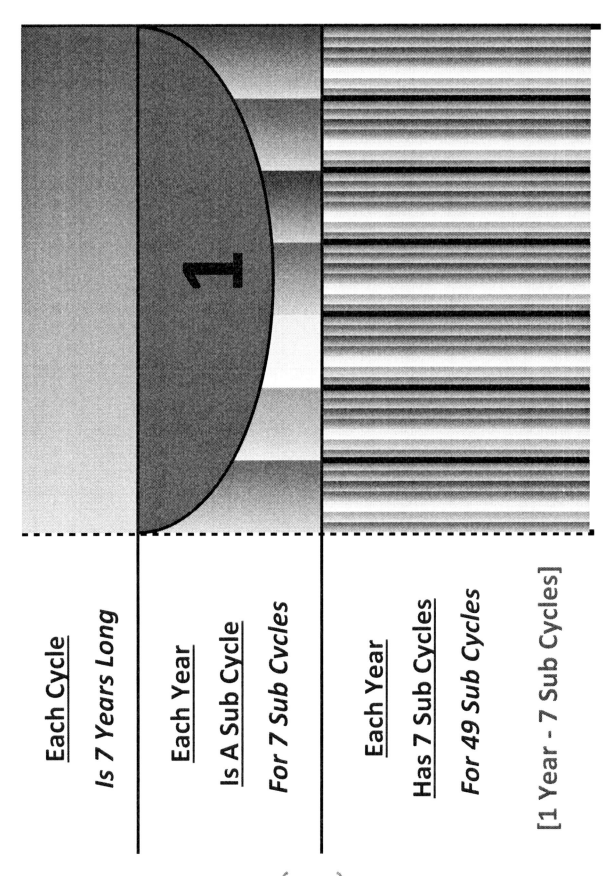

Each Cycle
Is 7 Years Long

Each Year
Is A Sub Cycle
For 7 Sub Cycles

Each Year
Has 7 Sub Cycles
For 49 Sub Cycles

[1 Year – 7 Sub Cycles]

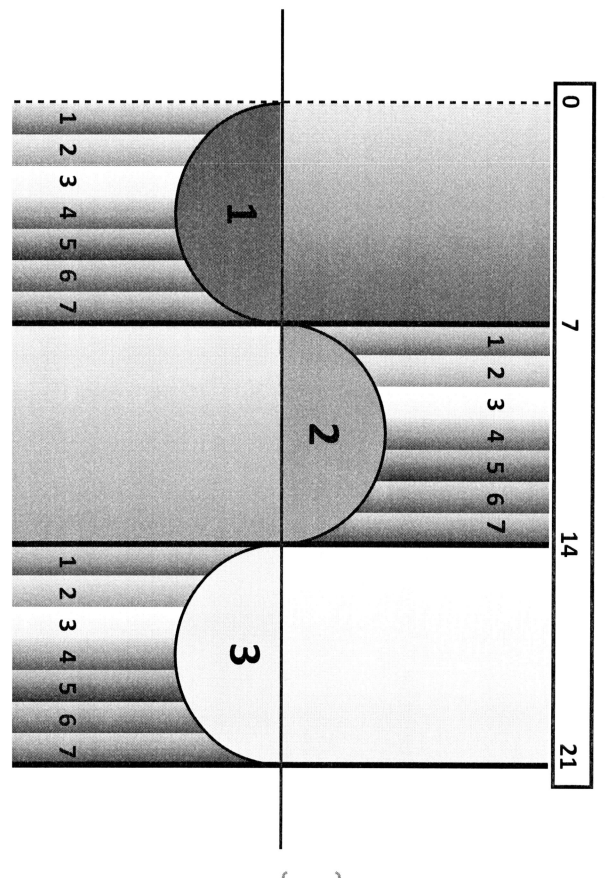

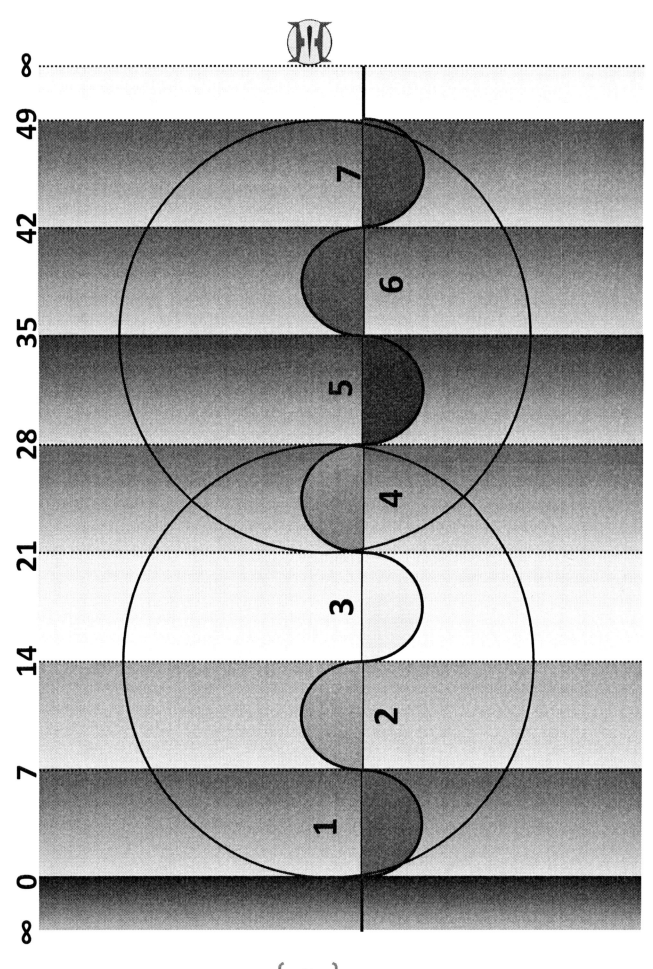

HUMAN BODY ENERGY FIELD CYCLES

The following pictures give a set of visual explanations that relate to human experiences in life.

PICTURE # 5 (Page 84)
Illustrates the 7 colors, 7 cycles, and the 7 human energy fields with the 4th color green as the center.

PICTURE # 6 (Page 85)
Illustrates the human experience relative to the conscious mind, unconscious mind, and time.

PICTURE # 7 (Page 86)
Illustrates the human being standing with the ground below and the sky above.

PICTURE # 8 (Page 87)
Illustrates the difference between high and low energy vibration frequencies plus the hour glass of time.

PICTURE # 9 (Page 88)
Illustrates the hour glass as an energy focal point making the human heart an energy lens for the body

PICTURE # 10 (Page 89)
Illustrates the energy lens activated. The energy lens is what powers the body's ability to emit, transmit and receive energy vibration frequencies.

PICTURE # 11 ((Page 90)
Illustrates cosmic energy entering the human body through the top of the head where the human's 7th energy field is located. The higher energy flows downwards to the heart energy field.

PICTURE # 12 (Page 91)
Illustrates the cosmic energy moving through the human body with energy moving out the hands and feet. The full visual light spectrum inside the human is constantly receiving this cosmic energy.

PICTURE # 13 (Page 92)
Illustrates the effect of the 4th human energy field with the significance and meaning of the primary color green and the secondary color pink. The 4th energy field is the only energy field that has a secondary color. This is all the more important to understanding the human relationship with nature.

PICTURE # 14 (Page 93)
Illustrates the male and female side each human has and their relationship with the gray color scale.

PICTURE # 15 (Page 94)
Illustrates details that are related to natural and unnatural romantic human relationships.

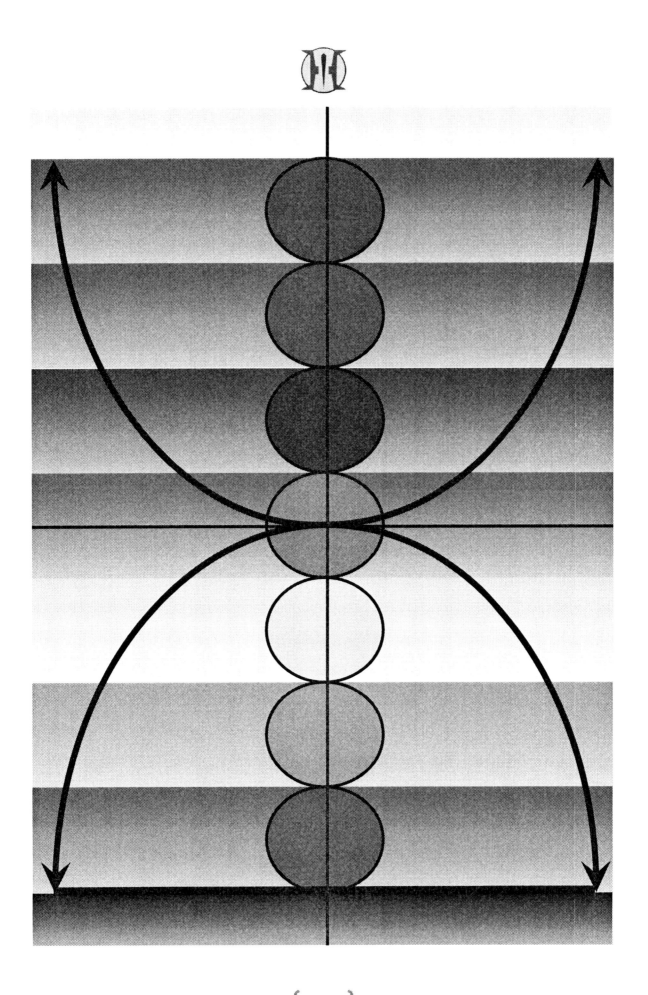

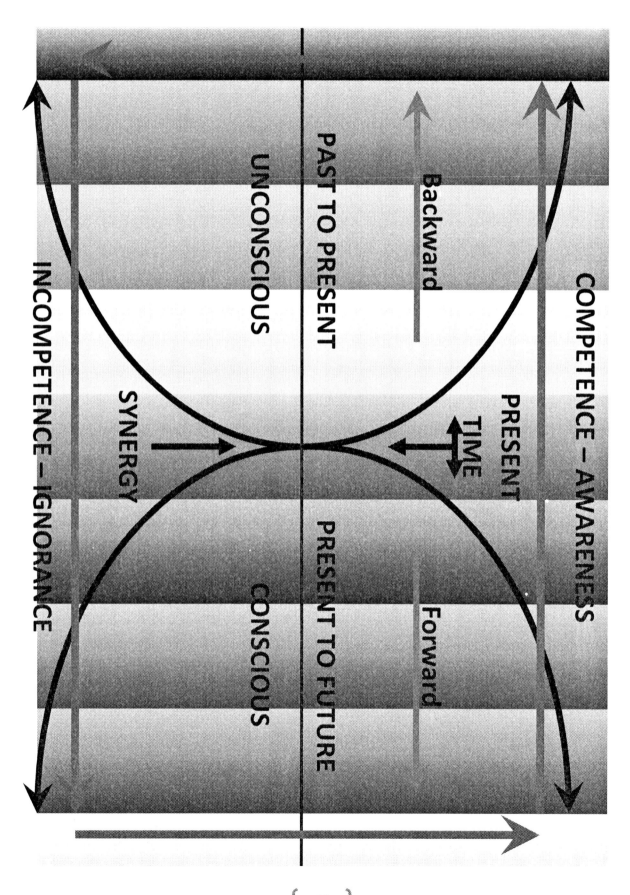

SKY – WHITE – LIGHT – HIGH VIBRATION

EARTH – BLACK – DARK – LOW VIBRATION

SKY – WHITE – LIGHT – HIGH VIBRATION

EARTH – BLACK – DARK – LOW VIBRATION

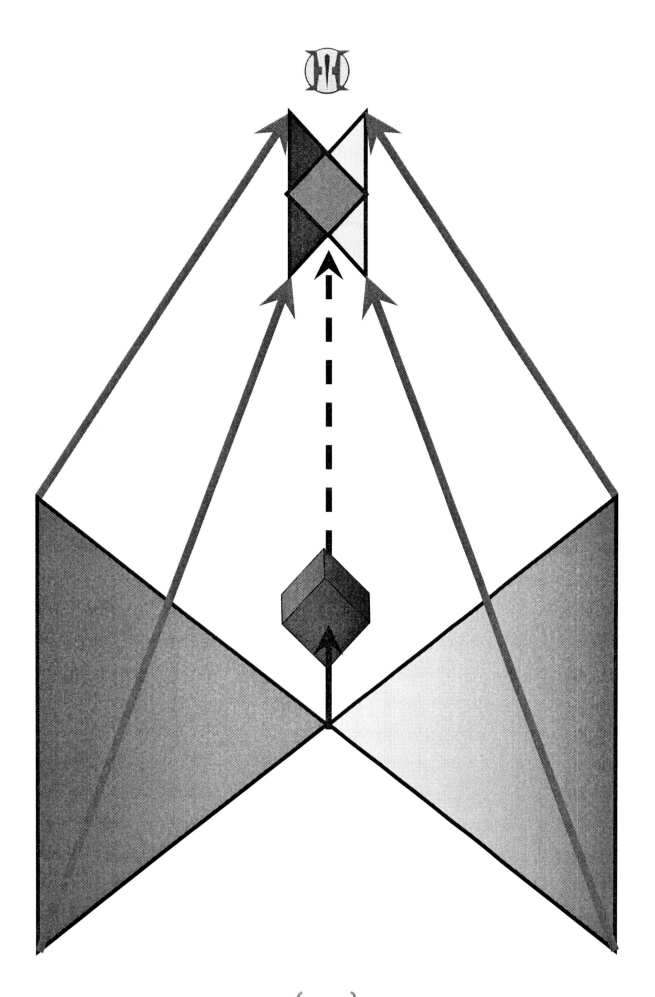

SKY – WHITE – LIGHT – HIGH VIBRATION

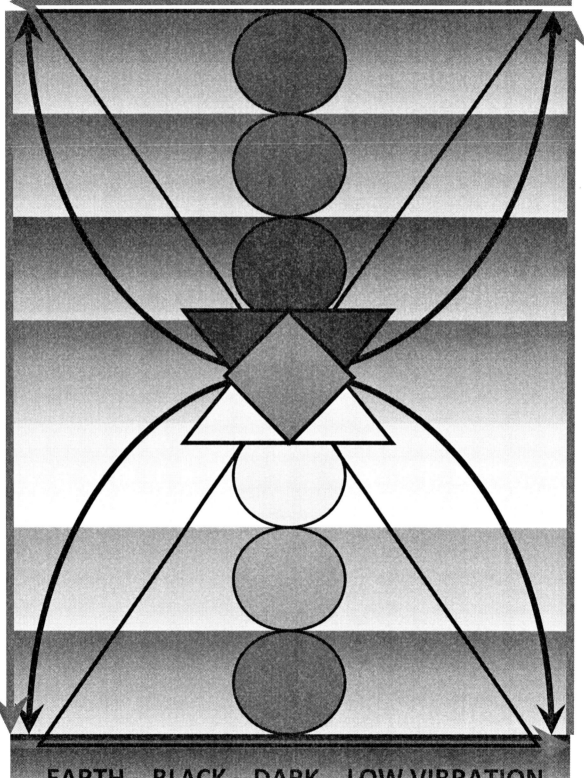

EARTH – BLACK – DARK – LOW VIBRATION

SKY – WHITE – LIGHT – HIGH VIBRATION

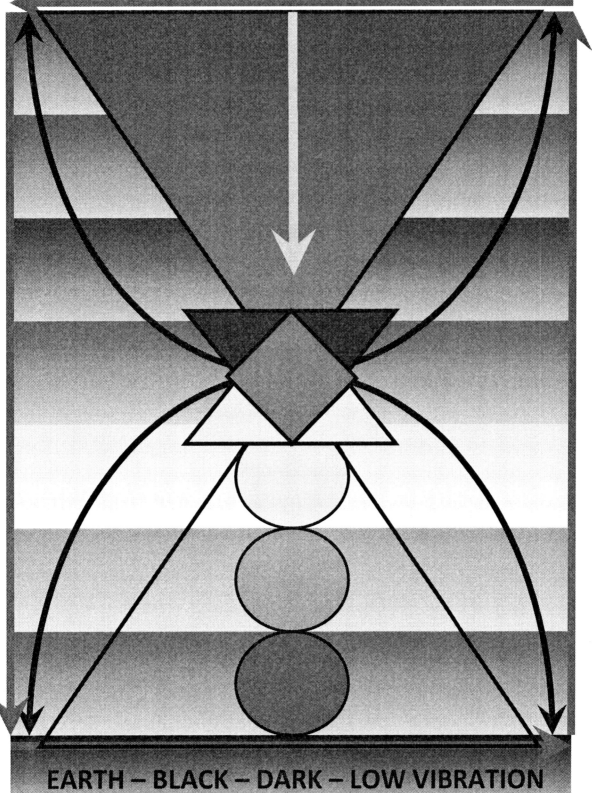

EARTH – BLACK – DARK – LOW VIBRATION

EARTH – BLACK – DARK – LOW VIBRATION

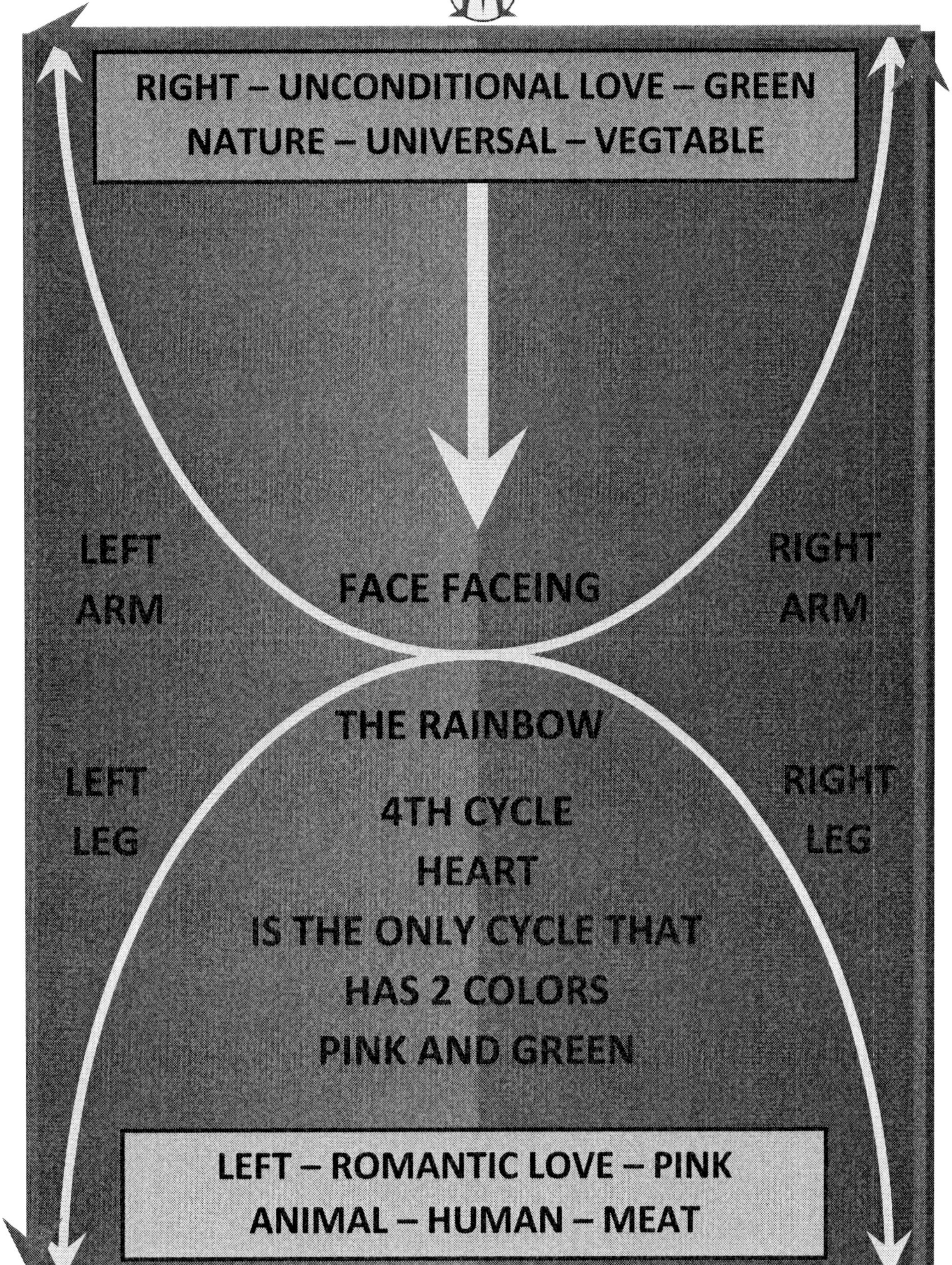

RIGHT – UNCONDITIONAL LOVE – GREEN
NATURE – UNIVERSAL – VEGTABLE

LEFT
ARM

FACE FACEING

RIGHT
ARM

THE RAINBOW

LEFT
LEG

4TH CYCLE

HEART

IS THE ONLY CYCLE THAT

HAS 2 COLORS

PINK AND GREEN

RIGHT
LEG

LEFT – ROMANTIC LOVE – PINK
ANIMAL – HUMAN – MEAT

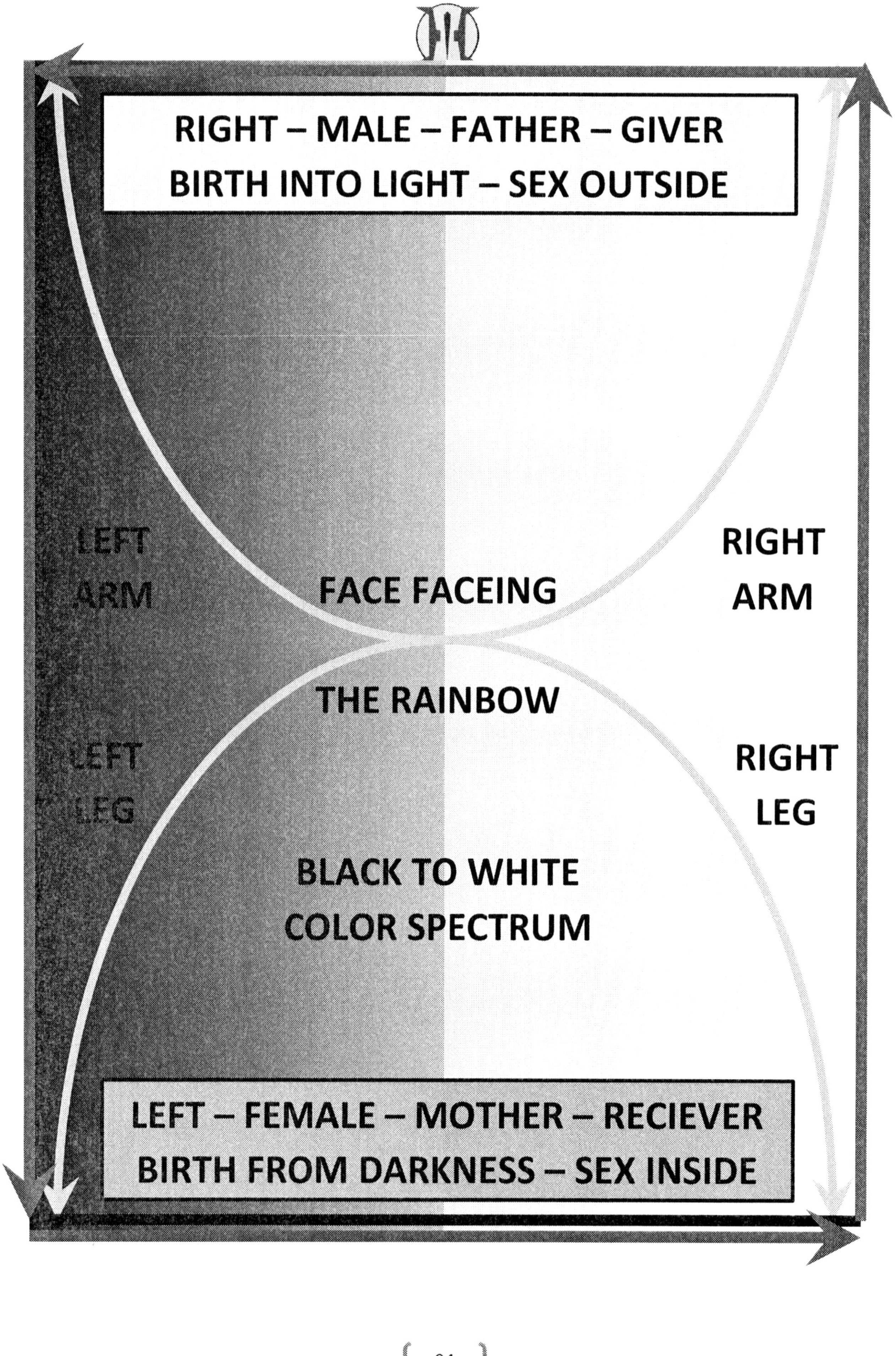

RIGHT – MALE – FATHER – GIVER
BIRTH INTO LIGHT – SEX OUTSIDE

LEFT
ARM

RIGHT
ARM

FACE FACEING

THE RAINBOW

LEFT
LEG

RIGHT
LEG

BLACK TO WHITE
COLOR SPECTRUM

LEFT – FEMALE – MOTHER – RECIEVER
BIRTH FROM DARKNESS – SEX INSIDE

Humans have 11.5 (12) body systems. Coupled, a shared compete sex for 12. Duality gives 2 chromosomes for each system 11x2, 22 plus 1/2 x 2 = 1 For a total of 23, Each 23 x 2 = 46 {22/7 = PI} 1 Egg + 1 Sperm

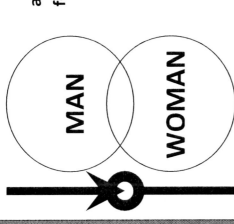

Unnatural Relationships

Result of an unnatural flow, *UNREAL LOVE*.

This unbalances the quarters into unequal halves. This depolarizes the man and woman, making an unbalanced hole of a half that holds both of them at odds.

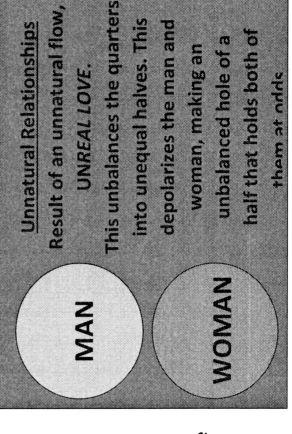

Man and Woman are facing Each other.
Both are 2 halves of a hole. Both are half halves complete.

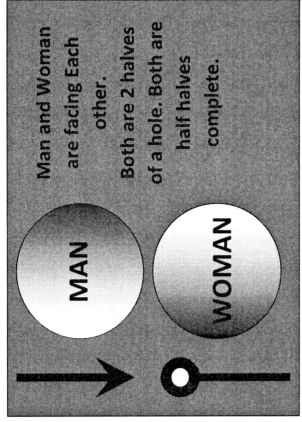

Natural Relationships

Result of natural flow and *REAL LOVE.*

This balances the quarters into equal halves. This polarizes the man and woman, making a complete hole of a half that holds them together.

LIFE CYCLES and COLOR

PICTURE # 16 (Page 96)
Illustrates a life cycle over 98 years. The life starts at point zero and ends at 98 for this example.

PICTURE # 17 (Page 97)
Illustrates the color spectrum. 7 cycles are half completes at 49 years then completes at 98.

PICTURE # 18 (Page 98)
Illustrates the cycles as markers in red. The cycle circle loop at year 21 signifies the adult stage of human life that generally declines in the late 70s. The half circle on either side are before and after cycles that connect to each other through the infinity of death to new life cycle.

PICTURE # 19 (Page 99)
Illustrates the continuation of the previous picture with the addition of "Links". These links start with orange, go to yellow, and to green. This balances the cycle circle with yellow and green. Now the first 4 colors of light are represented with red being markers that ground the linkages.

PICTURE # 20 (Page 100)
Illustrates the next progression of adding in the remaining 3 colors of light. The significance of there being 2 shades of blue become apparent as the sky blue and dark blue mix. In the human energy field these 2 cycle represent the air and the ether with are both invisible frequencies. The red links are added but note that the red link grounds the living live to the afterlife. The previous red marker are now black and white. Notice that the black is below and the white is above for the first 49 years and flips for the remaining 49 year to 98. This flip signifies what humans do not deal with in the first half of their lives will become the focus in the second.

PICTURE # 21 (Page 101)
Illustrates a 180 degree shift with time to show the way life and death are connected. If you take the previous picture any connect the infinity signs this is what you get. Meaning the cycles are part the bigger cycle or the torus of time as if both ends of the picture were connected, as you were to take a copy of this or the previous picture and tapped the paper's ends together

PICTURE # 22 (Page 102)
Illustrates the resolved upper and lower halves of the 7 colors. The first 4 colors represent the colors of earth and the remaining 3 colors represent the color of the sky. The rest is duality.

PICTURE # 23 (Page 103)
Illustrates the larger significance of theses cycles in the human life cycle brining the internal INSIDE-OUT experience with the external OUTSIDE-IN experience explaining the coexistence and significance in a human's life cycles. The growth of humans goes from grounding the body individually to the growth of a human with the larger role of their life with other humans.

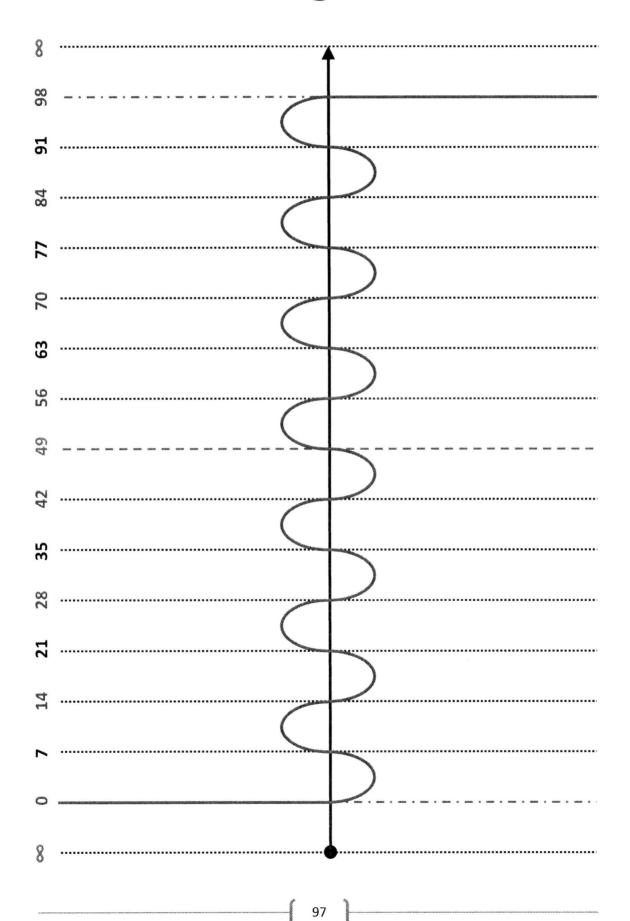

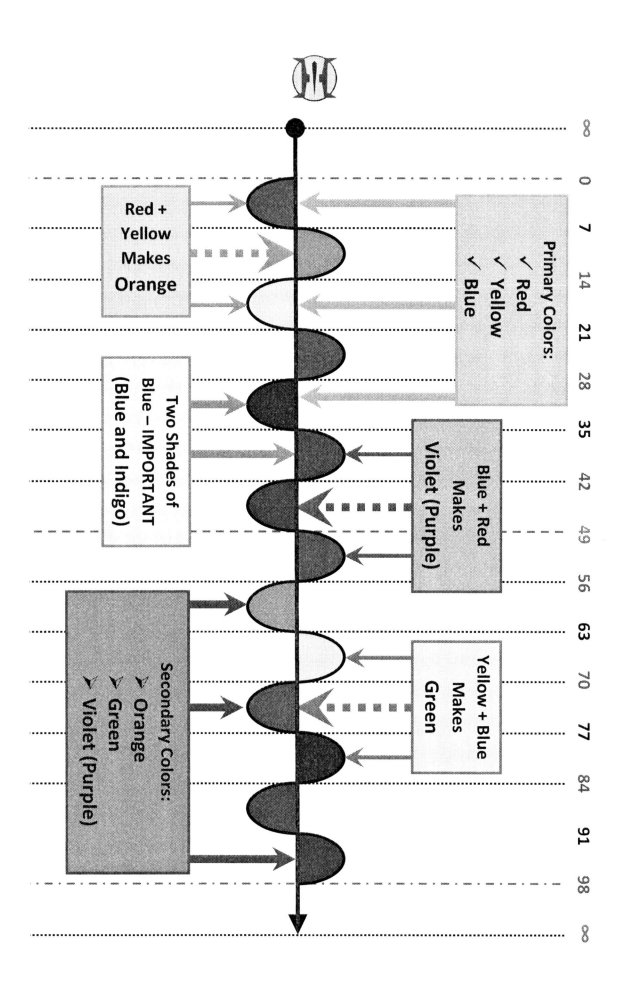

Primary Colors:
✓ Red
✓ Yellow
✓ Blue

Red +
Yellow
Makes
Orange

Two Shades of
Blue – IMPORTANT
(Blue and Indigo)

Blue + Red
Makes
Violet (Purple)

Yellow + Blue
Makes
Green

Secondary Colors:
✓ Orange
✓ Green
✓ Violet (Purple)

∞ 0 7 14 21 28 35 42 49 56 63 70 77 84 91 98 ∞

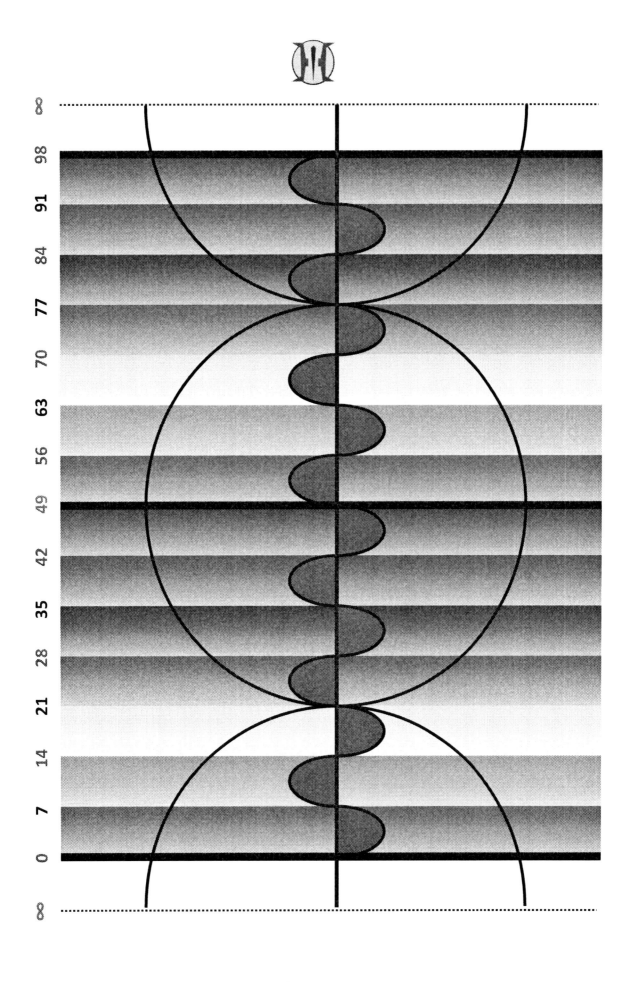

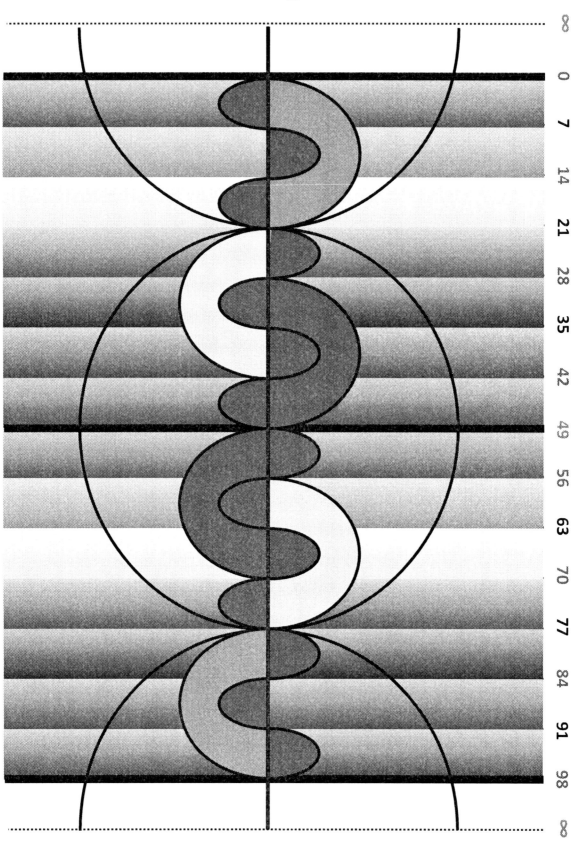

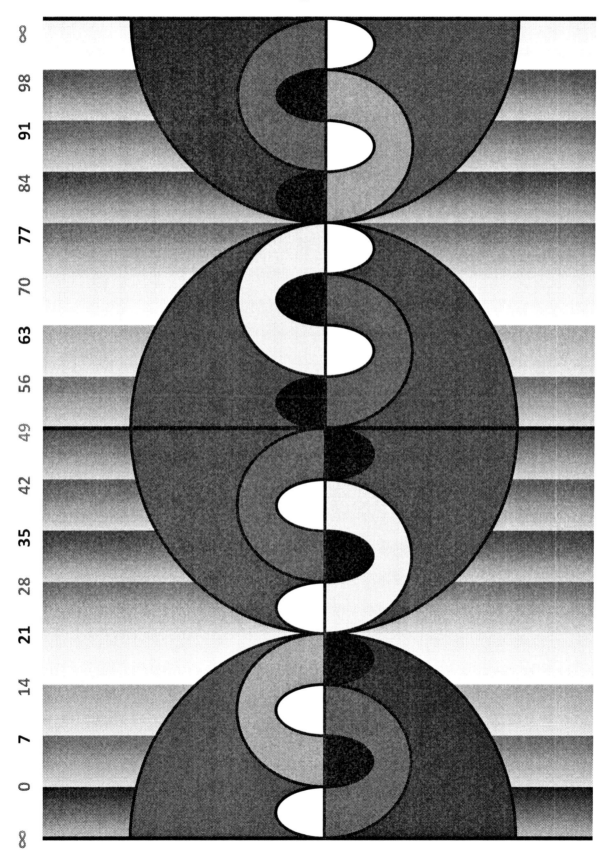

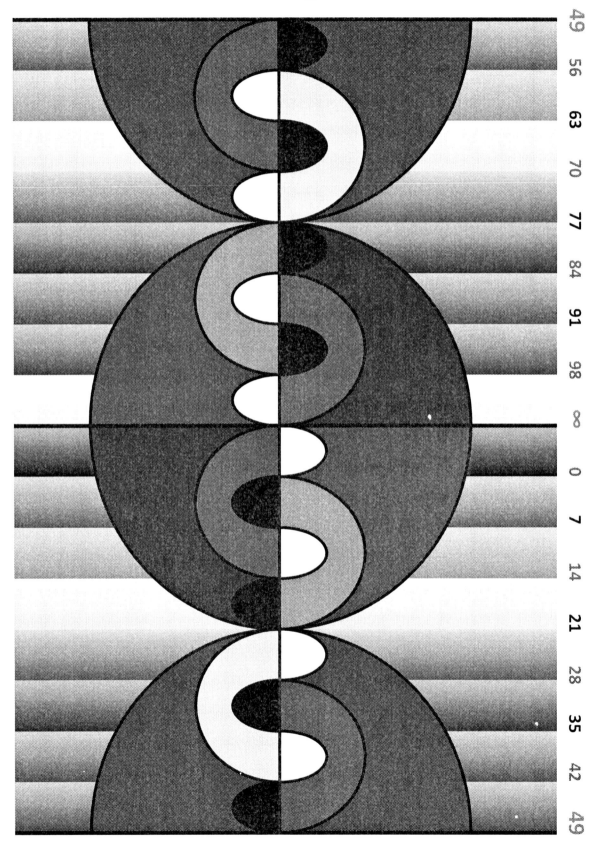

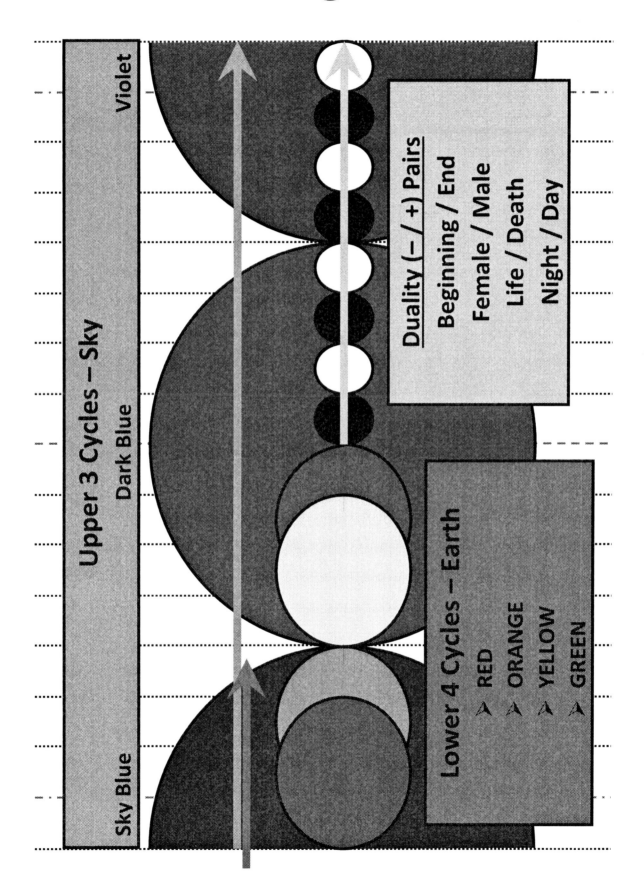

Upper 3 Cycles – Sky

Violet

Dark Blue

Sky Blue

Duality (– / +) Pairs

Beginning / End

Female / Male

Life / Death

Night / Day

Lower 4 Cycles – Earth

RED

ORANGE

YELLOW

GREEN

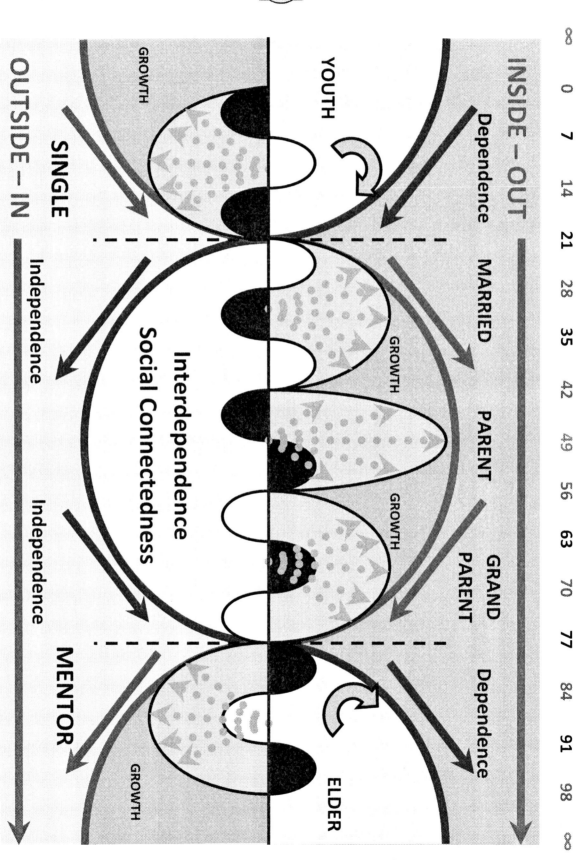

"The BRIDGE" and "The WALL"

There are three parts that make up the hole of human experience: mental or thought level of consciousness, emotional feedback component, and physical connection. The nature of duality creates the internal and external aspects of experience. There is a bridge between the external and internal worlds of reality that are naturally built to balance duality. Metaphorically that bridge is built in 7 stages, of 7 cycles, each stage having 7 bricks connected end to end with each stage lasting one year. After 7 years the bridge is as long as it is wide.

However there are blocks! The blocks are bricks that never made it to the building of "THE BRIDGE". The blocks are used to build "THE WALL" Have you ever noticed that about half of everything you were taught in life/school looks, sounds and feels backwards? Did anyone ever warn you about "The WALL"? Some life answers can be very elusive. Much of life does not make sense until you understand the reason for The WALL and why you built it.

Consider for a moment that during life you have only two options. It is simple really. Option one is to build a bridge between the cliff of your inner and exterior experiences by developing your mental and emotional maturity at least equal to physical maturity. The second is to build "The WALL" that blocks all your potential in life. You chose the building material: Bricks for the bridge or Blocks for "The WALL". As you age one grows larger than the other. The good news is a block can always be removed and made into a brick.

Typically sometime between the ages of 18 to 24 most people begin to notice "The WALL" is larger because it gets in their way. People will either back up against "The WALL" while facing that cliff in fear or will run and smack right into "The WALL" while trying to avoid the cliff. The WALL is nature's attempt to get your attention and acts like an alarm clock to tell you something is out of harmony with you. Either "WAKE UP" to start building that bridge or you will only be "DREAMING" of your potentials.

The WALL is the biggest elephant in the room and people rarely talk about it. Why? Because most people think that the experience is only happening to themselves. People feel trapped and it can be scary. It can feel like having the rug pulled out from under you, as your head falls between your legs, you are left wondering what happened, as all you thought you knew appears upside down. The majority of your dreams, desires and wants seem thrust up in the air becoming distantly elusive. That is what happens when you cannot develop your mental and emotional potentials. Build a wall or build a bridge. Learn the way to build your bridge and bring down your wall.

Next is a metaphoric depiction of what happens to humans when building the BRIDGE and the WALL. This metaphor helps humans understand the process that links cycles to bricks.

THE BRIDGE CONSTRCUTION

STAGE / CYCLE BRICK = Colors

| # 1 | # 2 | # 3 | # 4 | # 5 | # 6 | # 7 |

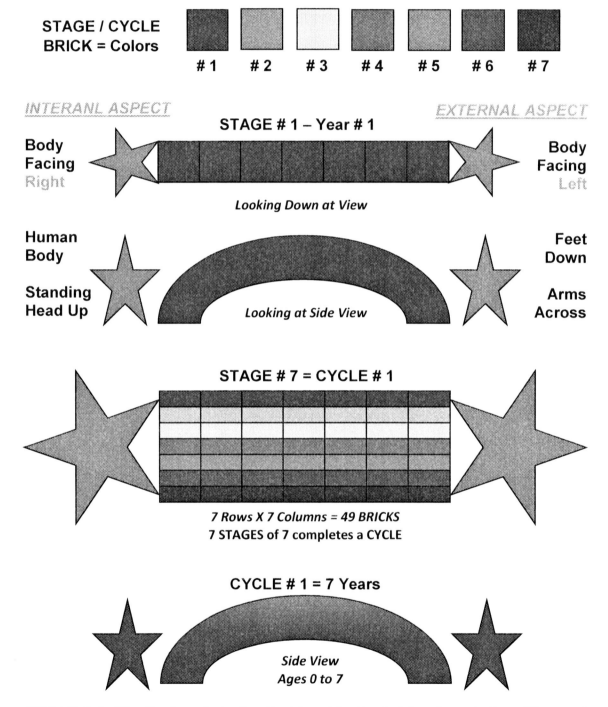

INTERANL ASPECT   *EXTERNAL ASPECT*

STAGE # 1 – Year # 1

Body Facing Right

Body Facing Left

Looking Down at View

Human Body

Standing Head Up

Feet Down

Arms Across

Looking at Side View

STAGE # 7 = CYCLE # 1

7 Rows X 7 Columns = 49 BRICKS
7 STAGES of 7 completes a CYCLE

CYCLE # 1 = 7 Years

Side View
Ages 0 to 7

CYCLE # 1: The first cycle is the first level to the bridge foundation. The next cycle builds below the existing level as understanding is created. This adds strength to the level above. This process continues till all 7 cycles are complete. The

THE BRIDGE CONSTRCUTION - CYCLES

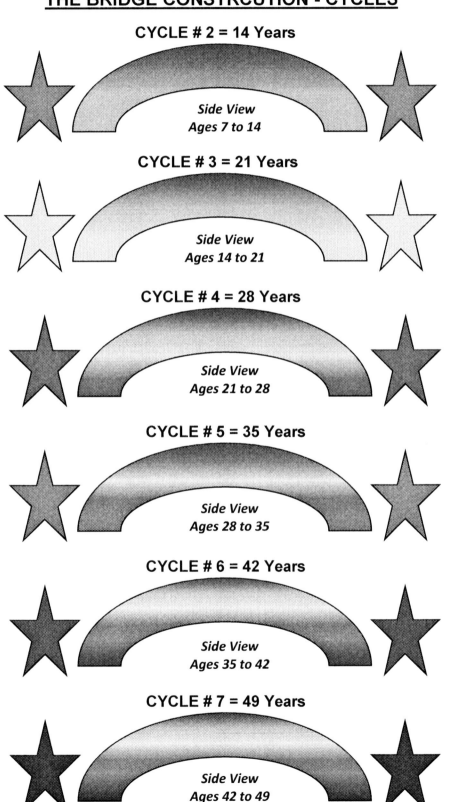

CYCLE # 2 = 14 Years

Side View
Ages 7 to 14

CYCLE # 3 = 21 Years

Side View
Ages 14 to 21

CYCLE # 4 = 28 Years

Side View
Ages 21 to 28

CYCLE # 5 = 35 Years

Side View
Ages 28 to 35

CYCLE # 6 = 42 Years

Side View
Ages 35 to 42

CYCLE # 7 = 49 Years

Side View
Ages 42 to 49

CYCLE # 7 completes the bridge. Making the entire bridge 7 bricks long, 7 bricks wide, and 7 bricks deep. The bridge is completed after 49 years.

THE BRIDGE CONSTRCUTION – BRICK or BLOCK

STAGE # 7 = CYCLE # 1 COMPLETE

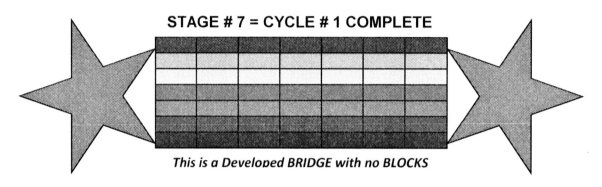

This is a Developed BRIDGE with no BLOCKS

During Bridge Construction
Some BRICKS Become BLOCKS

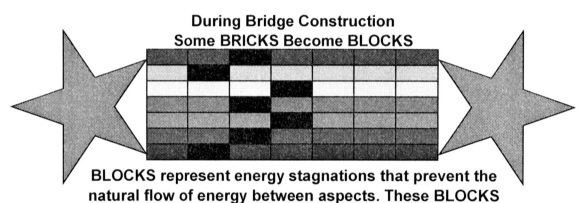

BLOCKS represent energy stagnations that prevent the natural flow of energy between aspects. These BLOCKS create ANTI-BRICKS that are used to build a safety WALL.

The BRIDGE is built LONG and DEEP

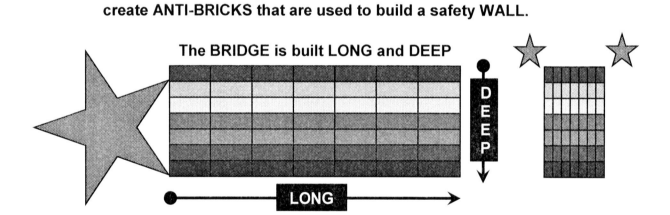

The WALL is built WIDE and TALL

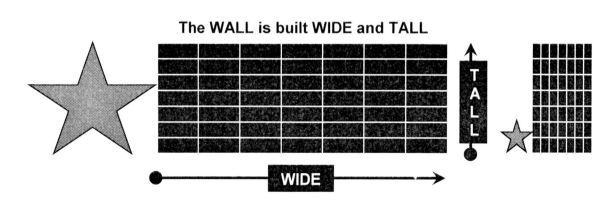

THE WALL CONSTRCUTION

INTERANL ASPECT

**Human
Body**

**Standing
Head Up**

EXTERNAL ASPECT

**Feet
Down**

**Arms
Across**

*The WALL is built from the BRIGDE base at 7 years old.
The WALL prevents the External Aspect from developing with
the Internal Aspect. BLOCKS are what build the WALL.*

The WALL builds one level per year or equal to the number of BLOCKS

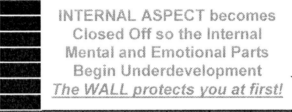

**Under
Developed
Aspect
begins
to fade**

INTERNAL ASPECT becomes
Closed Off so the Internal
Mental and Emotional Parts
Begin Underdevelopment
The WALL protects you at first!

**Over Development
Aspect
physical body
matures and
ages faster**

*The WALL pictured is 7 years of growth on top of the single
CYCLE # 1, in other works this human is 14 years of age*

*The WALL pictured is 16 years of growth on top of the single
CYCLE # 1, in other works this human is 16+7= 23 years of age*

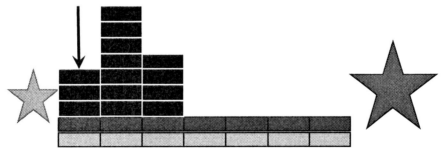

*The WALL pictured is 18 years of growth on top of CYCLE # 2,
4 levels of BLOCKS that are fixed start to fill in the built BRIDGE*

Awareness

"Becoming consciously awake to the true facts free you."

By understanding the process of perception within yourself and others, you can gain insight into the way others influence your thoughts and decisions. *Maintaining a consistent level of focus with regards to your perception will open the door to becoming aware of the world around you.* This will require that you always keep an open mind when considering information and ideas that come your way. Think of your mind as a parachute – it only works when it is open!

You must also remember that <u>*you don't know what you don't know*</u>. Your mind, your emotions, and your body are all working together to fill in the pieces to formulate what you believe to be true. *However, the total picture (as you believe it to be) may not always be completely accurate. You must be willing to accept that you may not know every aspect of what you see and believe as truth.* Always consider that what you are being told (or shown or taught) may have some elements of truth and may have some elements that are not true. Being humbly honest with yourself about the information you receive (and that which you may not receive) is essential to becoming fully awake to your world and aware of your surroundings.

Nature, in its pure form, is logical, ordered and simple. Before the development of human societies, everything on our planet existed in harmony and balance. Everything in Nature has a purpose and exists to serve that purpose. As humans too are of Nature, this also applies to humans who simply forgot this.

Below, are the five basic and unwavering truths that exist in Nature. *By understanding and observing these "Laws of Nature" or "Quantum Laws", you will become aware of the way you can operate in a manner consistent with Nature, and thereby maneuver with ultimate effectiveness as you navigate through your life.*

PERSONAL LIMITATIONS
Emotions can restrict our abilities to function properly, thereby limiting our capacity to realize our full potential. Just as our own thoughts can influence the world around us, we can also develop emotional barriers that hold us back from realizing our full potential. *Emotions such as worry, guilt, remorse and shame can stifle feelings of self-worth and self-confidence.*

However, not all emotional barriers are damaging. Sometimes, they help to create a buffer to protect you from immediate emotional pain. Some barriers are natural and allow you a moment of rest, reflection and peace before jumping in again. Some may provide a time to find balance and become level headed.

Having emotions is part of being human and expressing them is natural. *The key is to first understand what within you is bringing them to be expressed.* Only then can you take control of that process and use them to their full advantage (*in the same manner as your thoughts*). ***Emotions by themselves are never wrong.*** *Understand them and utilize their energy to bring them into action.*

FEAR

Why do you fear? The emotion of fear plays a very important role in humans. Fear of personal harm is an instinctual mechanism designed to protect our bodies, thus promoting our survival. This *instinctual fear* is "hard-wired" into our primal survival mechanisms. Because the only purpose of this type of fear is to protect the body, it is the only worthwhile type, if the threat to the body is reasonable.

Most fear is learned and not actually real. Rather, it is our mind imagining something that has not yet happened. *If something cannot physically hurt you, you are allowing your mind to convince you that the emotion is beneficial, when in fact, it is not.* One should not downplay the serious nature of fear, in terms of its ability to incapacitate a person. For some, fear of emotional and mental abuse is as real and life-threatening as a knife at the throat.

To overcome fear, you must first understand why you are feeling fear. Try to determine the external trigger of the fear within you. Use your perception to discover the source within you that reacts to the trigger and separate the two elements. If something cannot physically harm you, then it is up to you to re-program yourself to not be controlled by it. For some, this will not be an easy or quick task. In fact, many may find overcoming fear to be a long and difficult journey.

LIES

Why do humans tell lies? Why do human lie to themselves? While not an emotion, a lie can have the same binding impact on us. Like the emotions, it can limit our ability to function naturally by manipulating our perception. A lie is an attempt to convince others of a fabricated truth for one's own benefit (Service to Self). Lies are a mechanism of influence. They support the pursuit of an unnatural attraction or a misdirected intention. When truth becomes blocked by lies, a "*False Self*" is projected. Lies loom over the "*True Self*" giving energy to the "*Shadow Self*".

Lies are always intentional, but one's awareness of the intent can be masked by the perceived self. Once we convince ourselves that a falsehood within us is justified, we must convince others to believe the falsehood in order to reinforce our own warped beliefs. *The stronger the falsehood, the more energy must be exerted to support the lie.*

What lies do you tell yourself? Humans lie to themselves to promote a perceived self that opposes the true self. Most of us lie to ourselves many times every day, but have mastered ways to convince ourselves that the falsities reflect our true selves. Rather than facing the truth about ourselves, and dealing with the underlying reasons why we lie to ourselves, we spend enormous amounts of energy propping up the lies.

The lies that we tell ourselves are the greatest lies. They are the lies that we are never taught to defend against. You must not lie about your true nature. Accept who you are. If you do not like it, change it. Pretending you are not who you are does not help anyone, especially you. To make matters worse, there are people in our societies that have noticed this and are more than eager to help us lie to ourselves (see "Service to Self"). Be aware of this potential influence.

The true you, is expressed by the truth you tell others. It is the pure self and is ultimately who you need to become. Expressing yourself as something you are not will always limit your ability to realize your true potential.

OVERCOMING LIES

Overcoming the false projections that you create can only be addressed by understanding and accepting who you truly are and what you truly intend. Once you have this understanding, and you have come to terms with your true self, then you can redirect your thoughts and actions from your true self. *By doing this, you will create a natural attraction of influence that can support and propel your true intentions.* This will also allow you to repel the unnatural influences that lead you away from your true intentions.

OBSERVER MODE

Once you have gained a clear perception of the way you operate within the world around you, and the way people and groups influence your world, you will need to master applying the Quantum Laws to ensure you can take full control of your world. The most effective way to accomplish this is by going into "The Observer Mode".

The Observer Mode is simply living in and interacting with the world around you, while considering the way you and others think and act. It requires you to observe the way others interact with each other and with you, both as they intend it and the way events, circumstances, and situations really occur. It also requires you to examine yourself in situations where you are interacting with others.

While in Observer Mode, you are constantly considering all concepts found in the ***Choice, Perception, and Awareness*** sections of this book. You are making immediate analysis and also post-situation reflections within moments afterwards. *While in the Observer Mode, you are constantly refining your comprehension of what you observe, what you think you understand and then reconciling the two.*

Interacting with the world is not sitting in front of a television, computer screen, or any other electronic device. Even though a large part involves personal reflection, *you cannot enter into the Observer Mode in solitude.* Rather it involves actually engaging with other people (ideally people that are somehow physically interacting with each other).Being in the Observer Mode requires conscious application of *The Quantum Laws* described above. It demands constant, consistent and repetitive application until it becomes a normal part of your consciousness.

Initially, you will apply the Observer Mode as you reflect on the thoughts and actions you make. You may question which of your actions represented "Service to Self" or who influenced a decision you made. You may challenge yourself to prove if you are judging another based on your own expectations or if you are measuring another from a reference of yourself.

To be effective in the Observer Mode, you must be settled within yourself – you must be a "perceiver", not a "judger" and you must be "comfortable in your own skin". Drink in the scenery; taste the experiences around you; live in that moment; see the world through your eyes and others' at the same time. The Observer Mode can be applied to the remaining concepts in this book as well. We introduce it here to stress its importance in **_Awareness_** and to lay the foundation for **_Application_**.

PHYSIOLOGY

Change the physiology of your body. Become aware of the way you hold yourself in your own body, these actions change everything about the way you feel. This goes both ways.
The mind affects the body and the body affects the mind. The resulting emotions follow.

Feeling Pleasurable – Way One:
  – When you feel extremely pleasurable your body and posture changes
  – You stand tall, your heads up, you smile, shoulders go back, spring in your walk
  – You may skip, whistle, sing, and or hum along
  – Your body is energized with power and confidence

Feeling Pain – Way Two:
  – When you feel any type of pain your body and posture changes
  – You slouch, your head falls, you frown, shoulders get slouched, your walk slows
  – Your voice is depressed, goes lower, tired, annoyed, fearful
  – Your body is de-energized with low power and lack of self esteem

5 QUANTUM LAWS (The 5 Laws)

The 5 Quantum Laws are senior to the physical laws. The quantum level that these laws operate from is more powerful and supersedes all physical laws. Even physical laws have a hierarchy relative to one another. Surely humans are bound to the planet by gravity by way of the law of gravity yet birds and other creatures that fly are not bound by the law of gravity. This is because there is the law of lift that supersedes and is senior to the law of gravity. The law of lift simply defies and supersedes the law of gravity.

Once humans discovered this law of lift, flight was now possible and from it humans have helicopters and planes. Just because the more powerful law of lift is being used by an airplane does not mean the law of gravity goes away either. This is universal and part of the quantum energy field. The quantum energy field directly affects the physical and makes the physical laws happen. The 5 quantum laws are the most senior laws.

What science defines as laws are actually agreements between the ways unseen forces of energy vibration frequencies operate in the universe. Human belief works the same way. Humans make such agreements based the way they believe things work. At some later point in the future when there is evidence to prove the agreements incorrect; humans redefine their beliefs to suit the new evidence. All the while nothing has ever changed in reality.

The laws of science have been created by humans the same way. Humans have just created a set of laws for the way things work based on their understanding. So humans have a set of beliefs for the physical universe that they believe to be true and these are called laws. The Quantum Laws are senior to the Physical Laws. Quantum laws are the most powerful laws and supersede everything else. Quantum laws explain the way energy works in the unseen universe. Everything else humans believe goes away because no other laws exist by comparison when the quantum laws are being employed.

Nature, in its pure form, is logical, ordered and simple. Before the development of human societies, everything on our planet existed in harmony and balance. Everything in Nature has a purpose and exists to serve that purpose. As humans too are of Nature, this also applies to human who simply forgot this.

There are five basic and unwavering truths that exist in Nature. By understanding and observing these "Laws of Nature" or "Quantum Laws", you will become aware of how you can operate in a manner consistent with Nature, and thereby maneuver with ultimate effectiveness as you navigate through your life.

Law # 1 – Intention

PROGRAM: CREATION
In the beginning there is always a purpose, a meaning, and a reason before any physical action will become manifest. *Creation is the result of a thoughts and feelings in action.*

LAW OF INTENTION:
Intention is the seed of purpose or spark that triggers creative powers to manifest everything into existence. The intention defines the purpose and gives instruction for the purposes meaning. Everything in nature exists or occurs for a reason and serves a definite purpose. The purpose holds unlimited potential until it is de-fined or limited. *Creation is an action of choice directly initiated by intention.*

HUMAN HARDWARE CONNECTION – SENSE OF TOUCH:
Sense of touch is specifically the human organism's ability to feel internally and externally through the central nervous system. The spinal cord is the tree trunk and root system for the body. The brain's tree branches comprise the function and feedback system to operate the organism. The mind controls and commands the energy flow consciously and unconsciously. The body is the host computer for the experience. Feelings are the energetic interface that records the experience physically and ethereally. *In effect the human body is a movable sending and receiving information relay construct or living broadcast antenna.* The human nervous system acts as the battery and electrical information system relay for internal and external experiences.

FUNCTION:
Thoughts manifest the creative energy vibration and feelings are the signal amplification of that vibration. The cumulative resultant of focused thoughts and feelings generate the command to initiate the universal creative program and powers the creation signal to begin. Thoughts make things real and feelings give the human body an internal and external feedback system. The feedback system is the experience that is called life. The feedback system is also present to generate contextual information for continual guidance and ethereal growth.

OPERATION:
The human experience called life is a growth experience for the energetic ethereal mind construct. *Growth does not need to be painful but it often is for a reason. Pleasure and pain are the duality points that generate context or texture for the experience. Without feeling there could be no pleasure or pain interface.* The result is that human experience and memory is generated from emotional and physical feelings. Your feeling generate the living experience. The sensation of internal and external feelings allows the human to make decisions based off the feedback system.

The purpose of existence is to experience, to learn and to grow. All three are beneficial outcomes or results from life. Pleasure is the beneficial result and pain is the non-beneficial result. Between the two is a range of experiences that generate context or texture. Human feeling feel texture to relate to the context Over benefit or excess can occur and lead to non-beneficial results. The range from benefit to non-benefit is dynamic. The range is for information intake and provides motivation for more experiences. The motivation is to inspire a perpetual desire to live in pursuit of pleasure and the avoidance of pain. Remember too much pleasure will not always beneficial and the concept then loops back becoming pain. The reverse is true also. Pain can be very beneficial and loops back to pleasure. An example of this kind of pain is hunger. This means that there is beneficial pain and non-beneficial pleasure.

Humans have old, engrained, and well established patterns and habits that propel them forward or hold themselves back. The ones that hold humans back are non-beneficial. Many patterns and habits hold non-beneficial thought energies and result in non-benefit situations. These energies are activated when things occur in your life that make you feel uncomfortable or in pain. *Pain occurs as an energy restraint or point of blockage.* Acupuncture is a great example of a method for discovering and releasing physical blockages. There are also mental and emotional blocks. Techniques and powerful decision can change these pain events. Over time non-beneficial activities can diminish and become smaller. In many instances nearly all non-beneficial actions can be eliminated.

Consider energy polarity creation as an example. There is a positive and negative present in every electrical circuit. Remember the human body is made up of thousands of circuit connections. The transfer of energy flows from the negative poles to the positive poles. Energy desires to go from a non-beneficial state to a beneficial state. There is an energy build up and a release. Energy is built up and used. Energy is always in a flux of either being stored for use or being used. The human condition of experience is no different.

The human experience is like the negative pole that is discharging energy. You too will be able to expel the non-beneficial energy towards the positive pole or the beneficial side of life's experiences. As this takes place the non-beneficial side's magnetic pole will become weaker. Thus the human body draws less non-beneficial energy and more beneficial energy. All thoughts, feelings, and consequent actions generate patterns and habits. Inside of the human body these habits and patterns create neural pathways of energy flow in the brain and throughout the body. The human body is highly efficient and holds all memory related to these pathways.

The key is to alter and change the neural pathways away from non-beneficial thoughts, feelings, and actions and promote and create new dominate beneficial neural pathways. This makes the non-beneficial ones less used and thus weaker and weaker in their dominance over the human experience. The beneficial energy will become more and more dominate and bigger and bigger. Consider a total amount of energy as 100%. The two poles represent the sides the energy can build up on. If the pole size is equal then the energy is balanced out or neutral. When the ball of energy on either pole is larger than the other that is the dominate pole.

Energy holds potential for use in either the positive or negative state. When held in a non-benefit there is a lack of potential energy use because the ball of energy is too large to use or discharge its capacity. When there is a larger benefit ball of energy there is a greater ability to express and experience the potential stored within you. *The human body works just like energy in a battery because it wants to discharge itself. The benefit ball of energy wants to express its fullest potential and because it is larger than the non-benefit ball it has all ability to consume all the energy in capacity.*

If a human is held in negativity or non-beneficial pole dominance, and energy is built up but not released there is a suffering, pain or aches. With this condition the human experience is one of non-benefit because it is more negatively charged. Stated in another way there is too much negative energy that is not expelled and thus the energy circulates back making the experiences more painful and less pleasing. The object is to reverse such a condition. *The stronger and larger the positive or beneficial pole dominance is the more free flow of energy there is to create a beneficial experience.* This lack of free energy flow is called a block. With a larger beneficial pole the energy has a pathway to discharge and be used.

New neural pathways that are beneficial must be made to allow for a greater buildup of beneficial potential energy. They must become the dominate brain structure and focus of the mind instead of the non-benefit ones previously created. The intention to create the non-beneficial pathways was learned or formed based on opinion or theory information and not factual information. There is a certain time, which is different for every human, when the beneficial or positive ball of energy will grow to be larger, stronger, and more dominate than the non-beneficial or negative ball of energy. When this occurs humans become awake to their greater potentials and their self-esteem or self-belief increases.

Then and only then is the human experience a downhill one, downhill meaning specifically less resistance verses uphill where there is a greater resistance. *The momentum to use the potential energy that constantly builds is now on the human's side or control.* At this time everything starts going in your direction. After this is done for a while with practice the non-benefit side will diminish and fade in magnetism. The result is unconscious competence where the beneficial habits and patterns occur automatically into beneficial neural pathways by themselves. This is the energy shift that occurs when the blocks are removed.

Prior to the shift, the negative or non-beneficial energy flow instantaneously occurred or happened with no conscious thought or awareness. It was the habit and pattern. Now all of a sudden the human is instantaneously shifting into the beneficial habit and pattern creating potential energy flow. This is the way the human body was designed to function.
It is up to the human to use and apply this now. As you do apply it, you will experience more results that are favorable and beneficial to you. Use the power within you. It is very simple. This is the way the LAW OF INTENTION works.

When something beneficial happens in your life you can smile with knowing because this will be beneficial external reflecting the internal. *You will now know because this is the factual way energy works and functions.* Before the shift life looked to be getting more difficult now life will become progressively easier and more fulfilling. Now life can feel more exciting, secure, content and relaxing. Also you will experience levels of emotions with intensities that are beneficial more so then ever before previously.

Remember everything in nature exists for a reason and serves a purpose. *Every living thing and non-living things supports the existence and evolutionary growth of every other living thing.* Just as the intention of a tree exists within a seed, so too does the potential for a human's realized fulfillment exist within the human's intention. When we have an intention, *the power to realize it is always there*, if the human is willing to be patient to wait it through.

What humans hold in our emotional heart is their intention. Intention will aid in guiding you through the maze of mirrors experienced in life. This is because your intention is reflected back like a mirror to you. The LAW OF INTENTION reveals the energy and direction towards a focused purpose. The human body is a tool to be used for projecting the intention outwards. Like a mirror, human intention is reflected inwards until the human decides to act on the intention. Once a decision is made the intention is then projected outwards. Self-confidence and perceived importance of the purpose will determine the way the intent is focused and magnified.

When practiced beneficially intent of purpose brings situations, events, and circumstances into being. Stated another way, *when you are doing what you truly intend to do, you can and will accomplish it.* While that may sound easy, remember that nothing worth pursuing is ever easy. All pursuits require some type of growth and the ease of growth is different for every human. However, the more it is understood, the easier it becomes. *A seed has intent within itself and so do you.*

The focus of your intent will initiate the process that you desire. Therefore you must have a clear understanding of your intentions, and focus your actions to their achievement. This is not an effortless task, as distractions are everywhere and you will have to "swim upstream" to accomplish what you intend sometimes and pass them by on your journey.

Clear intention alone is not enough. Humans can intend to do something but never actually do it because of lack of follow through. A clear intention must be accomplished by a strong resolve and desire. Stated another way intention must be accomplished with a strong intensity over along enough duration to see its accomplishments. Resolve acts as the lens that focuses your intention. Focus holds your intention to the forefront of your thoughts. Your thoughts and feelings must have actions that resolve the energy flow conflict that can occur at any time if you start to develop non-beneficial pole or negative side tendencies. Whether the human consciously chooses to apply the LAW OF INTENTION or not it will occur anyway. It will operate in your life every day anyway till the moment of your death.

INTENTIONAL ENERGY DIAGRAM

ENERGY USE

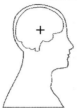 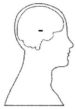

"Positive Energy"		**"Negative Energy"**
Beneficial Emotions		*Non-Beneficial Emotions*
Energy Ball Attracts		*Energy Ball Repels.*
"All" wants.		Attracts "NOT" wants

Electrical Energy Flow

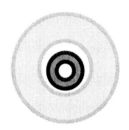  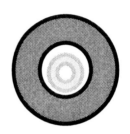

"+" Energy Ball uses the complete potential of all energy available in the "–" Energy Ball	The Natural Path of Energy Flows, Positive Terminals Draw Current from Stored Negative Terminals until the energy is Drained, the Dead Battery.	"-" Energy Ball blocks energy use and will drain other humans of their potential energy Ball

Law # 2 – Service

PROGRAM: GROWTH
The nature of creation requires value exchange of service to aid and help growth in all living forms. The energy for growth is a service that is provided for growth's attainment.

LAW OF SERVICE:
Learn and grow in physical, mental, and emotional health to serve your own health and relationships and to aid or help others to gain mastery of their own health and relationships. Basic survival requirements are meant to be meet first or "Self-Supporting" to ensure personal human growth and the ability to serve others comes second. Mastery of the first provides evidence for the second. The opposite too "Self-Supporting" is "Self-Serving". There are two forms of service towards others "Service to Self" (those that add value to society) or "Service to Others" (those that are parasites and live off the labor, production, and energy of others).

HUMAN HARDWARE CONNECTION – SENSE OF TASTE:
Sense of taste is specifically the human organism's ability to taste the service of universal abundance through the means of consumption. This concept is a bit confusing since taste is rarely expressed in terms of a service. The digestive system as a whole is the means by which all consumed energy is converted to useful body energy. The digestive system thus is the internal service system created for your life energy benefit. Without it there would be no ability to replenish energy for physical, mental, and emotional growth. Without taste there would be no desire to eat and the body could not grow. For the purpose of taste is to serve as a beneficial reason for eating. All forms of organic consumption is designed with the purpose to serve as an energy transfer. Energy gives aid or helps a life grow. All forms of life require of some type of energy as exchange to live and continue growing. Energy must be given to be received and must be received to be given.

FUNCTION:
This growth is primarily physical. In humans this also means mental and emotional growth as well. Sustaining energy services provides the energy that is required for physical growth and all human needs. Abundant energy exists to provide for sustainable energy requirements. Part of the purpose of organic life is to promote the life of others. Plants and trees grow to provide an ability to pass on their own life reproduction by the vegetables, fruits, and nuts they grow. All of which contain the seeds for new life packaged with enough energy to germinate new life. Animals that consume the energy giving substances do so for their own growth. Humans take full advantage of the various abundant energy sources and appreciate them all by way of the mouth specifically through the sense of taste. "Service to Others" promotes abundance whereas "Service to Self" creates the false reality of scarcity. There is more than enough and any apparent lack is by design created by the service to self-minded humans. Lack or scarcity is thus a purposeful action of mismanagement done to control resources and thus control other humans.

OPERATION:

"Service to Self" is rooted in scarcity and excessive desirers to control. "Service to Self" eventually harms other humans, nature, and the originator of the "Self-Serving" deeds. "Service to Others" is rooted in abundance and adds to the overall value of others by lifting other humans and nature to the level of the originator doing the service. In this way "Service to Others" is the benefit gained from the abundant use of energy. "Service to Others" expedites growth and "Service to Self " stifles growth.

Everything exists to support another part of the universal system found in nature. This support maintains balance, harmony, and abundance. Only humans have made the conscious decision to choose to be "Service to Self". All the pain that decision has brought and will bring to other humans will always connect back to the actions that arose from human thoughts, feelings, and consequent actions.

Humans have been entrained to believe and apply thoughts, feelings and actions with a "Scarcity Mentality" of viewing the natural world by the education system designed and controlled by the parasitic members of society who decided to become "Service to Self" oriented. *Because of this most humans believe most resources are limited and therefore create a false desire to horde.* This then leads many humans to becoming fixated on the accumulation of more than is needed in order to survive. *These reactions further perpetuate the illusion of scarcity in a world full of abundance as humans horde and accumulate more than what is needed.*

Humans are actually removing resources that would otherwise be available to others for their natural needs and use. All of which continue to further reinforce the "Scarcity Mentality". Nature is designed by the growth program to exist in abundance. The reality of abundance creates an obvious conflict to scarcity. When confronted with the flaws of scarcity the whole approach is completely false and is driven by persuasive opinions and wild schemed theories. When examined all of the persuasive opinions and wild schemed theories are created with more "Service to Self" objectives.

In a world where resources are believed to be limited, it can seem to be impractical to practice the "Service to Others" approach. When almost every human you observe or listen to is making their priority "Service to Self", practicing "Service to Others" may appear to almost guarantee certain self-destruction. For those who have rarely practiced "Service to Others", switching to this new mindset will be difficult to start and even more difficult to maintain. As long as the human longs to be in control, others are doomed to be suffering or in pain because of it.

The LAW OF SERVICE deals with unconditional love. Consider love as an energy that is expressed from within and done so without the expectation of receiving anything in return. In this regard, *"Service to Others" reflects a true expression of pure love*, while "Service to Self" reflects the absence of love. There can only be one master – the choice to serve others or serve yourself. Be honest with yourself about what path you have chosen currently.

When considering actions that relate to "Service to Self", it is important to distinguish between being "Self-Serving" and being "Self-Supporting". When actions are self-serving humans are being selfish in the traditional sense – putting their own interests ahead of others for the purpose of self-benefit instead of overall benefit. It is always short-sighted and misses the point, as the benefit being pursued does nothing to improve the true self. Consider "Self-Supporting" as in "Self-Love". Practice "Self-Love" by being true to yourself. Avoid being "Selfish" because those actions are petty and "Self-Destructive".

Self-supporting actions, on the other hand, are taken with the long view in mind, and reflect the desire to improve and grow through internal means and without interrupting the interests of others. A good example of being self-supporting is maintaining a healthy body. Being self-supporting means being true to yourself, your true self; pursuing your true intentions. For you are not being selfish or practicing "Service to Self" when you are expressing your true being. Having conviction and actively pursuing your desires, dreams, wishes, and wants reflects the LAW OF INTENTION and it balances with the LAW OF SERVICE.

You will ultimately learn that human desire to become blissfully happy with joy is your most important desire. *The fact is that when humans learn to add value to society and respect the natural world the energy return is the highest level of bliss possible. "Service to Others" is all about adding value to society. The LAW OF SERVICE adds value to your own life so that humans can become someone that other humans want to emulate.*

There has been entrainment to persuade humans form meaningful pleasure. Pleasure is a beneficial catalyst for continued growth. There is nothing wrong with feeling pleasure. There is something very wrong denying pleasure to one's self and others out of fear. Growing pleasing beneficial experiences that uplift one's self and others is the focus of living a joyous life. Seeking self-serving pleasure which is promoted by the entrainment is a human intention challenge.

Those who serve others best do so by being the example of what is possible to others. Humans naturally admire true genuine service and value those who provide it. For you will find out at a certain point it is not what you have but it is who you become that is the real value and is most important. Unfortunately most humans do not figure that out.

The LAW OF SERVICE help humans develops honesty, character of integrity, unconditional love, forgiveness, empathy, giving, appreciation, gratefulness, and thankfulness. Because life is about feeling good right now and helping others will help you feel good now. Every step of the living journey regardless of what you are looking at or situation, you will find yourself requiring your human needs to be meet and feeling wanted is one of them. Helping others can be the most blissful experience you can ever imagine. This is because the LAW OF SERVICE is designed for everyone and everything.

Law # 3 – Allowance

PROGRAM: FREEDOM

For learning to be an experience gained through growth it must be genuinely inspired. Freedom of will or thought and freedom of expression or action must be allowed to occur and guarantees each human the equal ability to think and act genuinely while living.

LAW OF ALLOWANCE:

Being more than just free-will or free-expression. Allowance guarantees the freedom to choose while also allowing others to have the same freedom. Too often the message has been twisted or confused to mean only freedom of thought. Even so the meaning has been lost to the degree the point is now dull. All living things are allowed and must be allowed to be completely free to think and act as they choose. This is not to say that these thoughts and actions must be agreed to or accepted. As all thoughts and actions have some form of consequences that result from choices made. Allowance to choose never states others must agree or allows others to take freedom from another. Allowance guarantees absolute freedom with the price that everyone and everything is also given the same right.

HUMAN HARDWARE CONNECTION – SENSE OF SMELL:

Sense of smell is specifically the human organism's ability to smell the uniqueness of an individual of anyone, any kind, and of anything. Just as a fruit holds the unique sent to its own creation and purpose, so too does each human to themselves and to each other. A banana smells like a banana and is never confused with the scent of a strawberry or an apple. The banana must be allowed to be a banana and cannot be anything more than what it is a banana. There are those animals that like bananas and those that do not. The banana is not offended, hurt, upset, self-abandoning, self-destructive, lacking in benefit or otherwise changed because of anyone, any kind or anything because of those thoughts or actions towards it. Something, some kind, or anything cannot permanently change its own sent because it must be allowed to be what it is without being altered in any way.

FUNCTION:

The sense of smell is the most acute of the senses. When a human smells anything it automatically determines the amount of agreeableness towards the scent. Things that smell unfavorable are repelling and those that smell favorable are more desired. Something's give off more sent then others do. Notice that no sent itself can be punished, taken away from, or hurt. The smell travels through the air and is completely free to be what it is and move about as free as the wind can blow it. The sent holds no resistance to itself and always is itself. Allowance works the same way. Notice the way humans accept the sense of smell because it serves them and works for them. The LAW OF ALLOWANCE is no different. No expectations can ever be levied on a sent so too must no expectation be made on other humans. Genuine choices that generate growth mentally, emotionally, and physically are beneficial. Any choice that limits growth or denies a creation its freedom to be is non-beneficial. Allowance's purpose is to ensure total freedom for growth in the living experience. Taking the freedom of any creation away from itself is not allowed. Such thoughts and actions result in non-beneficial experiences or pain.

OPERATION:
Expectation is a strong belief that something will happen, occur, or appear in the future. Allowance holds no expectation on thoughts or actions because it is there to guarantee freedom and must be absolute to do so. Expectation that something will occur is vital to the creation program because expectation is an intention of manifestation. Too often humans confuse the use of expectation of desire and its part of creation into existence with a force of will.

Humans have been entrained to believe that certain situations and certain circumstance allow them to project expectations on other humans. Humans have already been created and thereby must be allowed to make their own decisions and consequent actions. Humans hold endless possibilities to make choices and thus consequent decisions to take related actions. Just because a human can, does not make them subject to the expectation. Every human will decide or react to create the actions manifested by your own thoughts. For the actions to be genuine the human must agree to consciously have the thoughts that lead to their own decisions. Whether you want or expect something to happen, do not predispose another human to agree to the same choice. This means the introduction of possibilities holds the potential for an agreement but also at least a single if not more alternative possible choices. It does not matter if the others are implied, understood, or gives some clause or elements not involving alternatives. Allowance guarantees and preserves the right to have independent thoughts and actions.

Choice is more powerful than humans have been lead to believe. Belief is a personal choice and is completely independent of influence. Belief systems are created by humans to provide explanations where evidence does not provide any certain facts. Belief systems are allowance constructs or B.S. the mind creates to aid the mind in making decisions. Because there are no facts to hold evidence to the B.S., the B.S. is a self-creation made up of opinions and theories. Most B.S. sounds, appears, and feels good to the agreeing human. Humans must be allowed to make choices, as they have the right – the right to choose what to think, what to believe, and what decisions to make and the related ways or actions taken. You too have the right to make your own choices, you must decide to allow that which you want and do not want into your life.

The essence of the LAW OF ALLOWANCE is the freedom of personal choice while allowing others to have the same freedom. For the LAW OF ALLOWANCE deals with free will or free thinking and free expression or free action. Many humans give up much of their free will and free expression in exchange for the promise or perception of security or certainty. Others allow a majority of their free will or actions to become limited to satisfy the interests of a single human or a portion of society. Such choices are allowed but always accompany the price of limitations on choice. Agreeing to such decisions is allowed for beneficial and non-beneficial learning as part of the growth experience.

Because free will stems or originates from a human's thoughts, it is impossible to completely remove it from anyone. However, it can be dramatically limited forcibly, voluntarily or by influence. The LAW OF ALLOWANCE considers two aspects or perspectives within every human and living organism the external and the internal experience. The first relates to your ability to allow yourself to think, decide, or act. The second relates to your ability to allow another human to think, decide, or act for themselves. In many cases or circumstances, you are actually allowed to make any decision or take any action you want. Of course, you may personally choose to limit your own choices to those that allow you to function within society. The more challenging dimension for most humans is allowing others to make their own decisions and actions. As difficult as it is to accept for many, humans are allowed to generate their own thoughts, decisions, and actions and you are allowed to respond to them as you see fit.

Understanding allowance has a degree of frustration for humans. For as humans realize that each human is actually and completely powerless to change another. Humans cannot do more than suggest, advise or otherwise influence another human or humans to change, as only each human can only choose to change from within themselves. For these reasons the LAW OF ALLOWANCE is one of the most difficult of the LAWS OF NATURE to master, as it requires that humans do not pass judgment over other humans. Most humans have been taught directly or indirectly to form references towards other humans based upon our own belief systems, ideals, and societal norms. Removing judgment towards others takes a great deal of conscious thought and practice. If you want to make the best of any situation, you must learn to remove your judgment of others. After all humans are allowed to be who they are, and you are allowed to agree or disagree with them.

If you are truly interested in becoming aware of the real world around you, you must be willing and ready for internal conflicts related to change. Humans have been taught to lean on societal norms to help form references of ourselves. These references can be deeply entrenched in your psyches. The challenge arises when humans begin to accept the reality that humans may actually be different individually than what was previously aware or taught to believe. The conflict from breaking from this dependence may prove to be nearly if not impossible for some humans.

Take the example of a ship at sea. You can make the choice. Be on a ship without a rudder or any kind of engine. This ship will be tossed around by the waves and the wind. This is the state of the victim without any direction or focus. Or you can choose the other ship. Be on a self-generating nuclear ship with unlimited power. The ship can be steered by your own will of choice based on your own decisions. This ship has the power to be directed in any direction to go anywhere with purpose. The control of this ship is of any time or place you choose. You are allowed to choose but you must take responsibility for your choices that is the price for being allowed to choose.

Law # 4 – Balance

PROGRAM: CYCLES

For life to be self-sustaining and to experience growth a series of cycles governs all of nature. The cycles give the up and down changes that comprise nature of its harmony. Cycles are linked directly to growth, life and death. The balance between events can sometimes be measured where as other times there is no measurement. Cycles appear as wavelengths, frequencies, unbalance, rebalance, light, sound, and the concept of time.

LAW OF BALANCE:

Between any two unique events there is an unknown balance. Balance is perceivable and unperceivable, measurable and non-measurable, and is seen and tangible or unseen and intangible. The shifting of balance creates energies, events, situations, circumstances to occur. For anything to be created or manifested it takes some amount of balance to pull the resources together to shift the current state of one environment into the newly created environment state. A sense of harmony or music creates a symphony of new life, continued life, and the ending of life. There is a natural rhythm or flow that accompanies every cycle or set of cycles. Just a sound starts with a frequency as a set of repeating wavelengths that move in balance up and down outward. Balance is the controlling function that transmits the sound from one location to another.

HUMAN HARDWARE CONNECTION – SENSE OF HEARING:

Sense of hearing is specifically the human organism's ability to translate audible balance information into a sound. When the ability to hear is affected in any life form the life form will experience a state of imbalance. In humans this is called vertigo because the ability to find equilibrium is so out of balance that all sense of directions and the ability to navigate through them is nearly if not totally impossible. Lack of audible sound may not be present but an inaudible sound is always being transmitted through out nature. Light also has a frequency that is being picked up by the sense of hearing. The human body acts as a sender and receiver of transmitted sounds and energy waves. The broadcast is continual and constant as long as the human remains alive. The internal rhythm of the beating heart is the circulatory systems balance generator. The human sense of hearing uses the internal rhythm of the heart and its own voice as a built in calibrator or a feedback dampening system to modulate the internal balance relative to the external balance of the environment. If you go into a very quiet or nearly silent place three things can be heard. First is the internal beating of the heart, the echo or creation of sound do to the voice, and the third is the sound of the cycle program which can always be heard if humans attune there hearing to recognize it.

FUNCTION:

The sense of hearing functions as the synchronization or timing function that gives humans the impression of time. Without sound or the ability to hear or transmit sound the experience of living is dulled. Even humans who have lost their ability to hear still can feel the vibration of sound. The illusion of material existence is created by the vibration the cycle program generates. Everything in existence gives off a unique vibration of frequency patterns. These shifts of balance generate sounds that are picked up by the ears. Without speaking you can hear the voice of your own mind. This is because thought is sound and is part of the balance frequency each human transmits through the broadcasting body. Feelings are also sounds because feelings generate a raising and lowering of the heart rate and link thoughts to sensations. To hear the cycle programs sound is to hear the thought and feeling tone of nature. This is the sound and cycle that synchronizes our shared reality and sets up the balance movements that create cycles and thus the experience called life. Without sound there would be no material to make matter up with. Everything exists because of a thought, a sound or the balance shifting in between cycles.

OPERATION:
Everything in nature is ultimately seeking a balance. This may seem counter-intuitive when humans take a look around at their environments and see, hear and feel a chaotic world in many directions. The chaos that is viewed is imbalance and only time will bring it back into balance. Said another way the balance in-between the creation of imbalance and the eventual balance or the measure of the concept called time. Although things viewed from the "snap-shot" perspective of the moment often appears to be out of balance and chaotic, they must be viewed within a larger, "total" picture – seeking to align to the ultimate balance within nature.

To achieve balance is to become aware of all sides of that which you are focusing. This can be all of the elements to be considered when making a decision or it can be your awareness of your point of view and that of another. When something or a human is balanced, one is centered and comfortable in one's own being. When you are at balance you are at peace, while also being fully in control. The human body naturally is designed to stand in balance and its internal works are all in balance with each other. When these systems are out of balance that system and the related systems will signal an unbalance in the effected system or systems.

For humans time is the human concept that attempts to clarify and resolve balance to a measurable quantity. Time itself is the by byproduct of the cycle program running. Time must be allowed to play out so that balance can be reached. When applying the LAW OF BALANCE, remember that balance is not always achieved instantly. At least not the way humans and their concept of time will perceive time. But because no one knows the amount of time that is in balance between two or more events, there is no way to know the amount of time to achieve proper balance. This is why humans are wired to act and can recognize the necessity to act with urgency. Tap into the energy that the urgency provides to motivate you to achieve.

Notice the way humans use language with respect to balance. In a bank money checking account there is a balance. This is a quantifiable amount that is unique to each and every similar account held by a single bank. All banks have accounts with balances in them. The key point is to understand and relate that a balance is an unknown amount. Yet the balance is still an amount of some kind. Just because you do not know the balance of every single account, each account still holds a unique balance. The same analogy can be compared to a human life span. There is no way of knowing the balance of one's life but if they are alive there is still some unknown amount of balance left to be used.

Seek to achieve balance both within yourself and between you and your world. Humans can observe imbalance and the natural tendency to regain balance from the world around them. Internally, strive to reach balance within your mind, your body, and with your emotions. When seeking balance with the world around you, start by trying to establish harmony and peace between you and those most close to you. Then expand this balance to all those with whom you come in contact.

Notice the use of language again when using the word wavelength. Wavelength is the distance between crests of a wave, especially points in a sound wave or electromagnetic wave. Humans are transmitters and receivers of broadcast signals through a vibration or wave frequency. Wavelength is also a human's idea, thought, or way of thinking. The human wavelength frequency especially affects their ability to communicate with others or other things. The vibration frequency broadcast is in both the audible and inaudible range of heard sound.

Frequency is the rate at which vibration occurs that constitutes a wave, either in material as in a sound wave or vibration wave, or in an electromagnetic field. The human body is such a electromagnetic field. This also includes radio and light waves. Frequency is usually measured in a per second basis. Frequency is also the rate at which something occurs repeated over a particular period of time. A cycle is also loop that opens, closes, and repeats. These cycles are a series of events that are repeated in the same order. Although this sounds technical this is just a lot of language humans have created and use to try to comprehend the LAW OF BALANCE as it relates to the cycle program. The law is simple and is in constant use throughout nature.

Law #5 – Attraction

PROGRAM: MAGNETISM

For life to grow and multiply it must be drawn to a similar companion that can provide valued feedback to spark beneficial growth. The magnetism opens the possibility for greater energy flow through a larger connection. This energetic exchange is for more than reproductive purposes in design. For not all likes that are drawn to each other can or will reproduce. Magnetism provides acknowledgement to the source by the resulting feedback of what is being drawn in. Everything holds its own magnetism by vibrating a frequency that acts to repel dissimilar and attract similar. Magnetism attracts similar signs, signals, events, things, animals, materials, situations, and or circumstance to inspire growth.

LAW OF ATTRACTION:

Likes attract likes. All similar thoughts, feelings, things, objects, and materials contain sympathetic vibrations that are attracted to each other. Opposites are only attracted to each other relating to procreative means. However the respective male and female counterparts only form lasting bonds that support larger shared mutual attractions. Meaning outside of the reproductive attraction unless there is a mental or emotional bond animals leave each other after mating. In most animals the reproductive cycles are completely involuntary bringing the opposites together for the sole purposes of mating and furthering the species growth in number. This suits natures balance attraction requirements. In some cases more social animals mate for life. Attraction is more than reproduction. If an animal is hungry or thirst for example, the animal will be attracted to a food or a water sources because of the attraction to survive and continue living.

HUMAN HARDWARE CONNECTION – SENSE OF SIGHT:

Sense of sight is specifically the human organism's ability to translate visible light information into a rage of sight comprising the view screen projected from the eyes to the brain. The view screen is the total range of sight upward, downward, to the extent from both sides, and the near to distant ranges. Although sight is inclusive as to what can be seen in the range of sight, sight itself is limited beyond those ranges. Anything happening out of range is in the blind spot. Given the enormous size of the world and the vastness and far reaches of space and beyond most of what can be seen is not visually possible. To each human the range of sight fills their whole conscious mind. This is only a fraction of a fraction of what is visible in reality. Adding an additional layer is the larger range of non-visible light that is contained in the full spectrum of light and not seen by human eyes. Visible light gives the human the ability to navigate the living experience being attracted or un-attracted to objects living or nonliving. Take special note that just because something can be seen visually does not mean that it is seen by every human.

Although all senses utilize the LAW OF ATTRACTION the sense of sight is completely and exclusively directed to the purpose of survival, creation, and reproductive means. Also the human's thoughts and feeling are directly linked to the visual attraction mechanisms generated by the sense of sight. For all thoughts and related feeling that are generated result from a visual desire, dream, and wants in some capacity. All images that are seen when eyes are closed, are based on the original visual sense of sight attraction connections made first by images seen from the open eye.

FUNCTION:
The sense of sight functions as the video or radar screen in a movie theater. The screen by which all living life compares its internal experiences to the external surroundings that distinguishes it from itself. Much like a television projects organized light patterns into a picture on its own screen so too is the information seen externally projected to the eyes then projected internally to the human brain. The human experience is in effect a reverse television projection system to and from the human brain. Much like the internet is a common signal that is picked up by any electronic device with the matching software and hardware to decode it so too is the external living world seen by all living creatures through their sense of sight.

Sight normalizes and relates a common external environment that all living things experience so each individual can relate back to a known reference. Some animals see more or less of a visual spectrum than humans do. Visual light only makes up a small percentage of the entire light spectrum. Visual light makes up the color spectrum and it increases from a low vibration to a high vibration. These frequency vibrations generate the visual holograms known as matter. Although the visual screen is limited in range for each viewer the overall visual screen picks up the same matter because the vibration signals are universally the same for all living life and is programmed to be picked up by the same biological hardware or eyes.

The attraction component to sight relates to the magnetic vibrations each object gives off by way of a unique identifying frequency both generated and carried by light. Anything that is physical is the equal corresponding magnetic vibration held in tension for a specific frequency. This is the reason for light being a particle and a wave form at the same time because in effect light creates the physical hologram in form and the external reflection of light that is seen by way of the color vibration.

Although no physical touch is required or used to see. Past experiences of physical contact with objects links and matches sight to shape, texture, and density. Survival quickly encodes which physical items are to what visuals. In this way for example an un-ripened banana is more firm and green and a ripened banana is less firm and yellow. So if a human is hungry and attracted to a ripe banana the human now knows what to look for.

Sight allows for three major requirements to be created and used. Attraction is required to find and locate food and water for life, and comfortable and pleasing environments for shelter. Attraction is also required for wants and desires relative to comfortable and pleasing experiences. Lastly attraction is required to continue reproduction of organic life and in-organic objects; for production of in-organic objects requires the same conditions as organic reproduction. For example a table is not alive but humans are attracted to the use of a table so humans reproduce more tables for their use. Whether organic or in-organic attraction is the motivation to continue to do what is necessary to stay alive, reproduce, and experience life.

OPERATION:

Are we talking about the LAW OF ATTRACTION as described in other media? The LAW OF ATTRACTION so it is the same by definition. There are very clear distinctions in the use and application of it. This makes a huge difference in the effectiveness of it due to proper use. The LAW OF ATTRACTION does exist and does work all the time. For optimal results the LAW OF ATTRACTION must be used with the other four quantum laws.

The energy expressed by the body is a vibration wave. The human thought is broadcast as a vibration wave from the body. Every time you think and are feeling a feeling you are broadcasting this signal. Vibrations share in sympathy with each other and are attracted to each other. This calls fourth more situations, events, people and circumstances into your life that give you the same or similar feeling. Within nature, those things that exist for like purposes will naturally be attracted to one another. Thirsty animals (and hungry crocodiles) will naturally be attracted to the watering hole. Bees will be attracted to flowers. Humans will follow like purposes to support their instinct for survival.

In the simplest form those humans of similar thoughts, emotions, and actions will attract similar humans among other experiences. Attraction requires actions and can become realized by choosing to act upon those thoughts and feelings that generated attraction in the first place. A human of one interest, when discovering another with the same interest, will naturally form a connection. Usually this occurs with great comfort as long as the other human is aware enough to realize what is happening. Such connections tend to openly express and investigate the interest with the same amount of enthusiasm.

Conversely, dissimilar interests will not form natural attraction. Unnatural attractions result when humans become attracted to a projection that does not reflect a true self. This is also the reason why "Service to Self" is destructive because the "Self-Serving" motives force unnatural connections that eventually become evident. These projections are self-lies and self-deceptions. Although these unnatural attractions exist frequently, they eventually become and often are problematic and rarely productive in any way other than for apparent short term gains.

The LAW OF ATTRACTION holds a greater importance when the energy of intention is considered. This is because a human's intention is the true reflection of the "True-Self". It is impossible to naturally attract that which you are not. This is regardless of the amount of energy spent convincing yourself or others of a false you. Ultimately you will always be you. Become honest and just learn who that is and you will attract into your life that which is best for you.

Attraction also leads to growth. Growth is not always going to occur in a recognizable manner. Natural attraction that leads to a specific connection can bring about growth for each individual, the pair, and as a new or renewed set of life experiences. Think about the way the attraction of two people can lead to the birth of another. In beneficial ways growth connects to natural joy or bliss from creation. The same experience occurs in other forms of creation like those of artists, writers, composers, carpenters, painters, and even the gardeners. The joy of creation and the anticipation of the end result becomes a motivator.

H.I.M Part 2 – The Creation Program: Prelude

CONNECTING THE 5 QUANTUM LAWS

The Quantum Laws are all linked to each other. Each of them is a component of a holistic system and each can be explained and understood in terms of the others. All energy is controlled by the 5 Quantum Laws. Each Quantum Law is reflexive because each law is independent, dependent, and interdependent of each other. This make for the appearance of complexity but in realty there are only these 5 Quantum Laws affecting your human experience.

The way the # 1, LAW OF INTENTION, links to the other laws:

Law # 2*: Service* – If you focus your *Intention* toward yourself, you will experience Service to Self (and all that comes with it). If your *Intention* is practiced with the other human(s) in mind, you will experience Service to Others (and all that comes with it).

Law # 3*: Allowance* – You know your own *Intention* but not those of others. That unknown *Intention* must be taken into account as a function of the others' choice when making your own choices

Law # 4*: Balance* – Your *Intention* cannot be genuine if your inner self does not balance (reconcile) with the *Intention* that you project externally.

Law # 5*: Attraction* – Those of the same *Intention* will be attracted to each other.

The way the # 2, LAW OF SERVICE, links to the other laws:

Law # 1*: Intention* – Your intention determines whether you will be *Service:* "of self" or "for others"

Law # 3*: Allowance* – You must allow people to choose be *Service:* "of self" or "for others", as it is their choice (and their right), just as you must be allowed to practice *Service:* "of self" or "for others" as you choose.

Law # 4*: Balance* – By *Service to Self*, imbalance is created within others. By *Service to Others*, balance is made within you.

Law # 5*: Attraction* – Those of the same understanding of *Service* will be attracted to each other.

The way the # 3, LAW OF ALLOWANCE, links to the other laws:

Law # 1: Intention – You must <u>*Allow*</u> yourself to be true to yourself to find your true intention.

Law # 2: Service – You must <u>*Allow*</u> other(s) the choice – to be "of self" or "for others". This is the root of freedom of choice.

Law # 4: Balance – Balance can only be achieved by <u>*Allowing*</u> forces to seek an equilibrium.

Law # 5: Attraction – Those who agree by way of <u>*Allowance*</u> will be drawn to each other.

The way the # 4, LAW OF BALANCE, links to the other laws:

Law # 1: Intention - If one's intention is not in <u>*Balance*</u> with one's surroundings, either the intention will not bear fruit or the surroundings will not support it.

Law # 2: Service – Your rewards in life reflect the <u>*Balance*</u> of Service: "of self" or "for others" and those rewards are always in exact proportion (balanced). The more "Service to Others" you have in your life, the less "Service to Self" you need.

Law # 3: Allowance – People will either agree or disagree. Even in choice there is a <u>*Balance*</u> that is struck.

Law # 4: Attraction – Explains the process by which <u>*Balance*</u> is visible, as in all sides or points of view.

The way the # 5, LAW OF ATTRACTION, links to the other laws:

Law # 1: Intention – Those of the same intention will be <u>*Attracted*</u> to each other.

Law # 2: Service – You can only have one master (yourself or others), so you will <u>*Attract*</u> people who have either one or the other, directly related to your own level (of understanding "Service").

Law # 3: Allowance – Your freedom of choice will make it easy to decide that which you want to <u>*Attract*</u> and that which you do not want to <u>*Attract*</u>.

Law # 4: Balance – The very nature of balance requires two opposing forces to repel or cancel each other, while two <u>*Attracting*</u> forces will come together to promote growth. Just like two personalities that come together make a new and separate identity (of the couple). In terms of growth, two mentally, emotionally, and physically <u>*Attracted*</u> individuals will come together to promote a healthy pair.

YOU DID IT

Congratulations you read the whole book!
Now read it **AGAIN**!
Enjoy learning with a new perspective on life!

"In order to get the most out of this book, it is highly suggested that you, read the Human Instruction Manual Part 1 completely two times before reading Human Instruction Manual Part 1 Part 2."

Get ON 2 IT!

"Engineered Mentoring For A Fulfilling Quality Life"

3D SUCCESS:
<u>D</u>iscover Clarity
<u>D</u>evelop Self-Esteem and Confidence
<u>D</u>efeat your Shadow-Self

Go from **"Zero-to-Hero"**

GetON2it.com ● 216-496-9494 ● Don@GetON2it.com

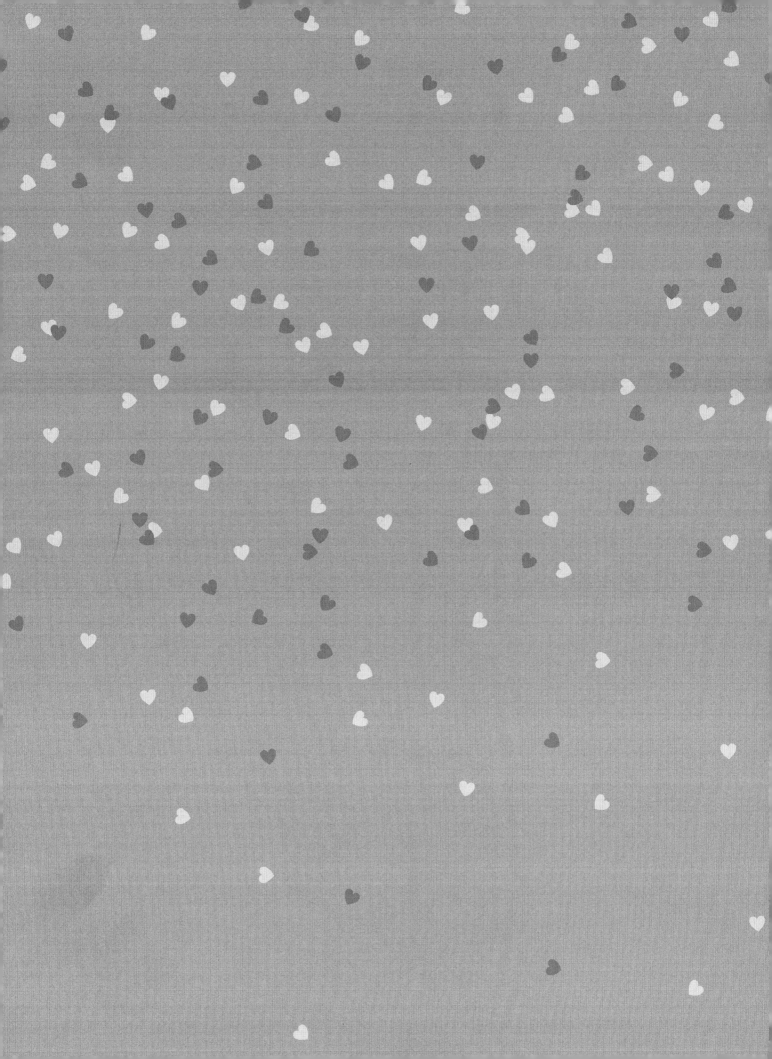

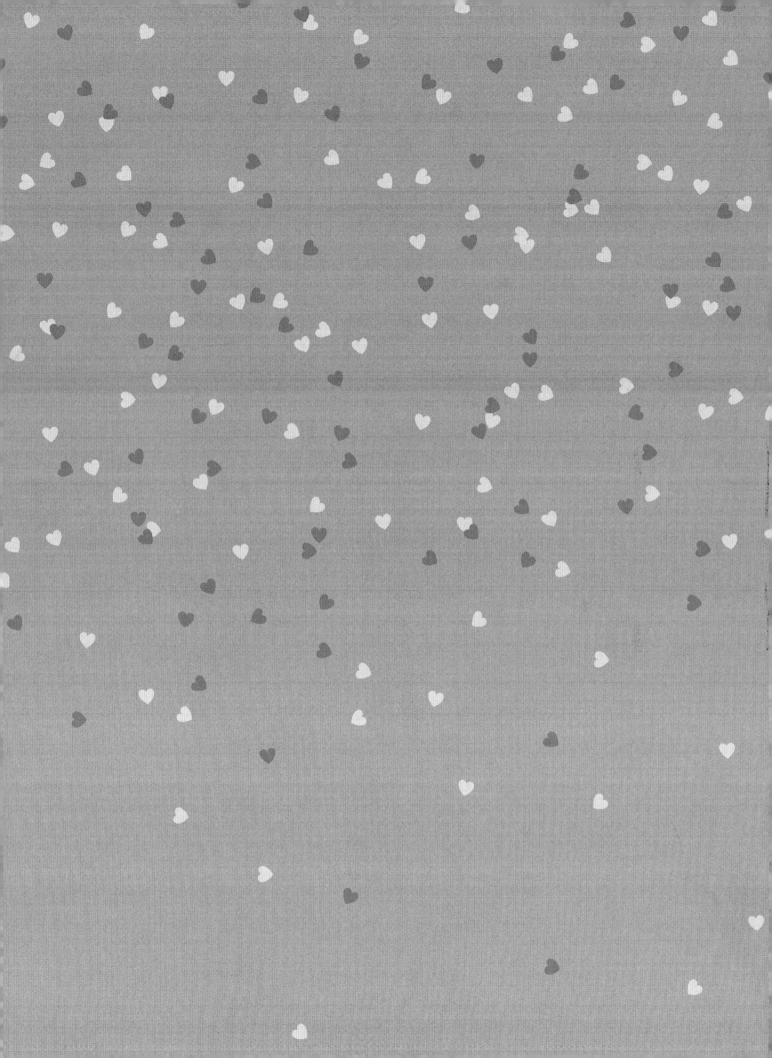

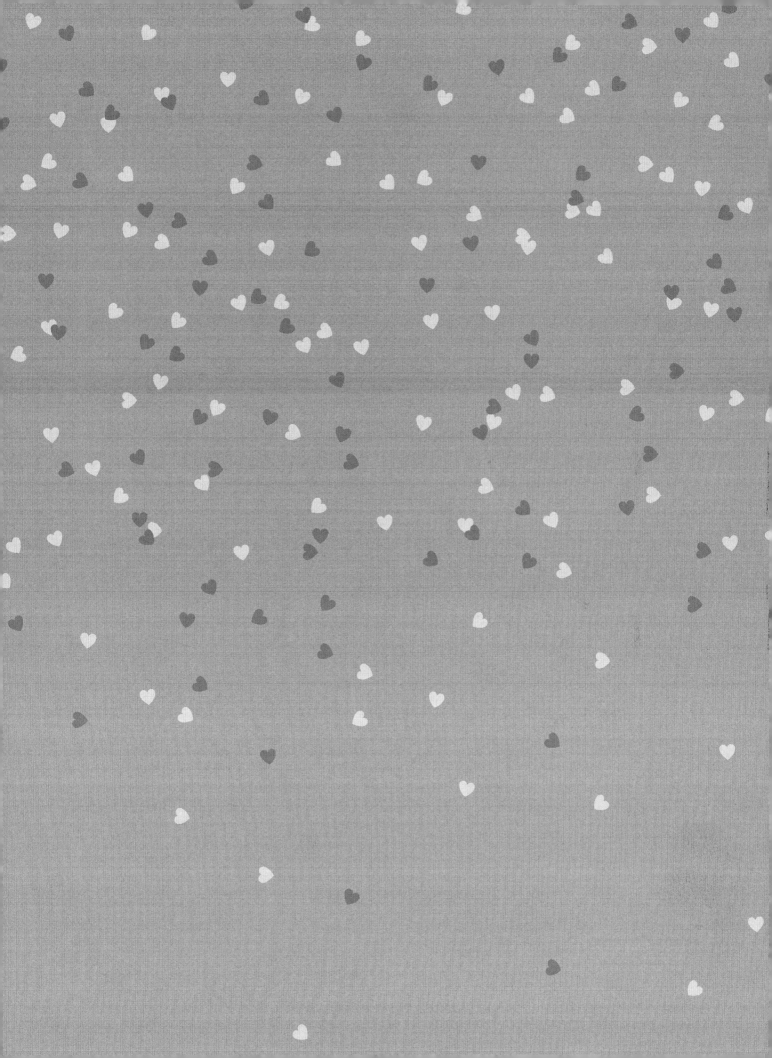

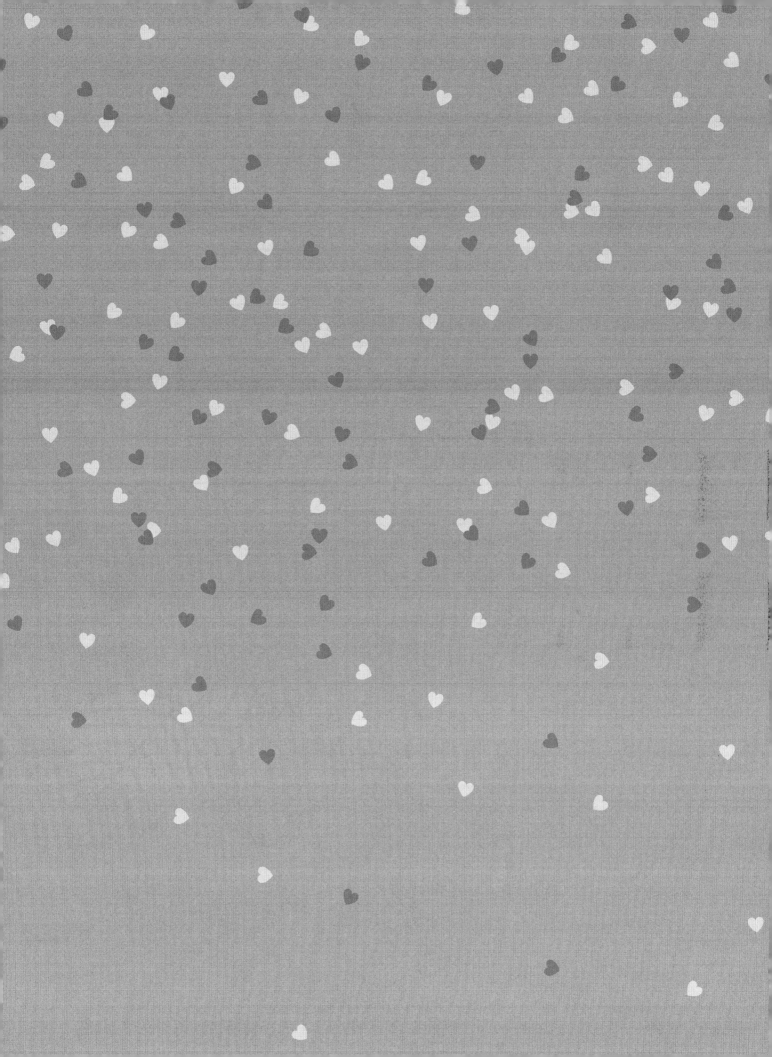

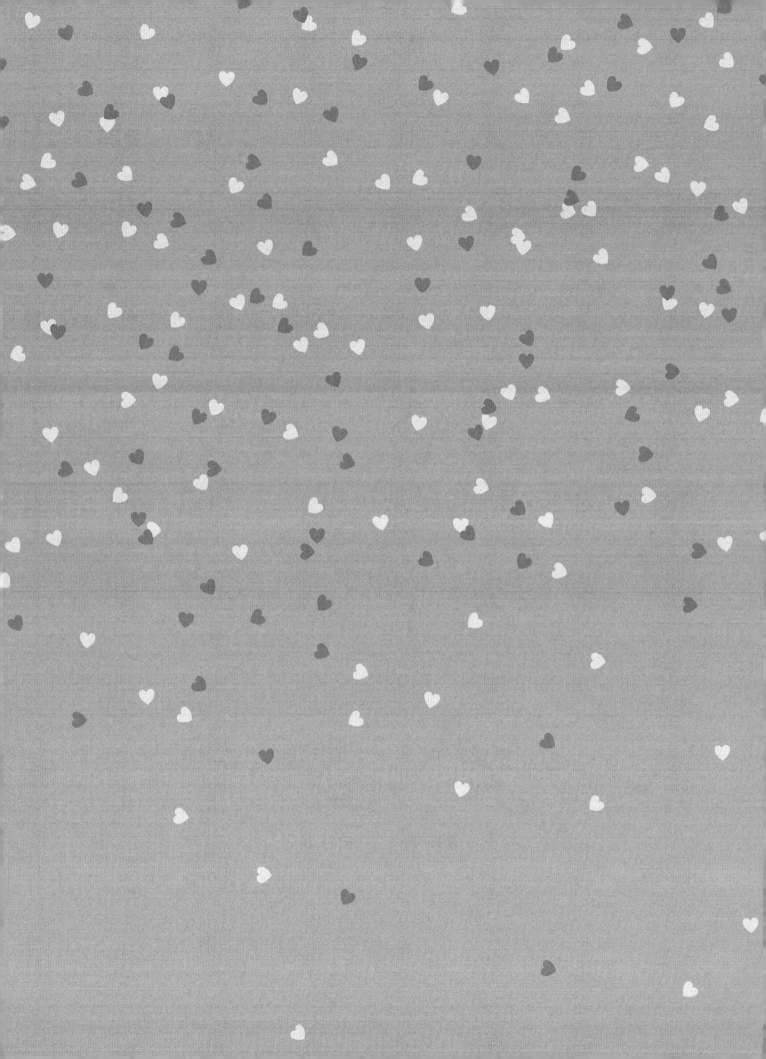

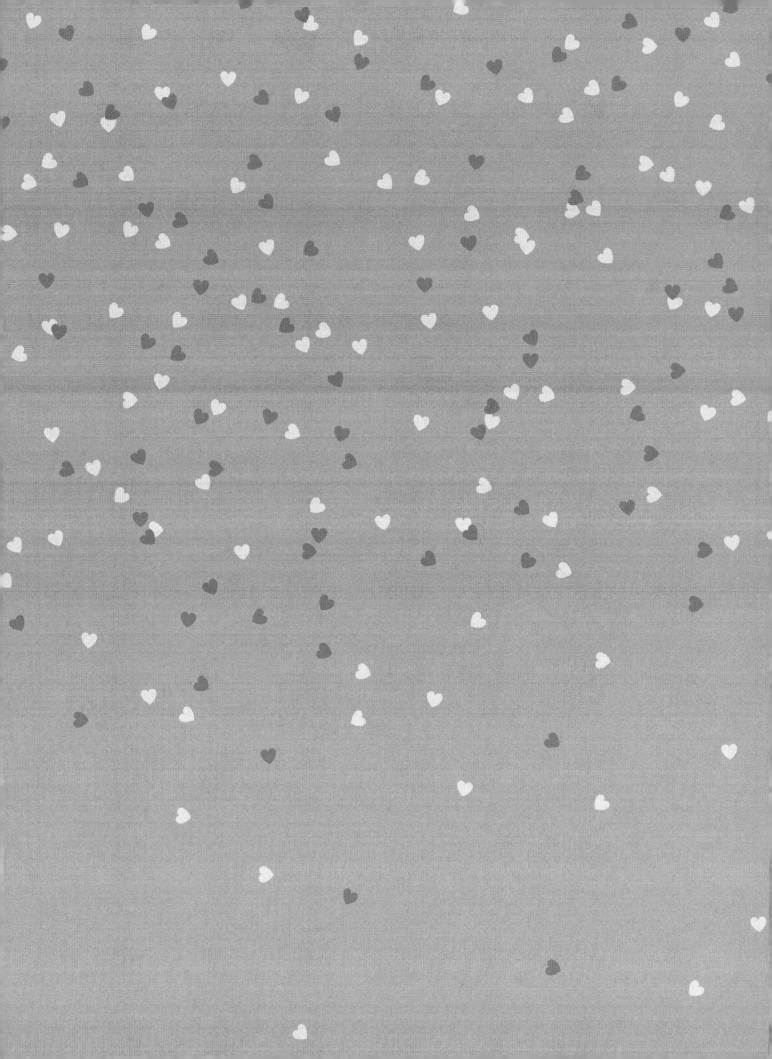

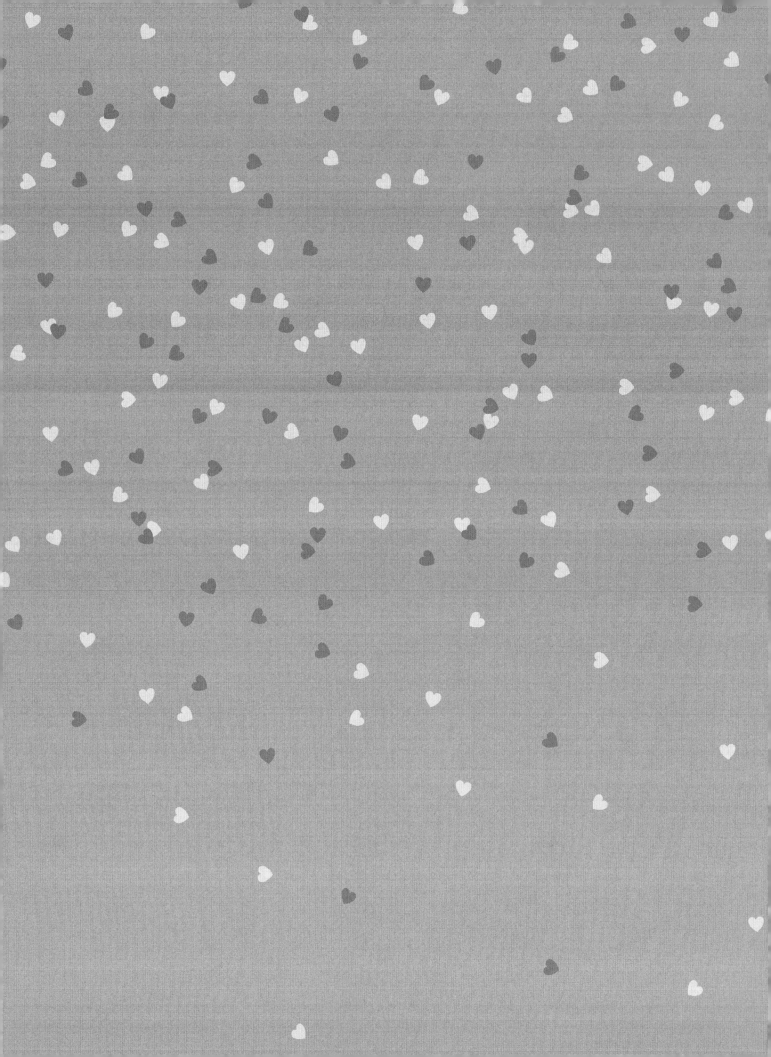

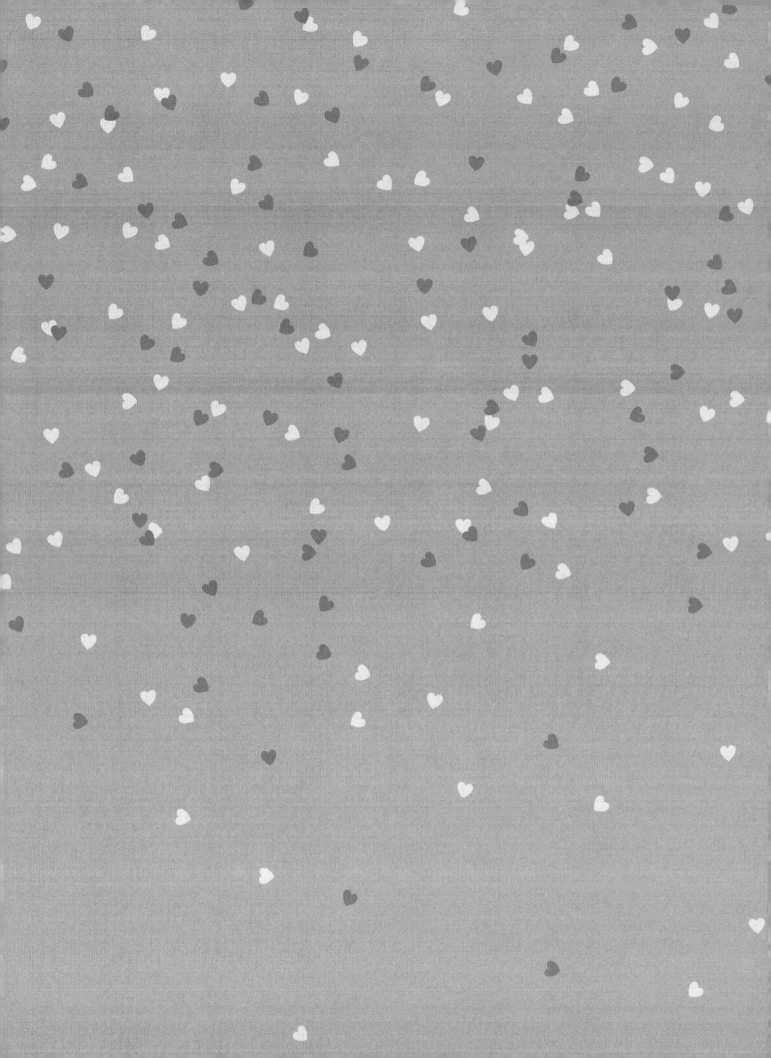

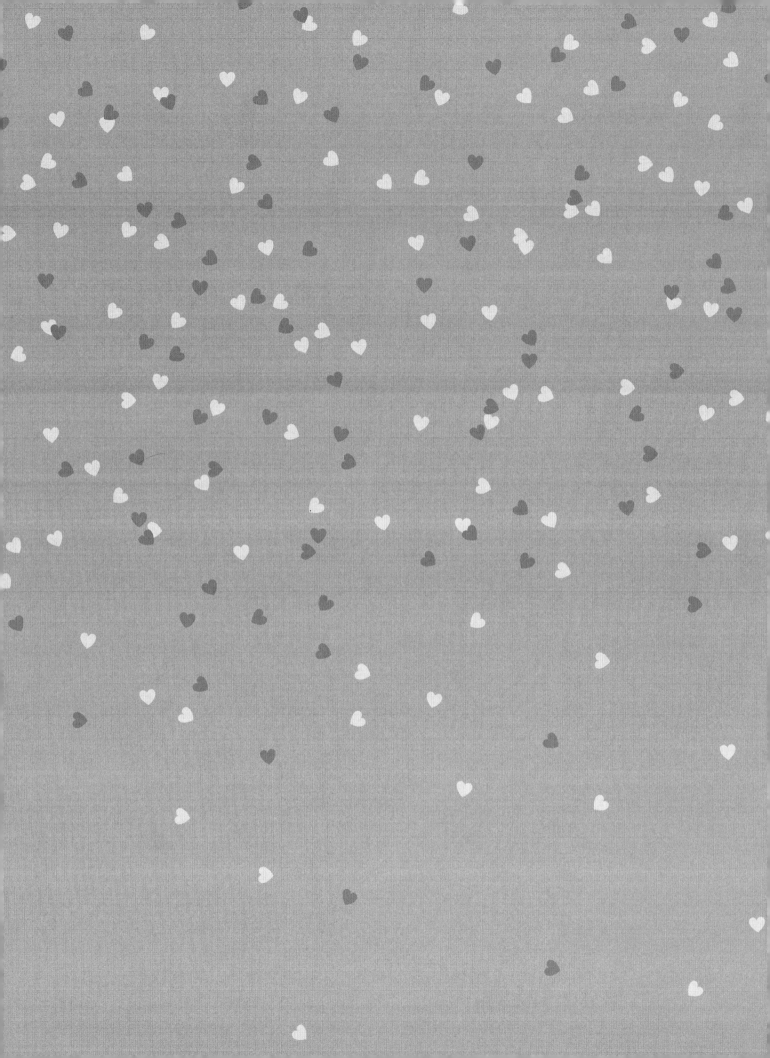

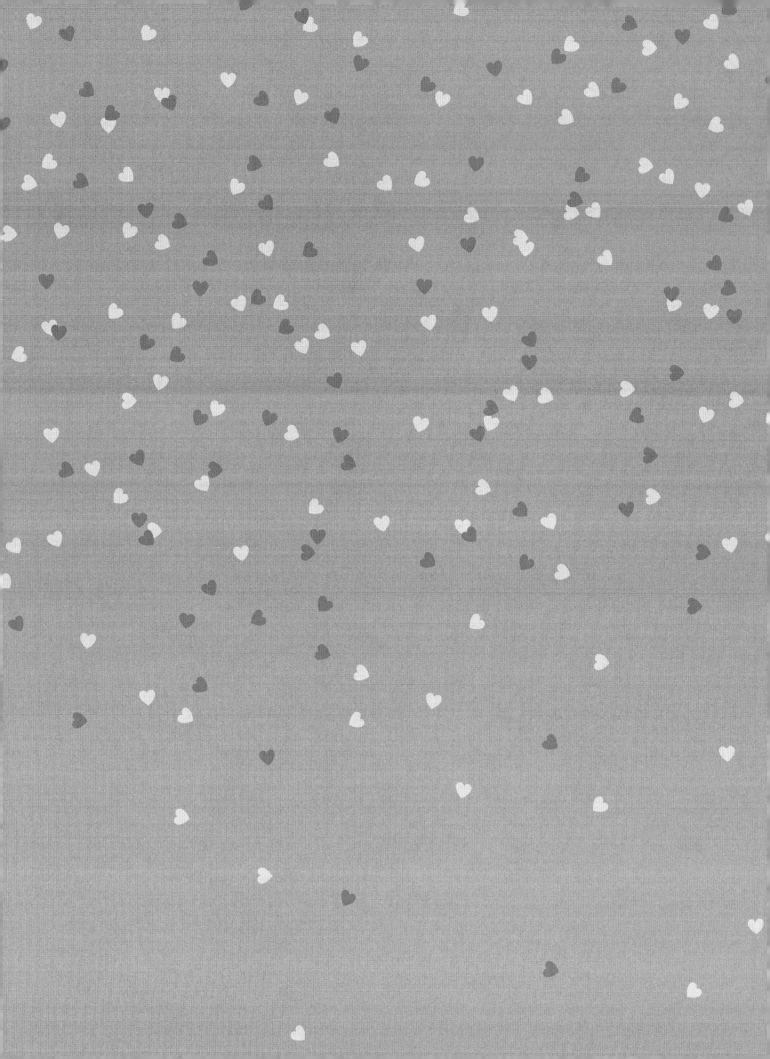

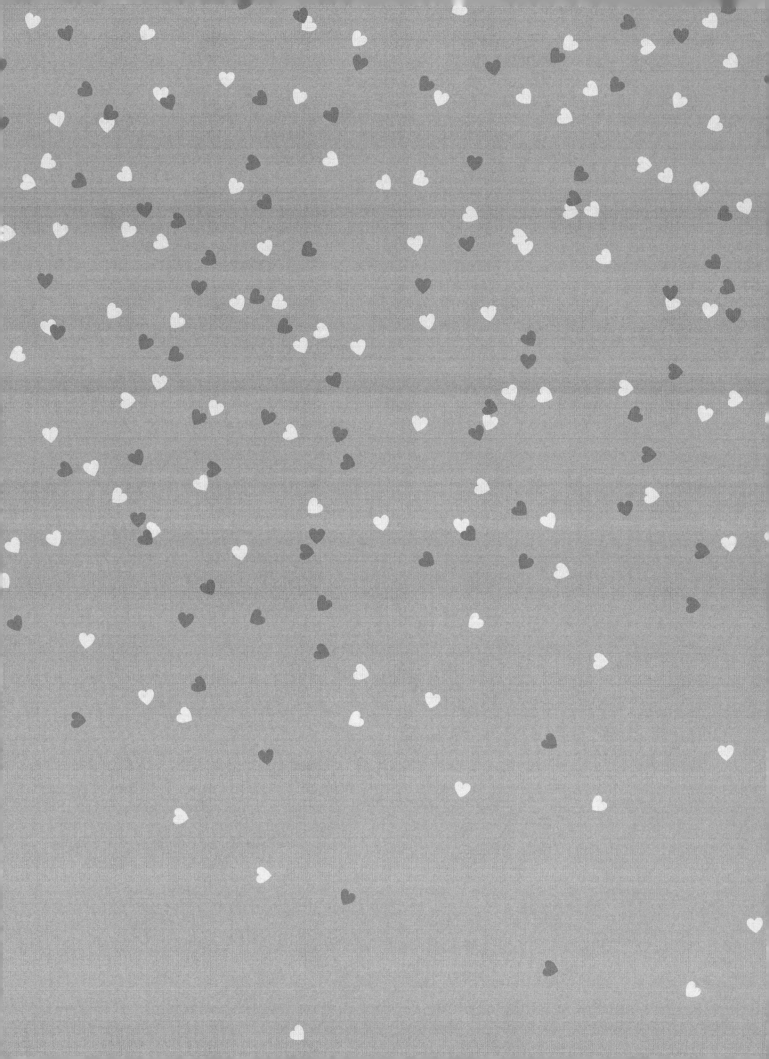

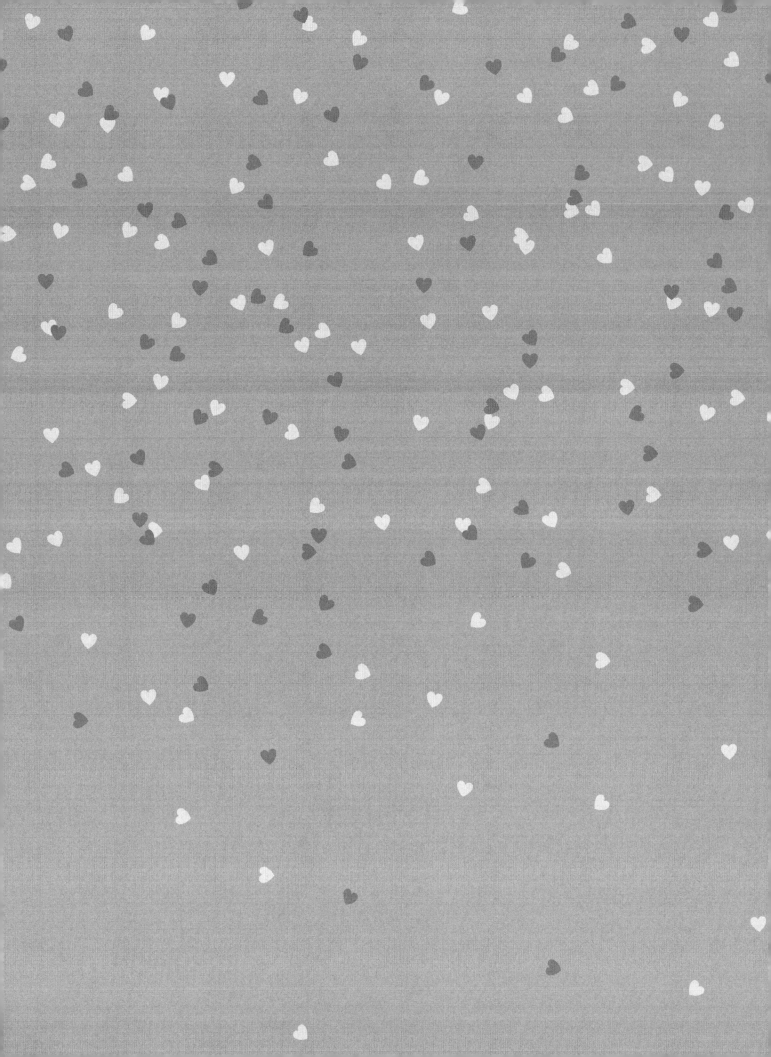

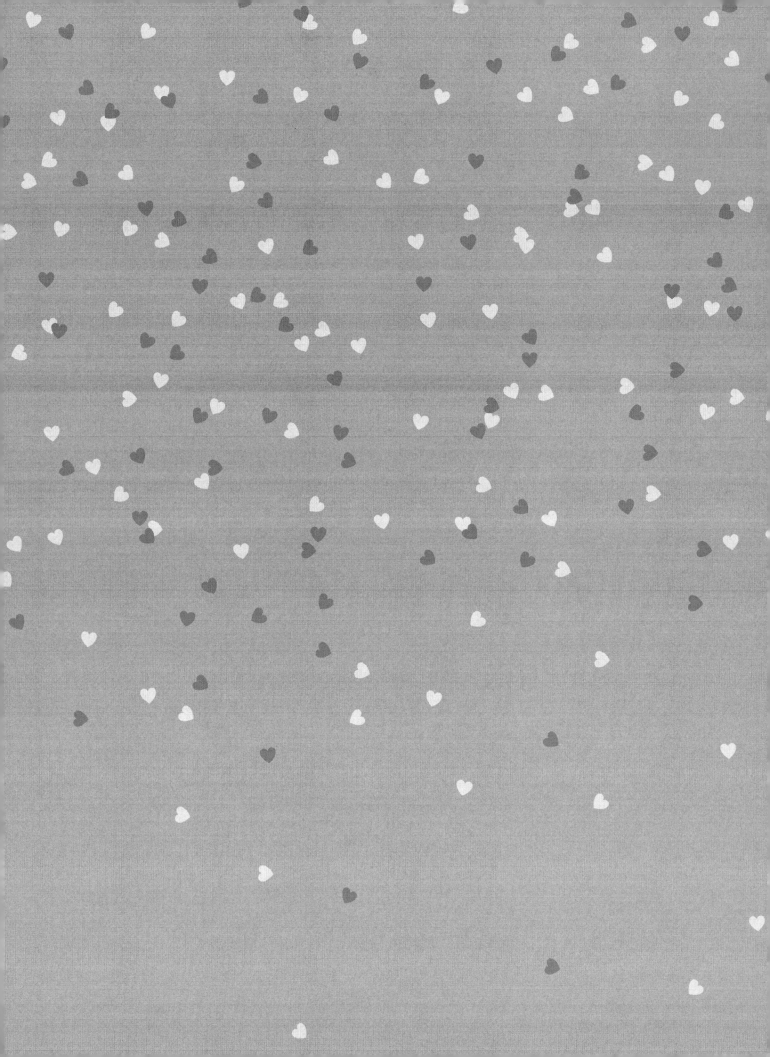

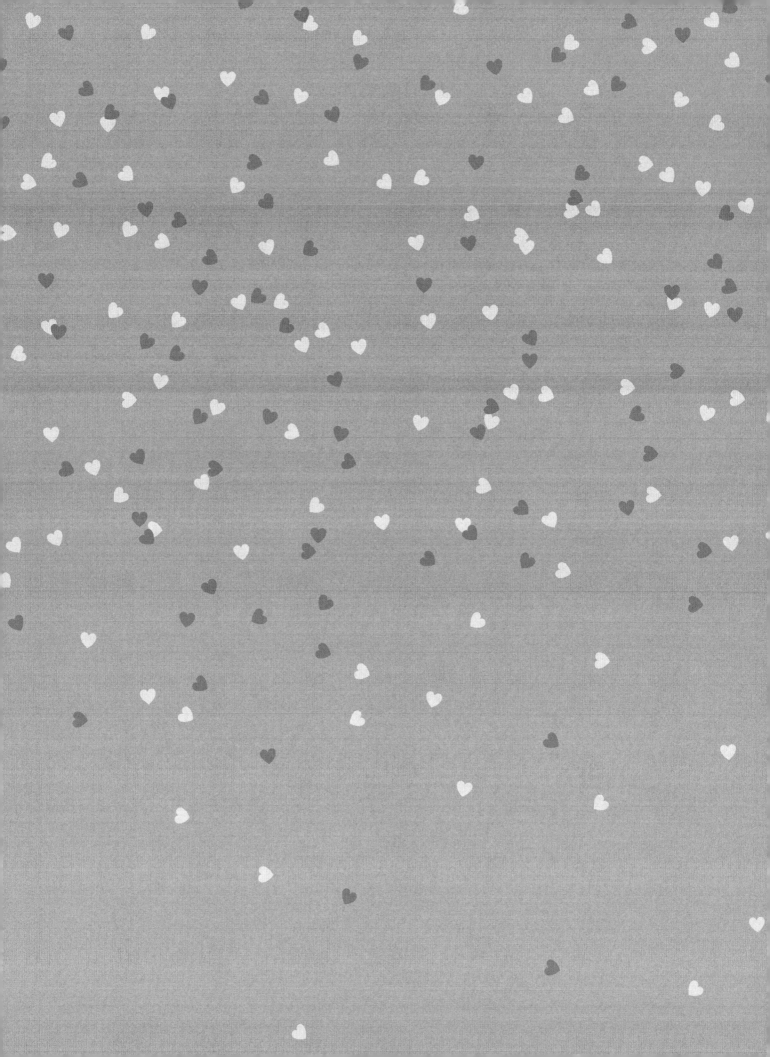

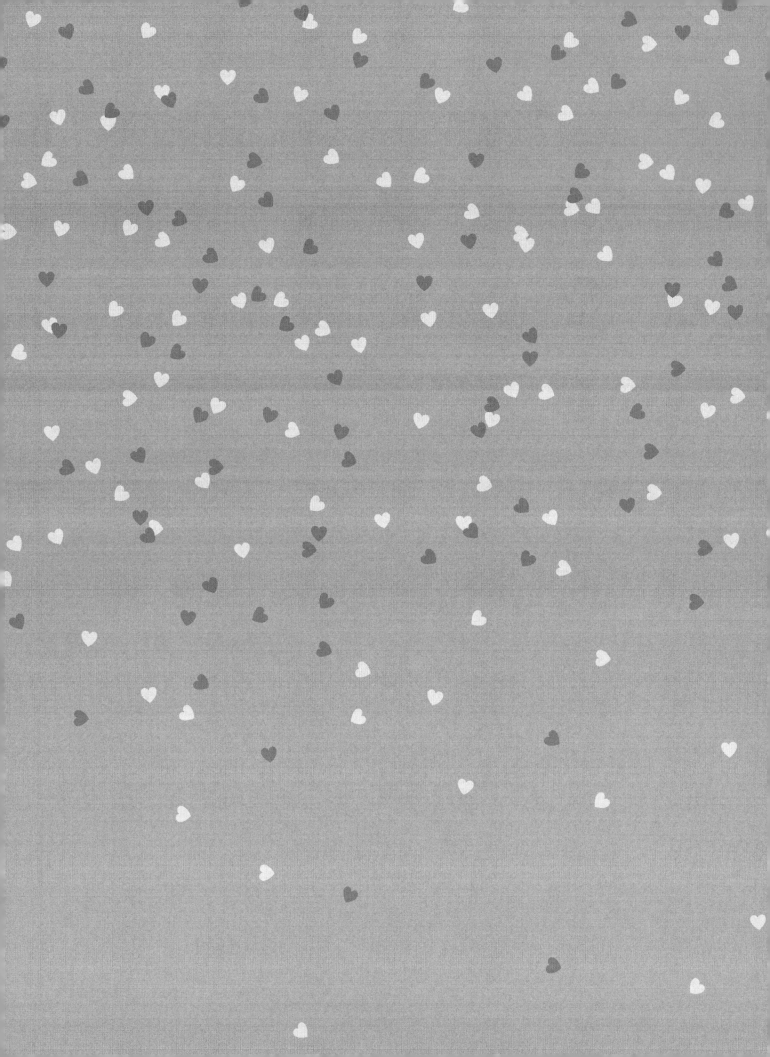

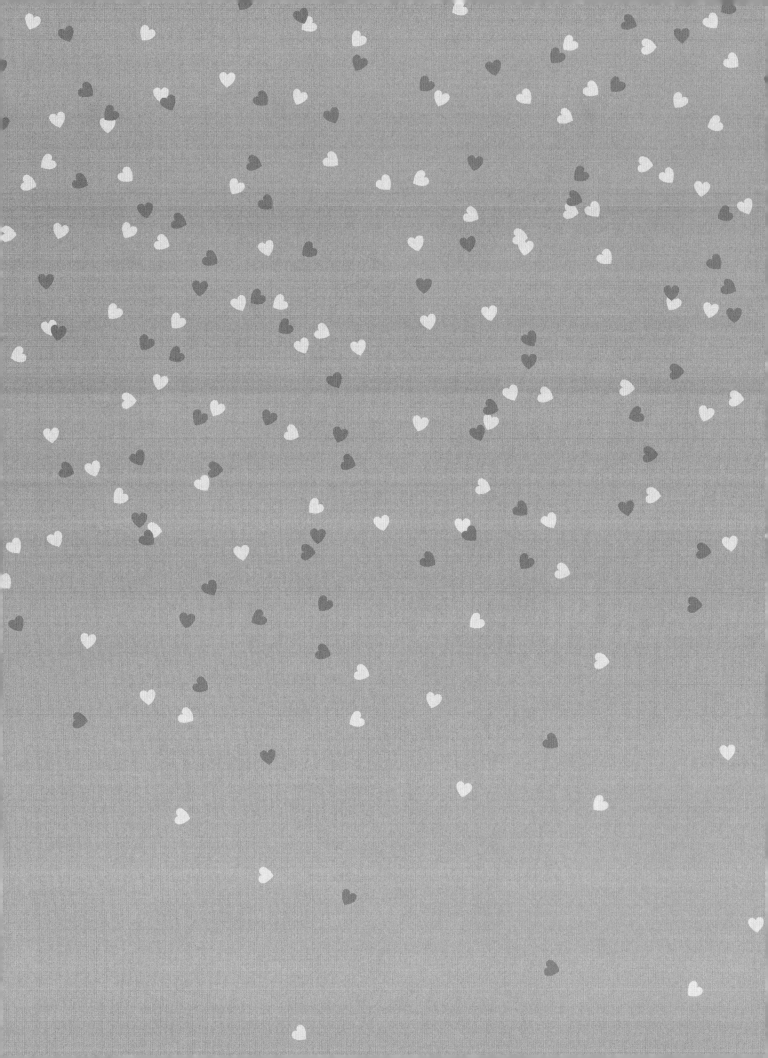

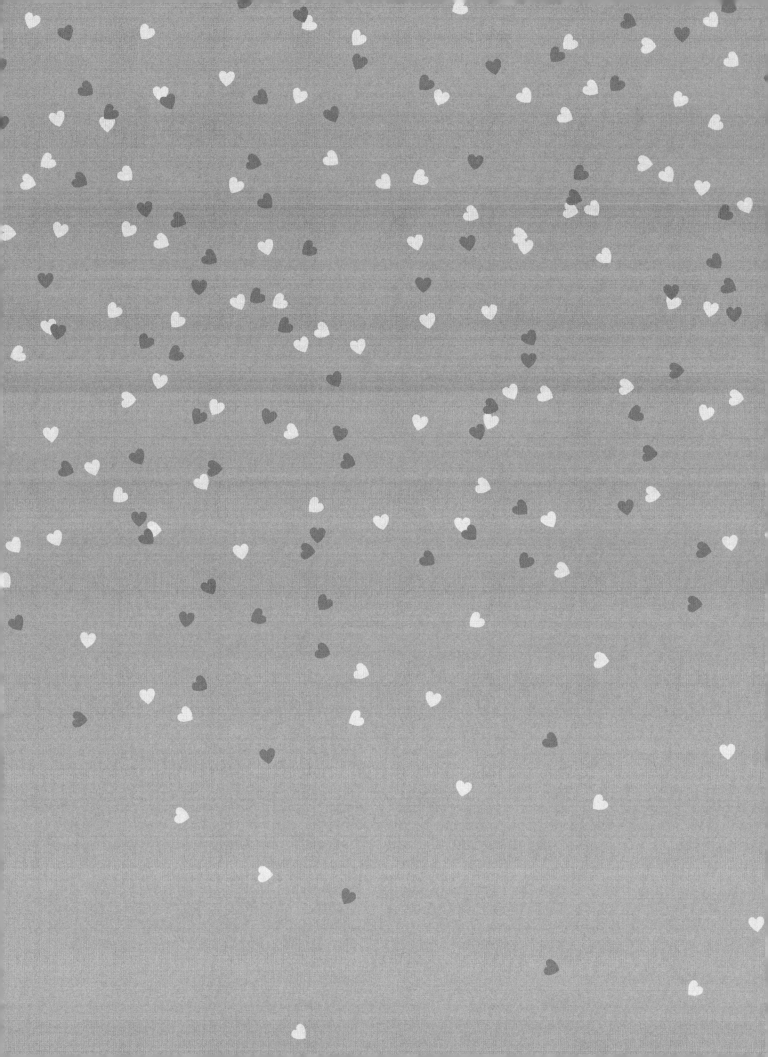

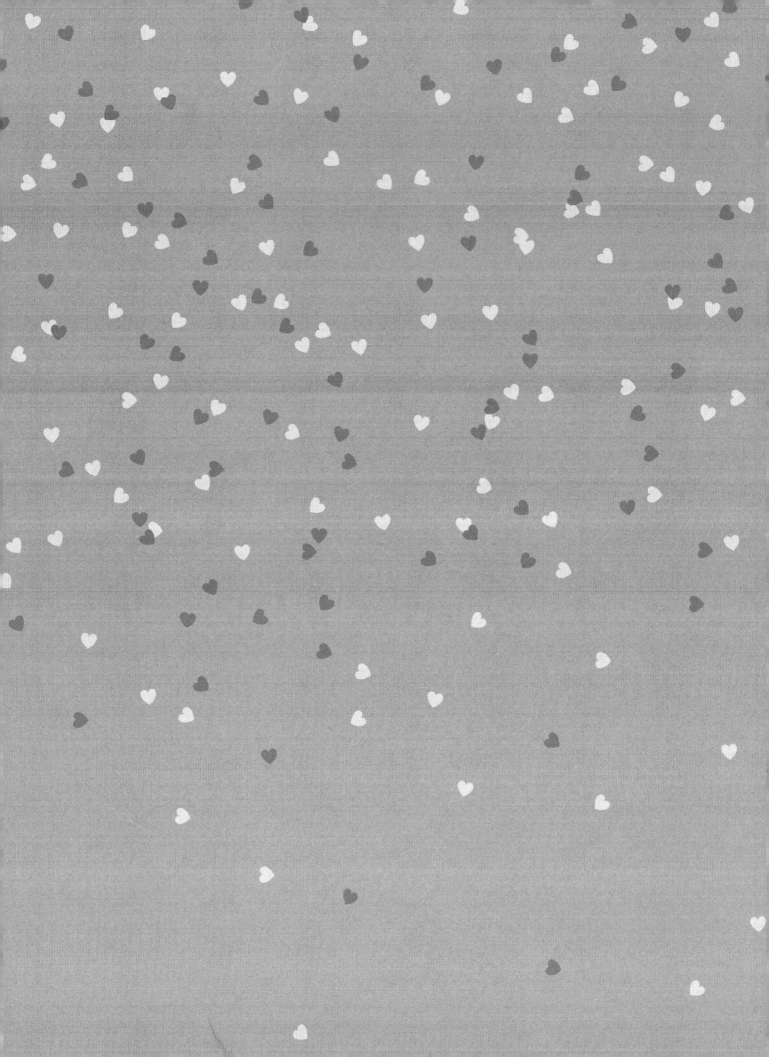

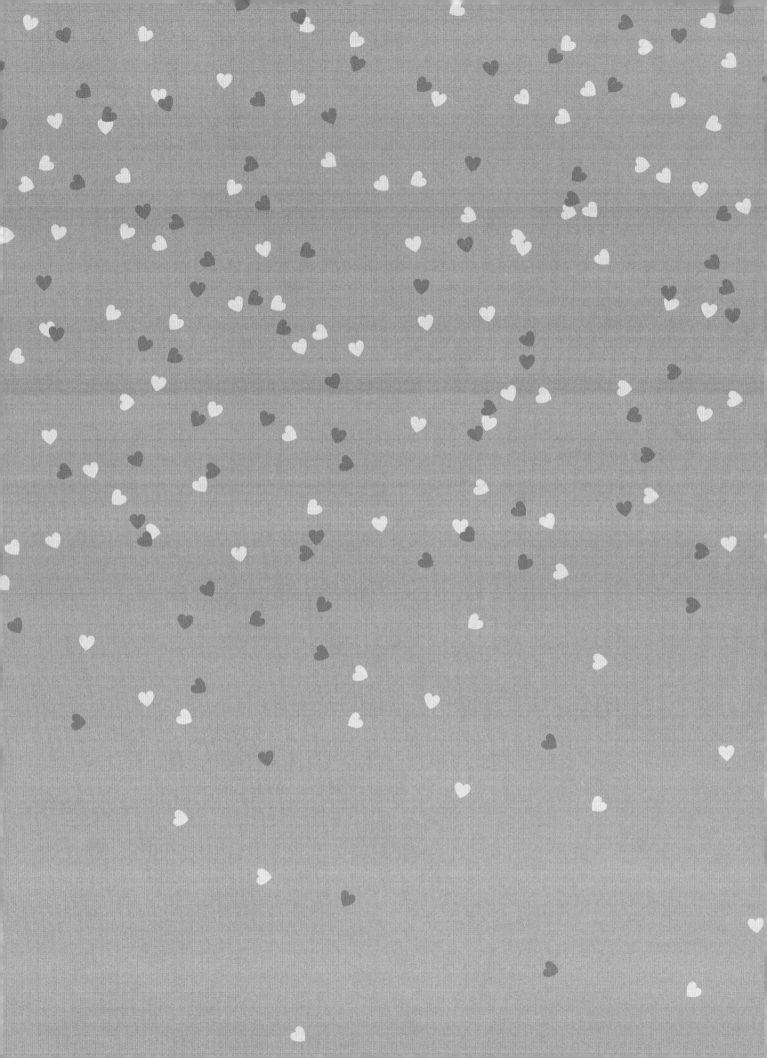

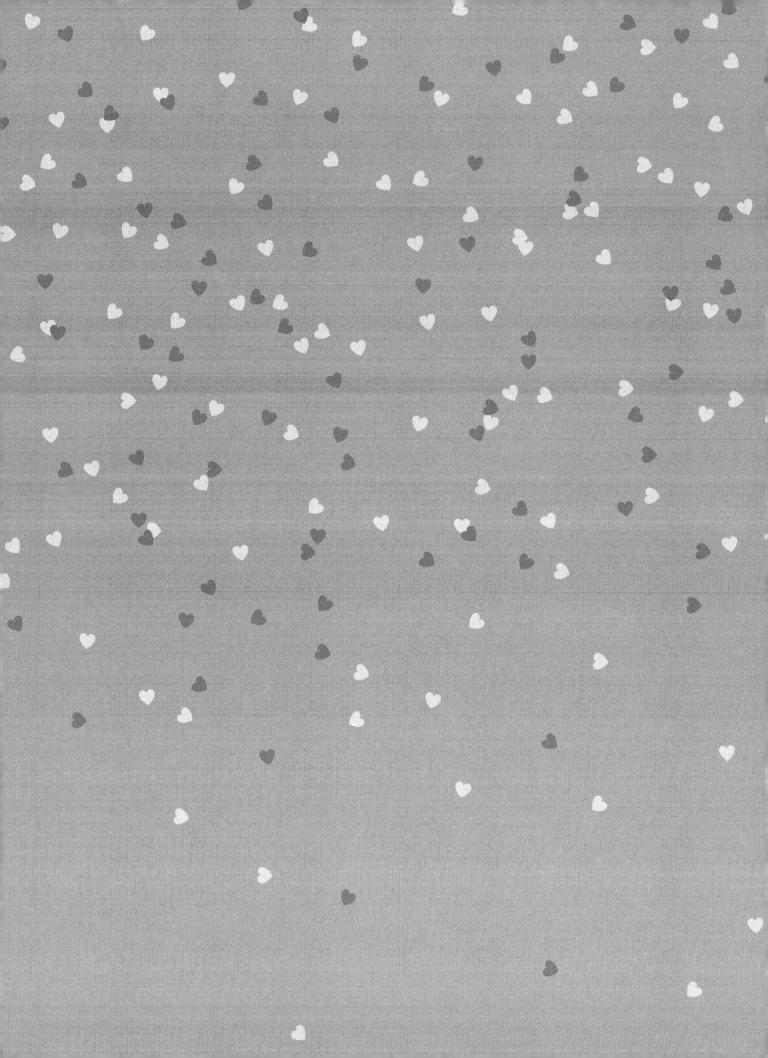

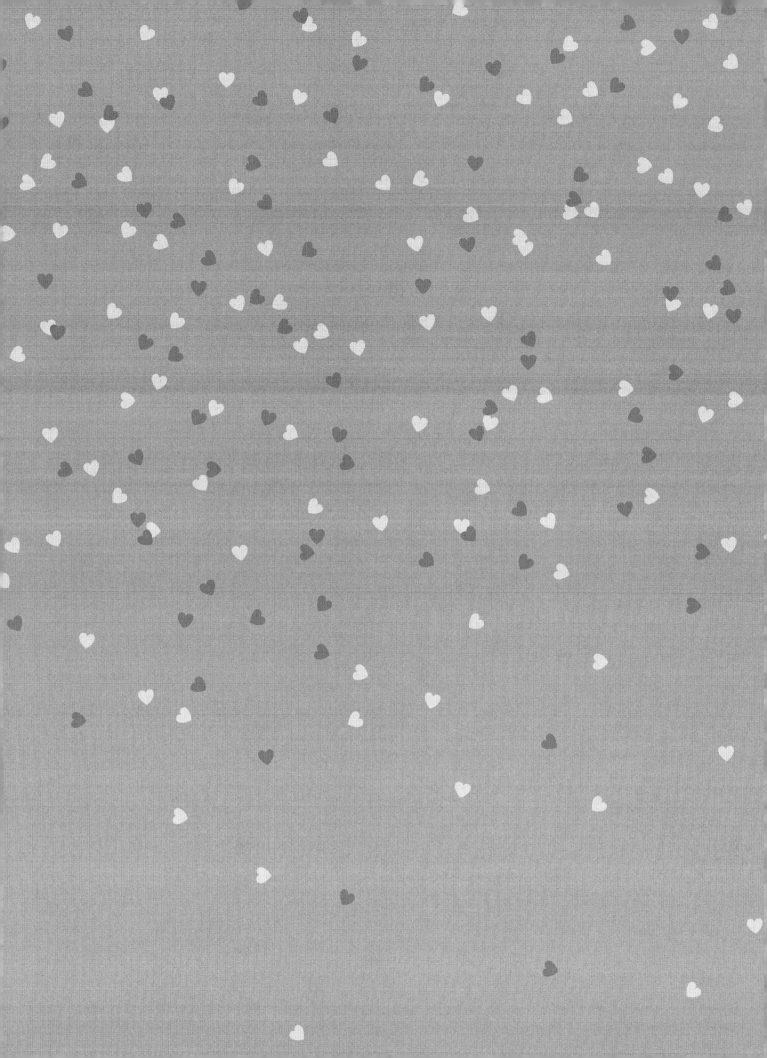

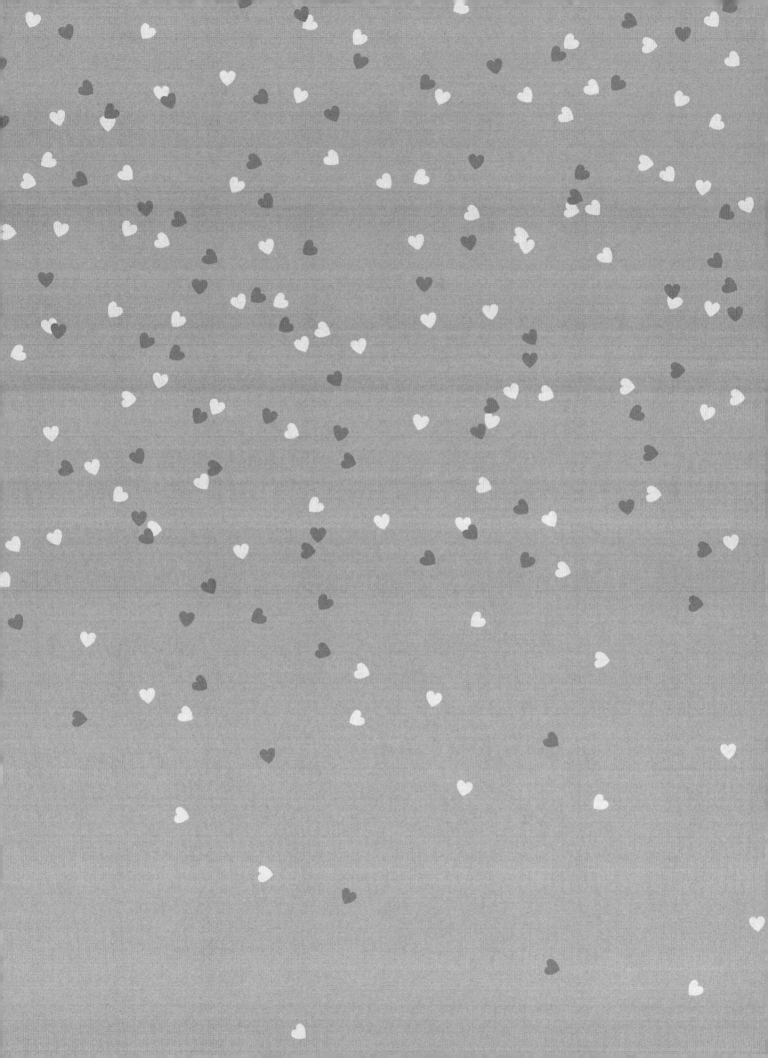

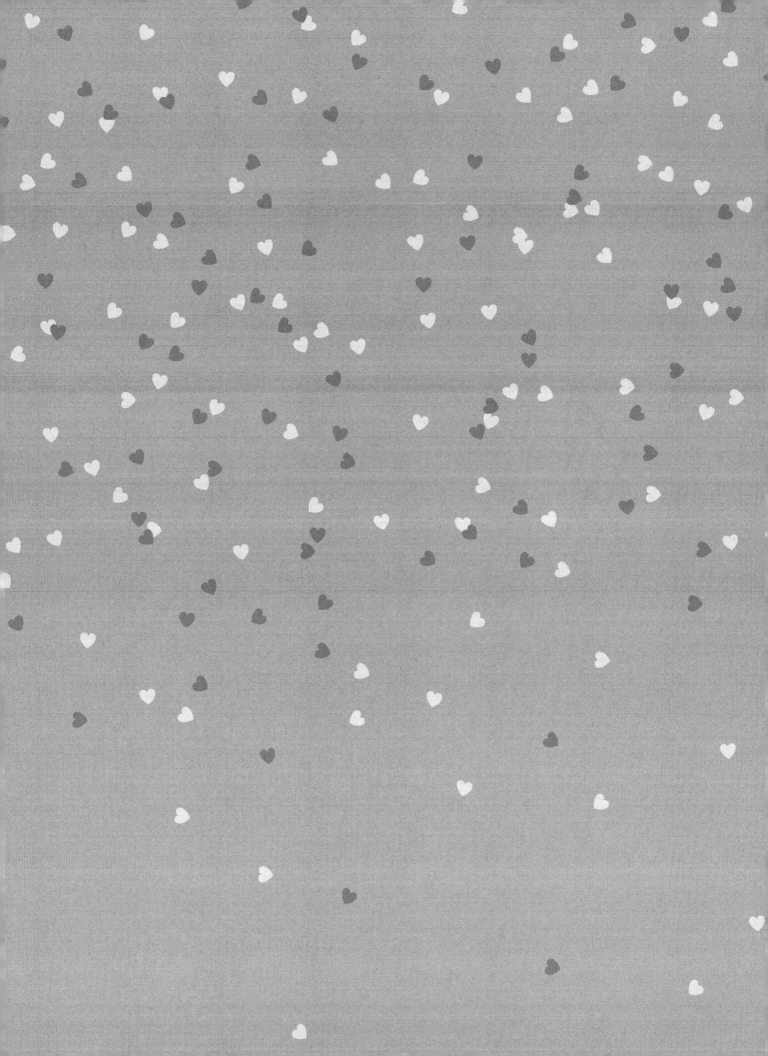

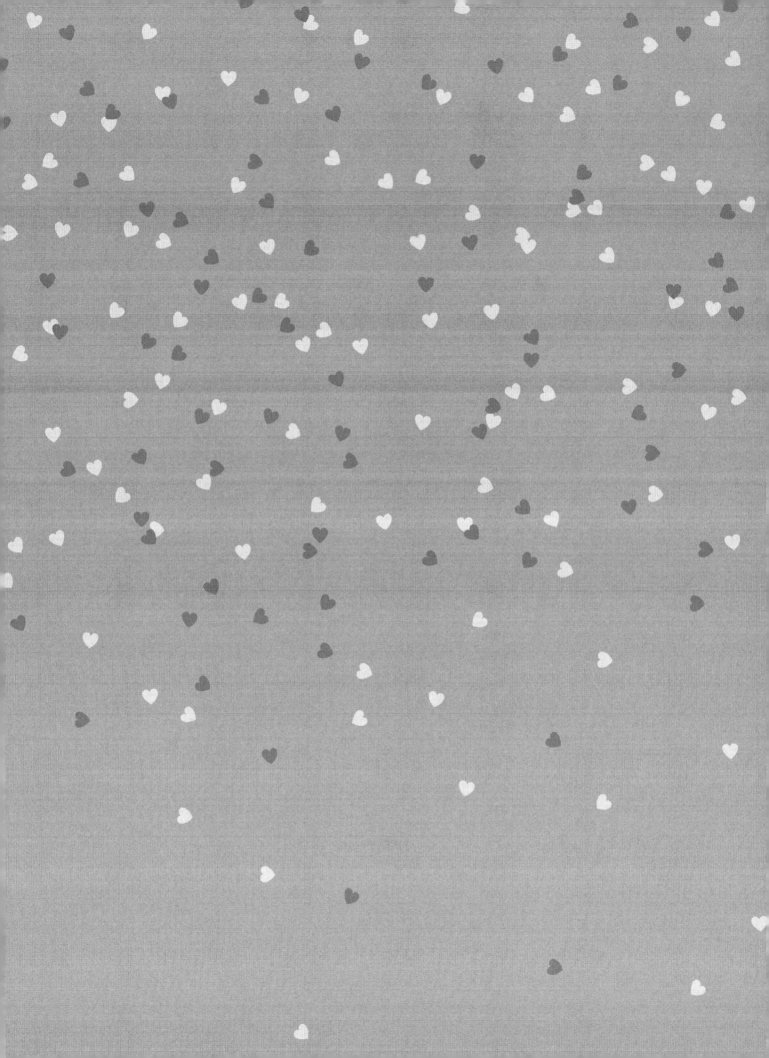

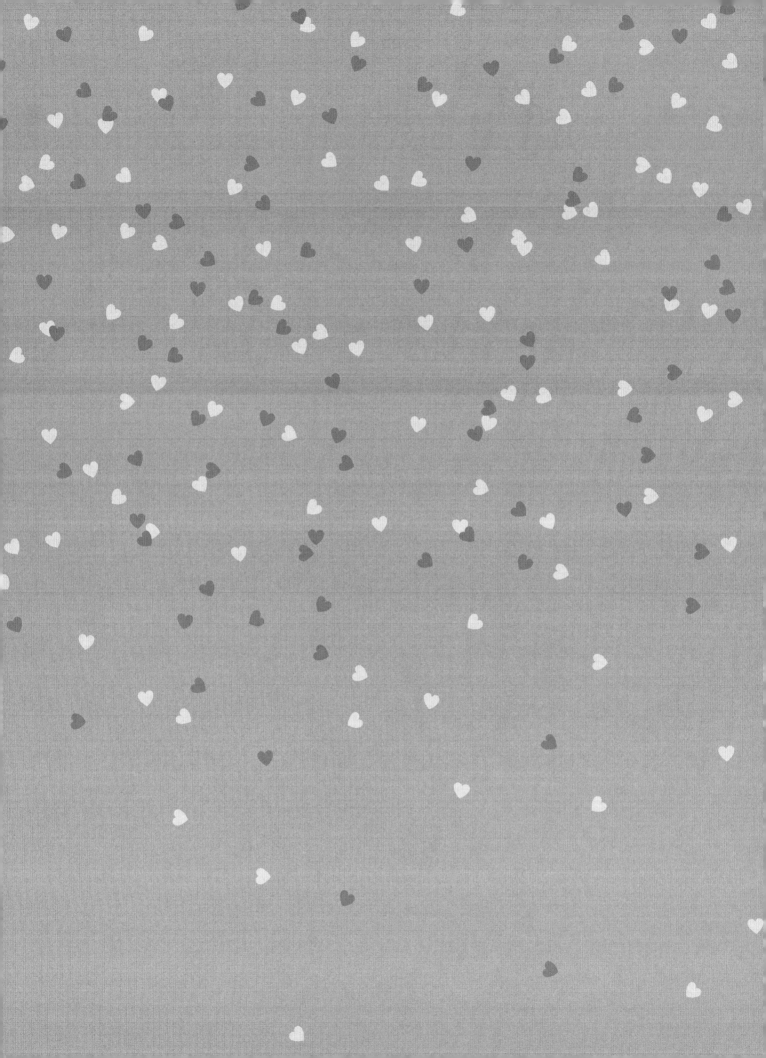

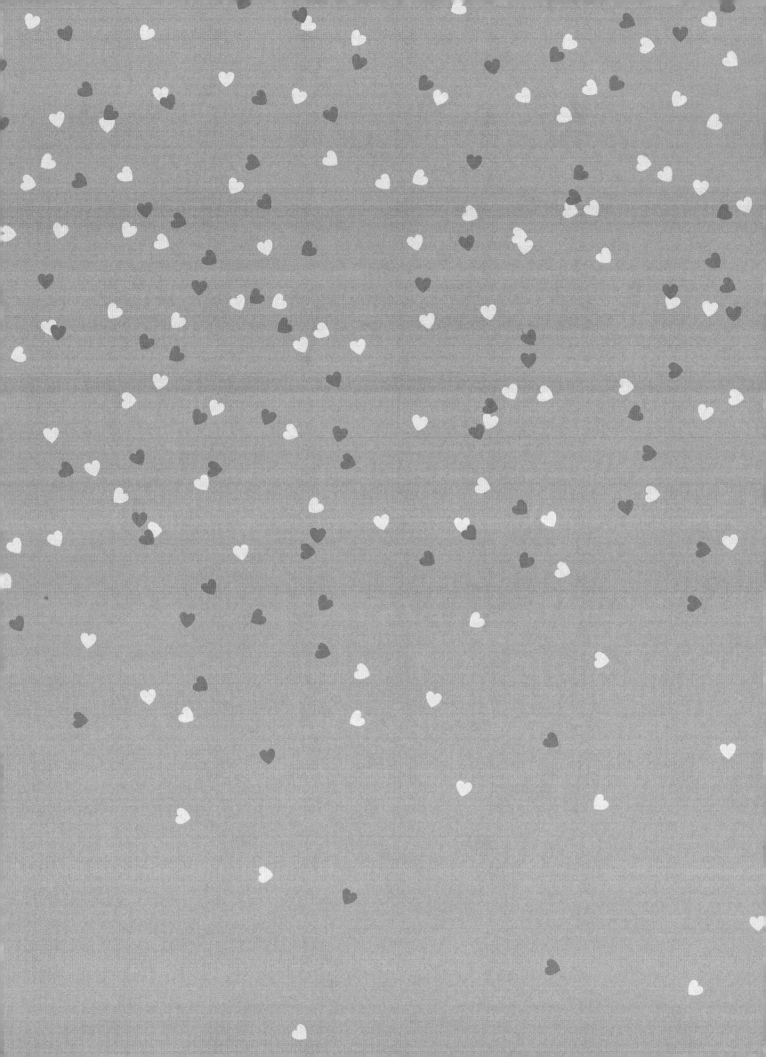

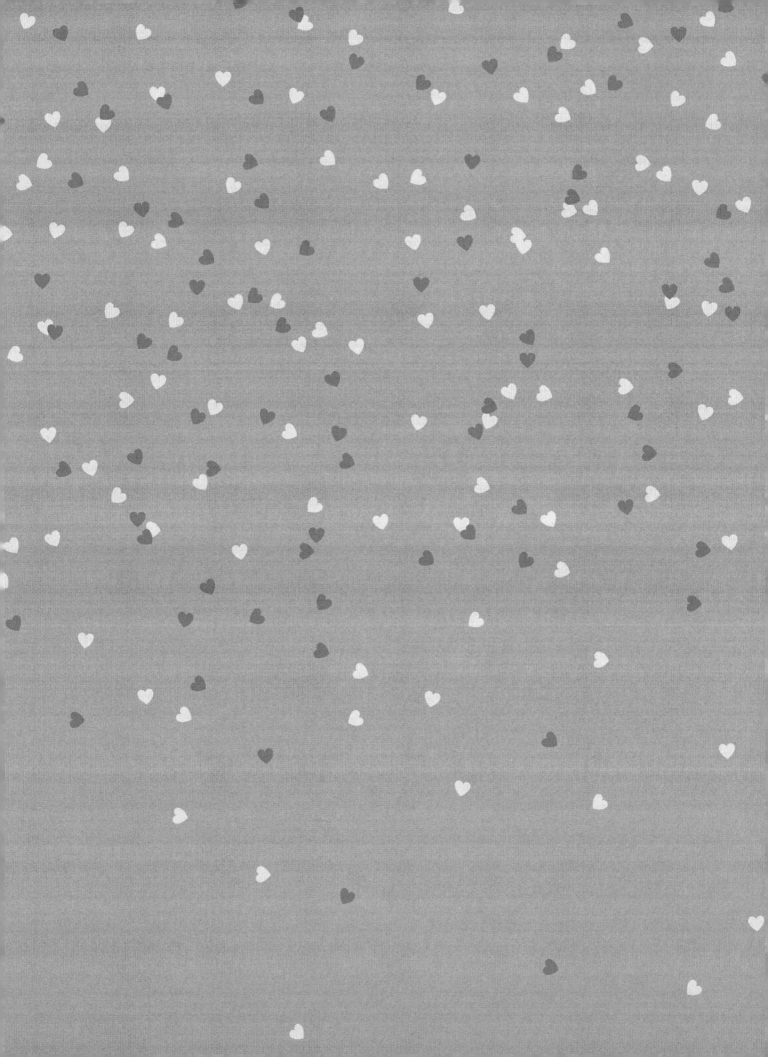

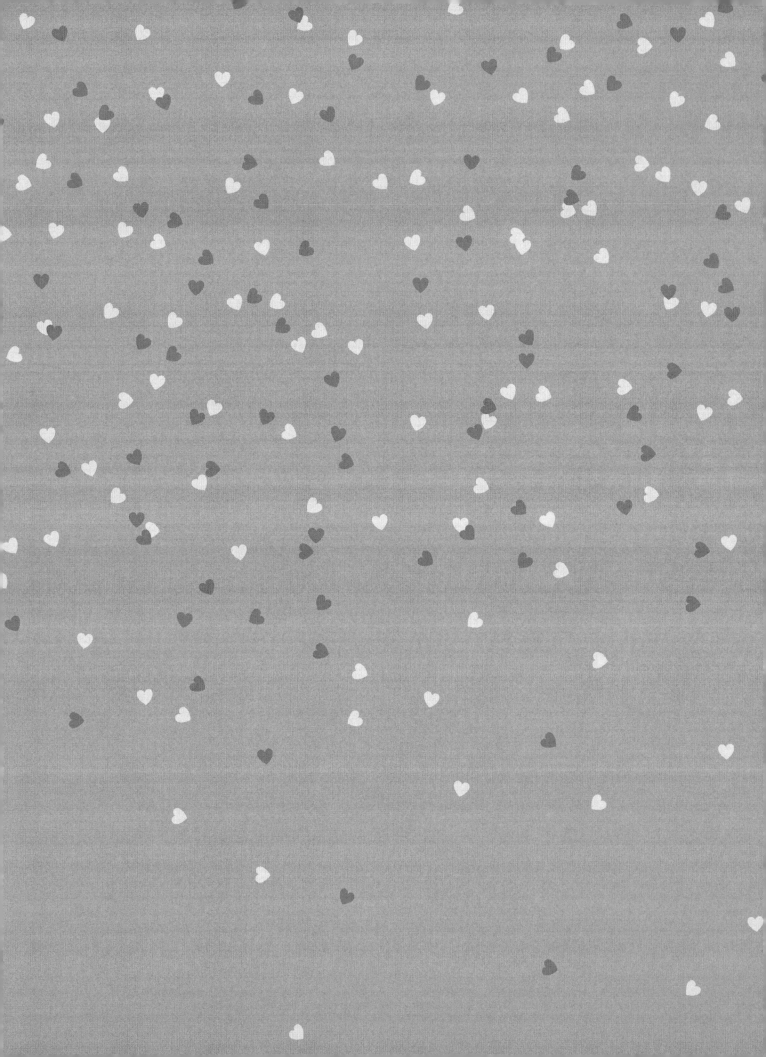

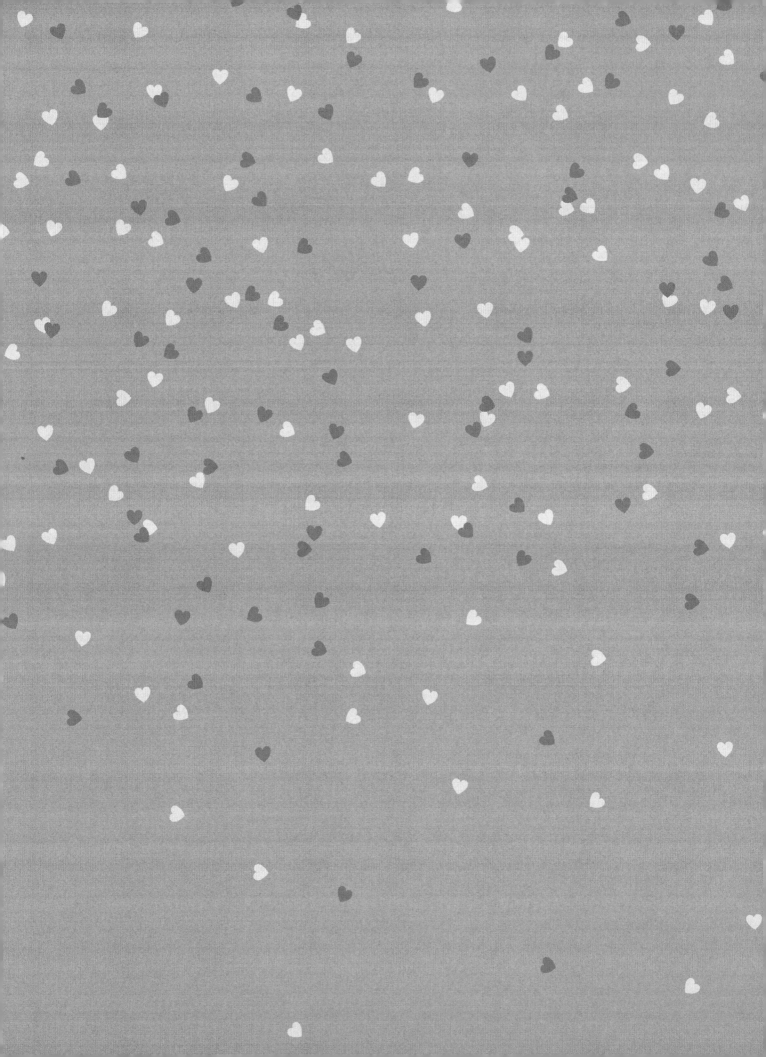

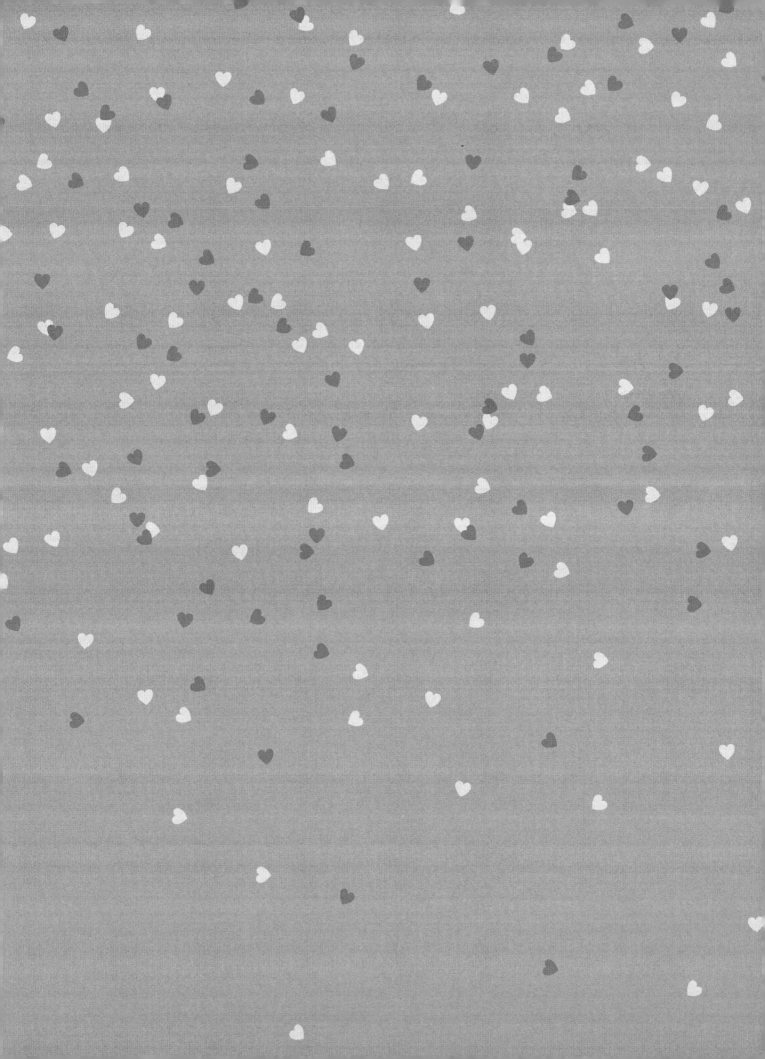

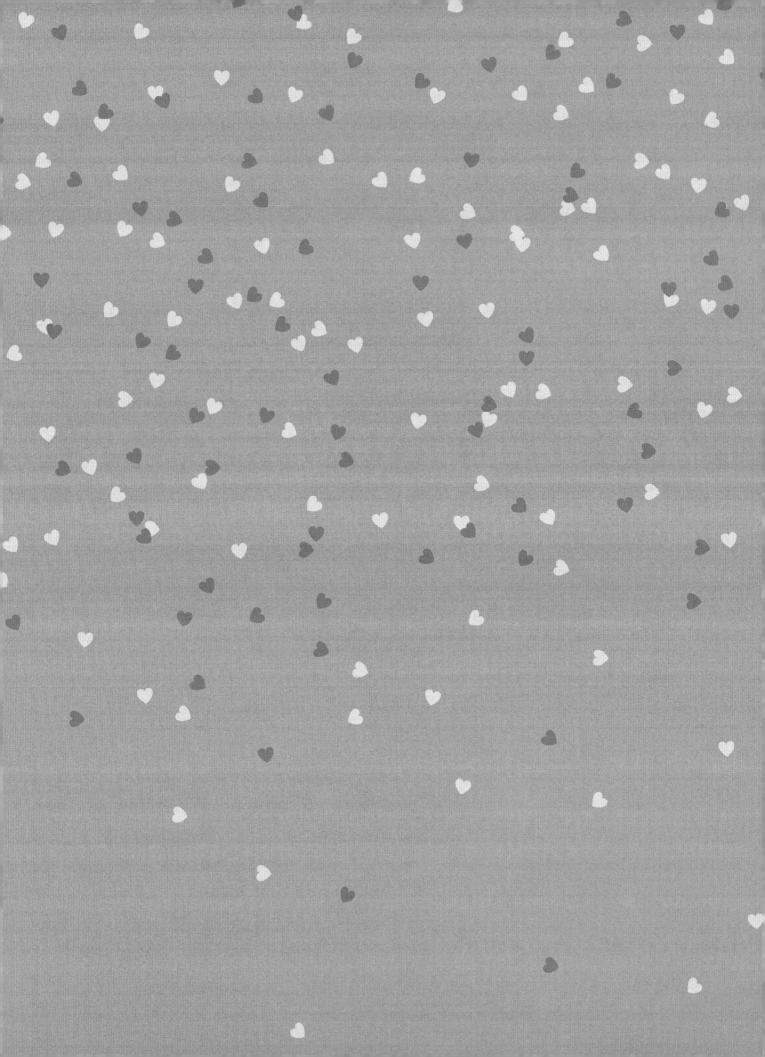

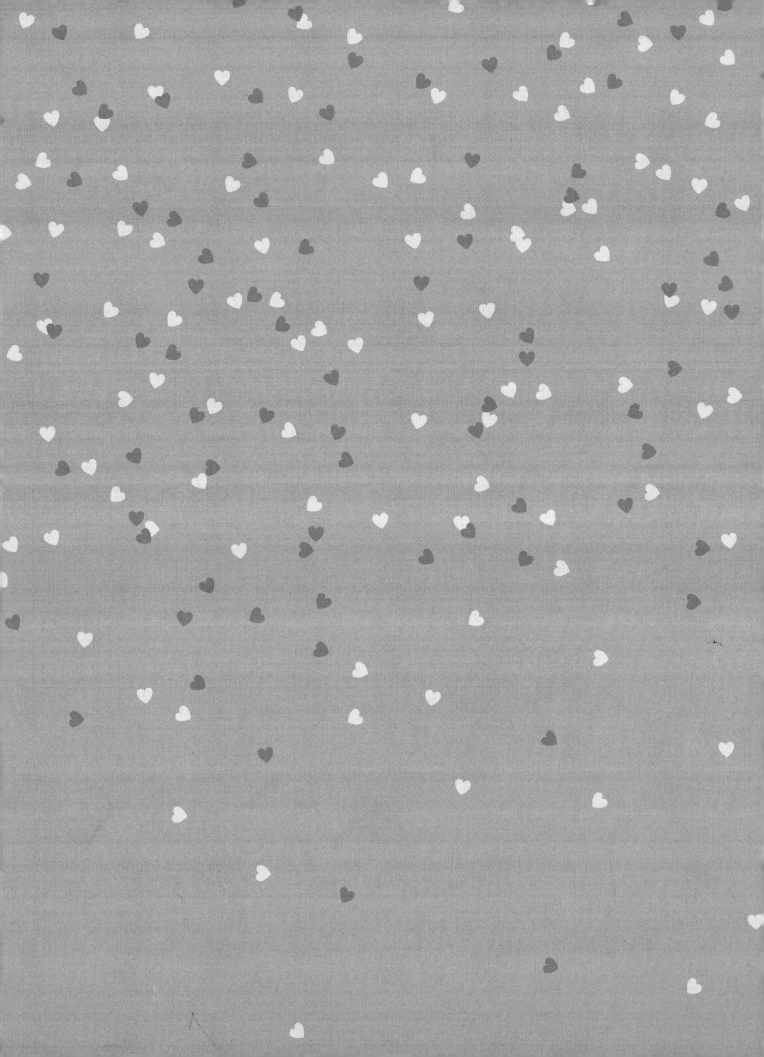

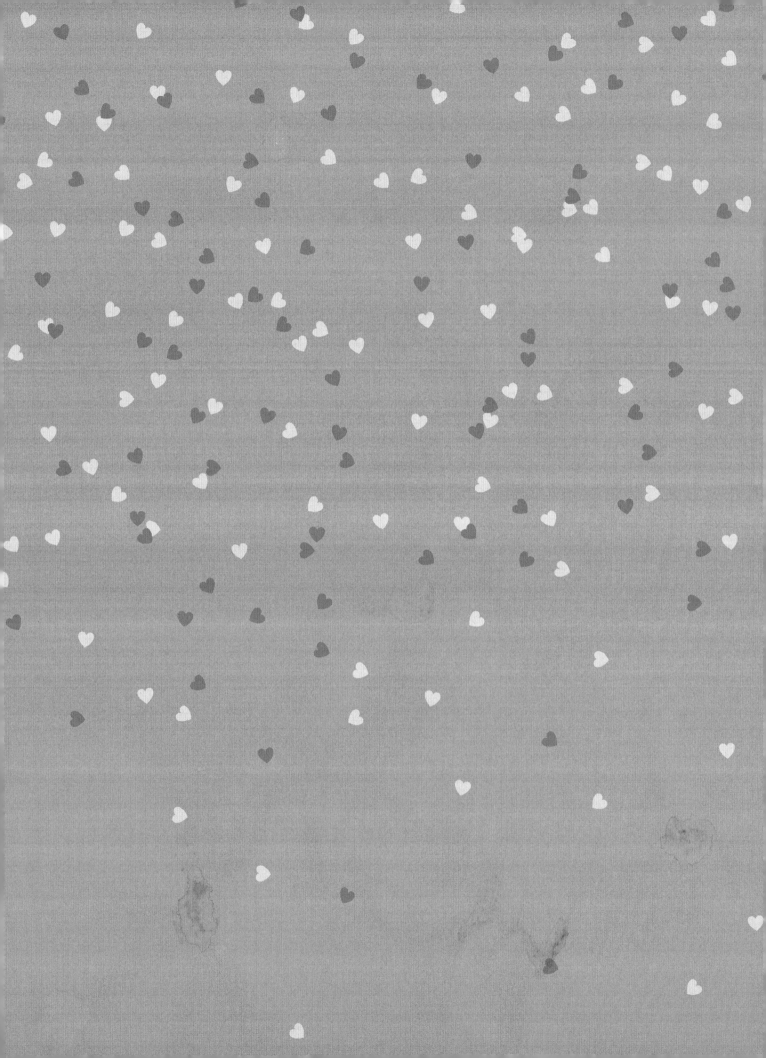

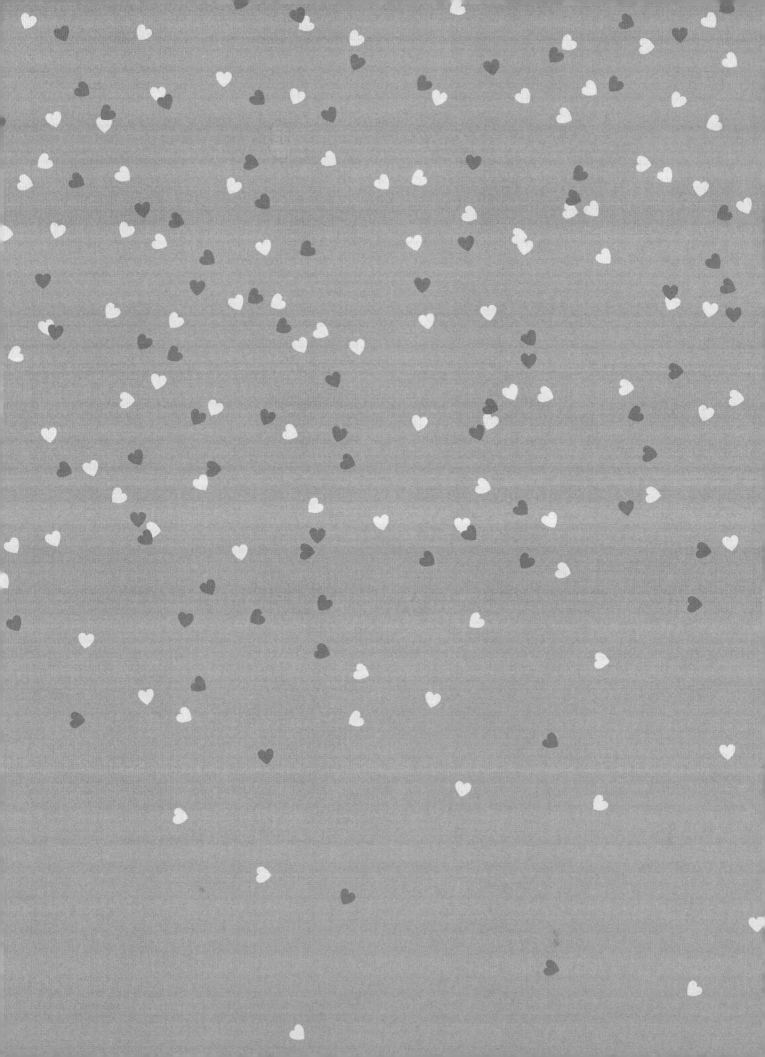

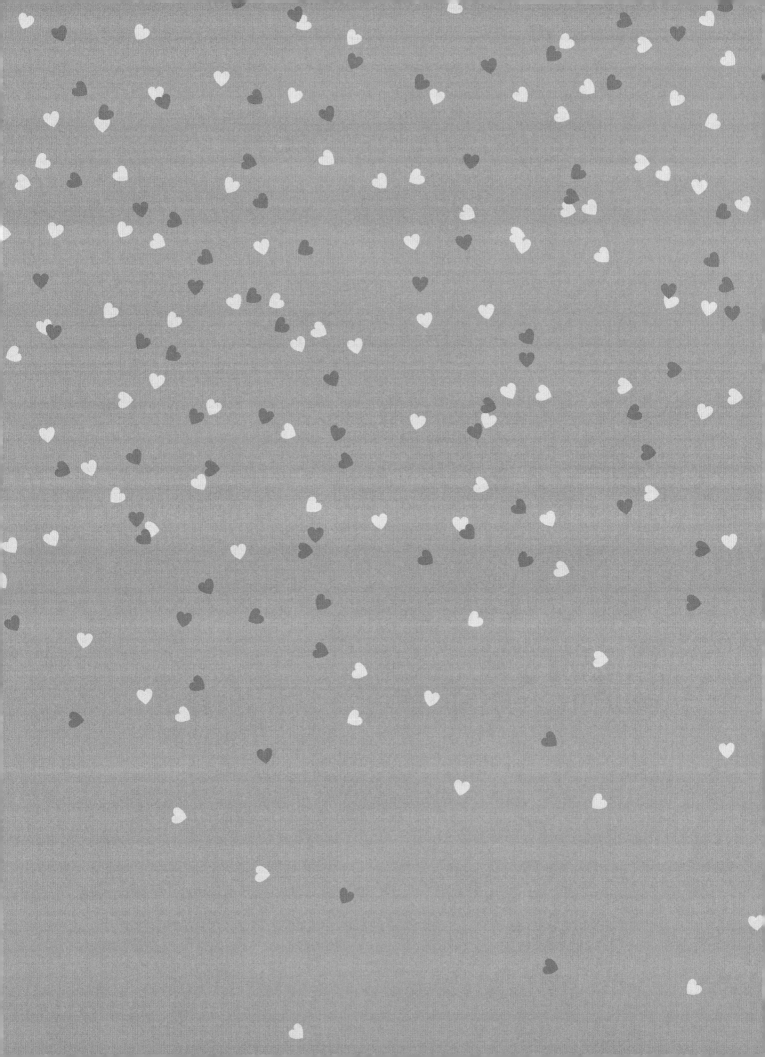

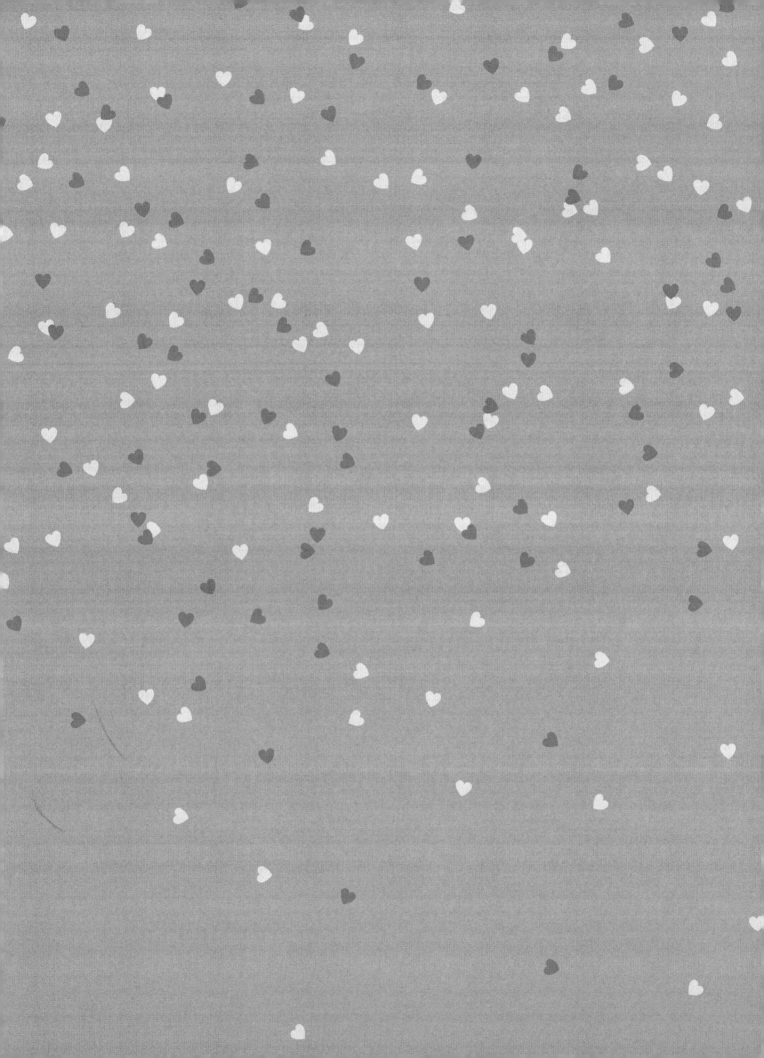

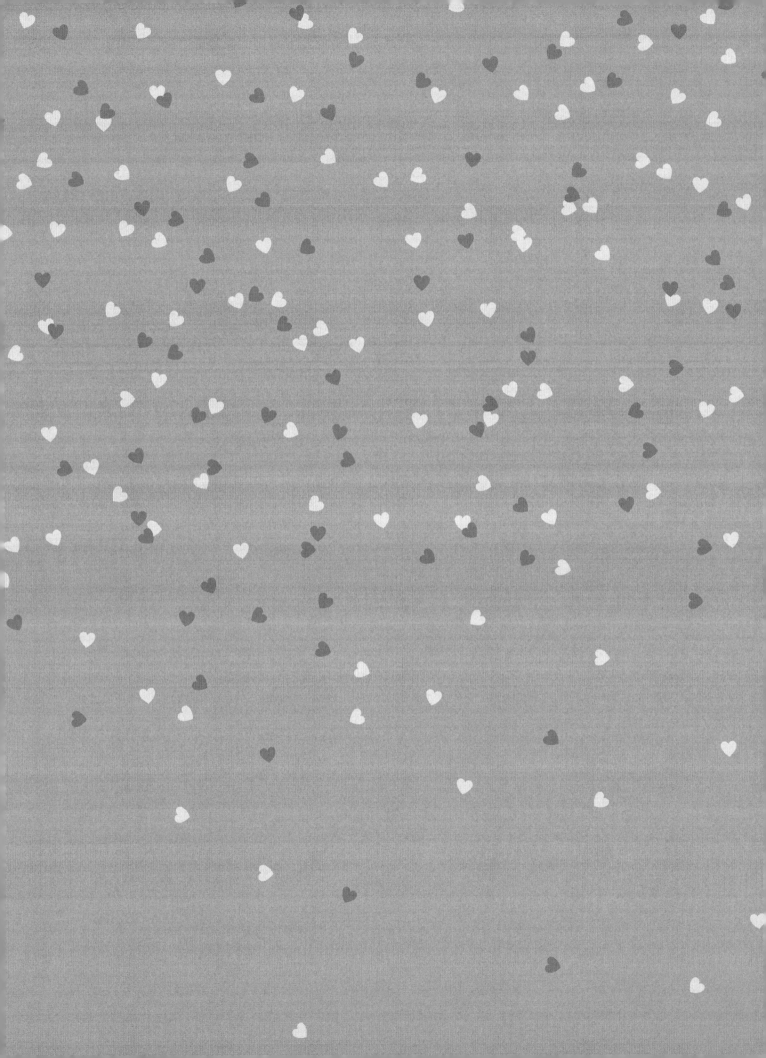

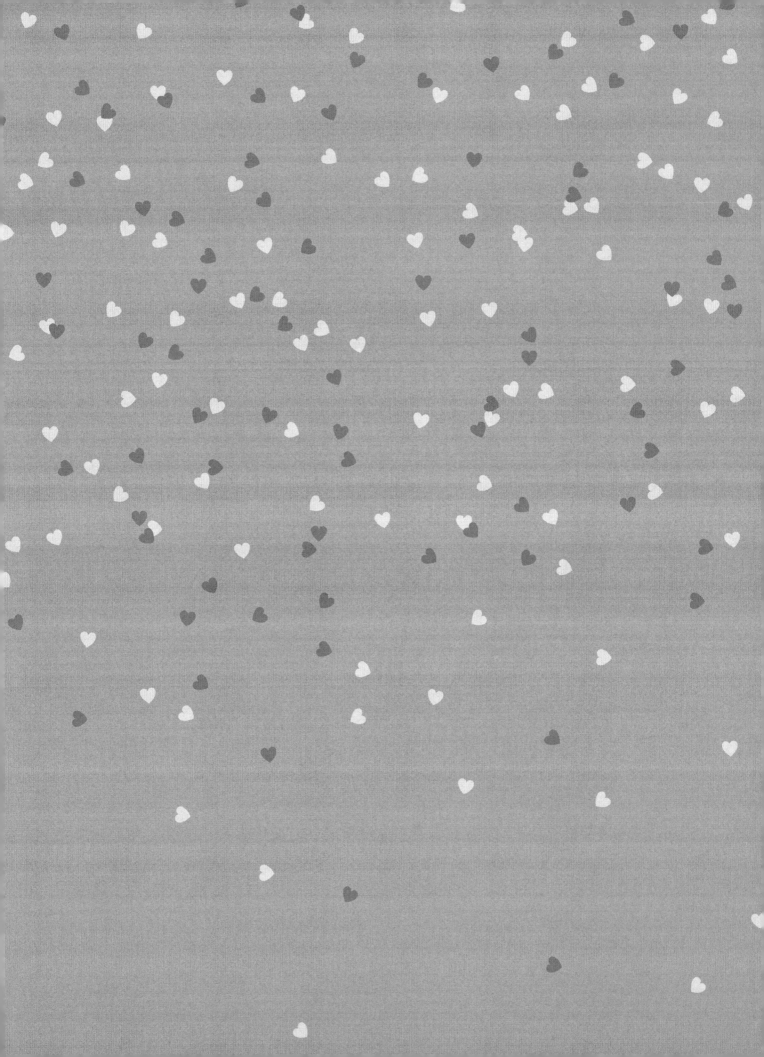

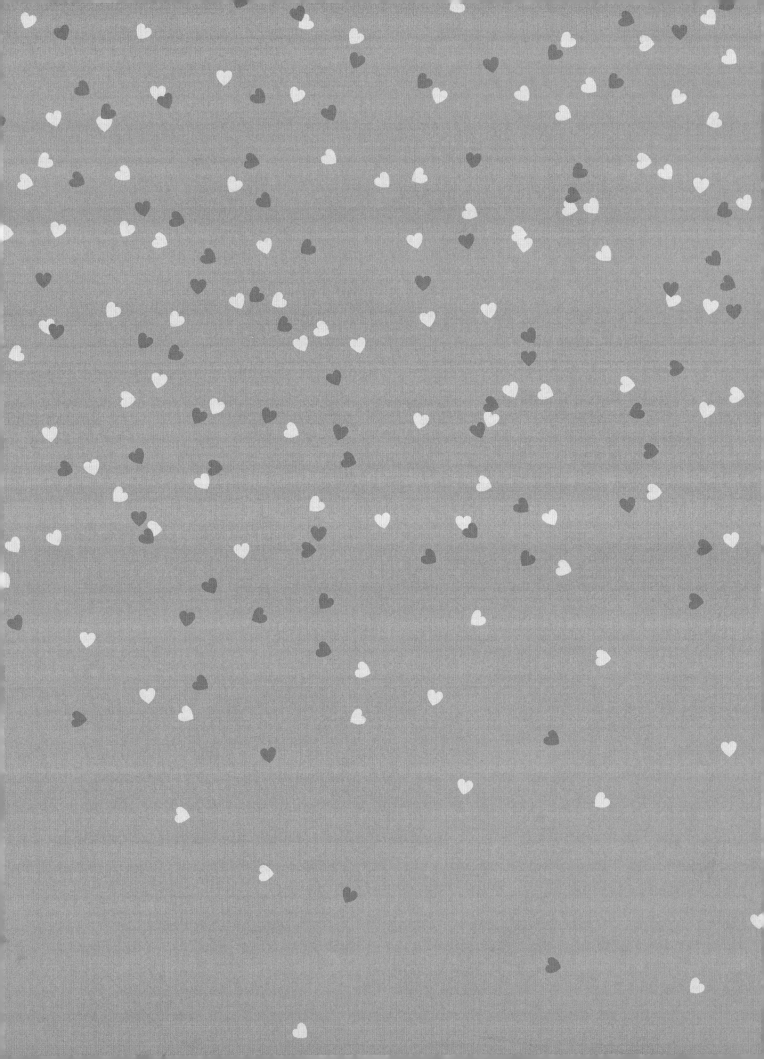

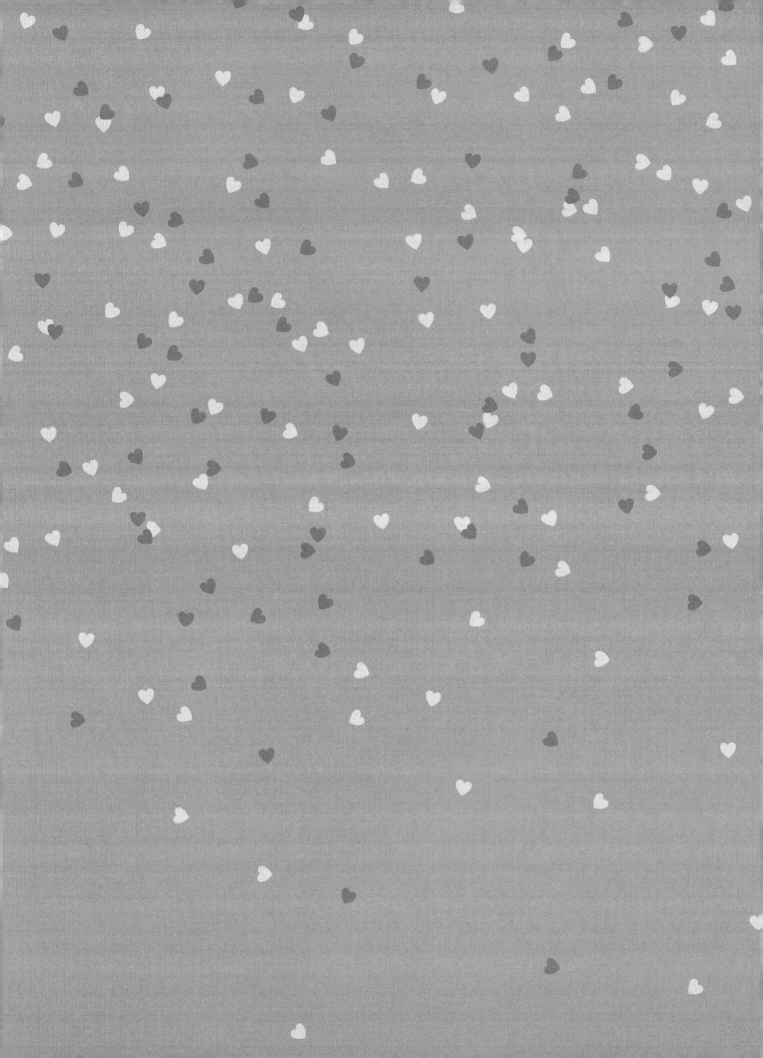

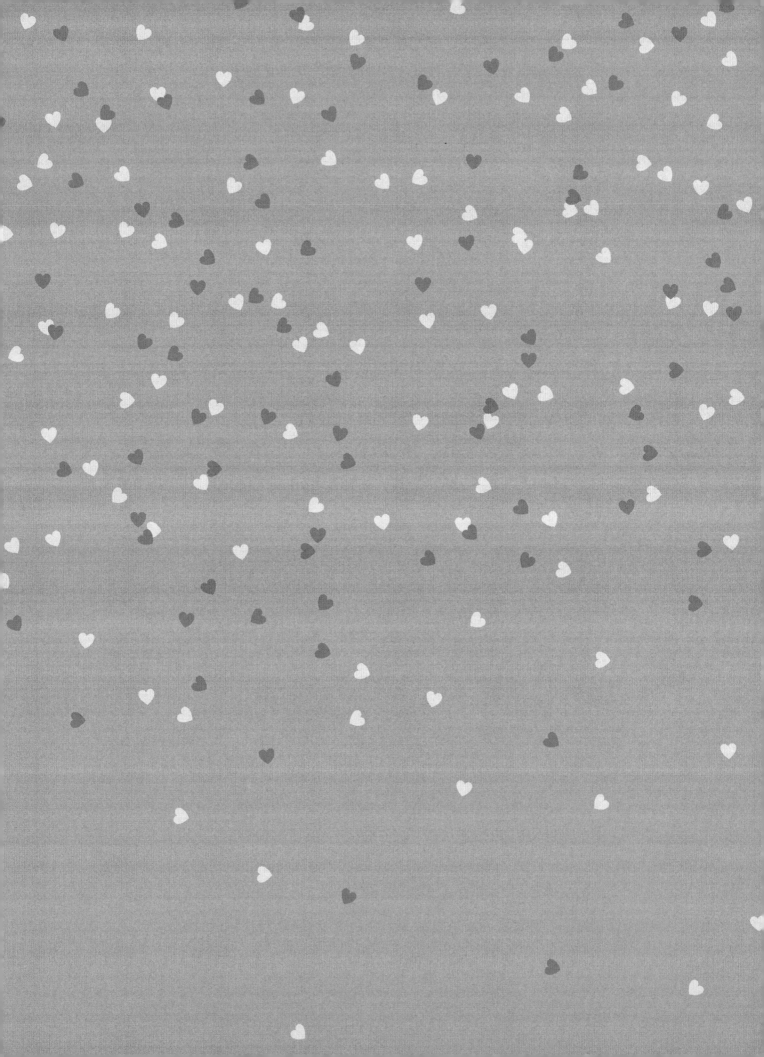

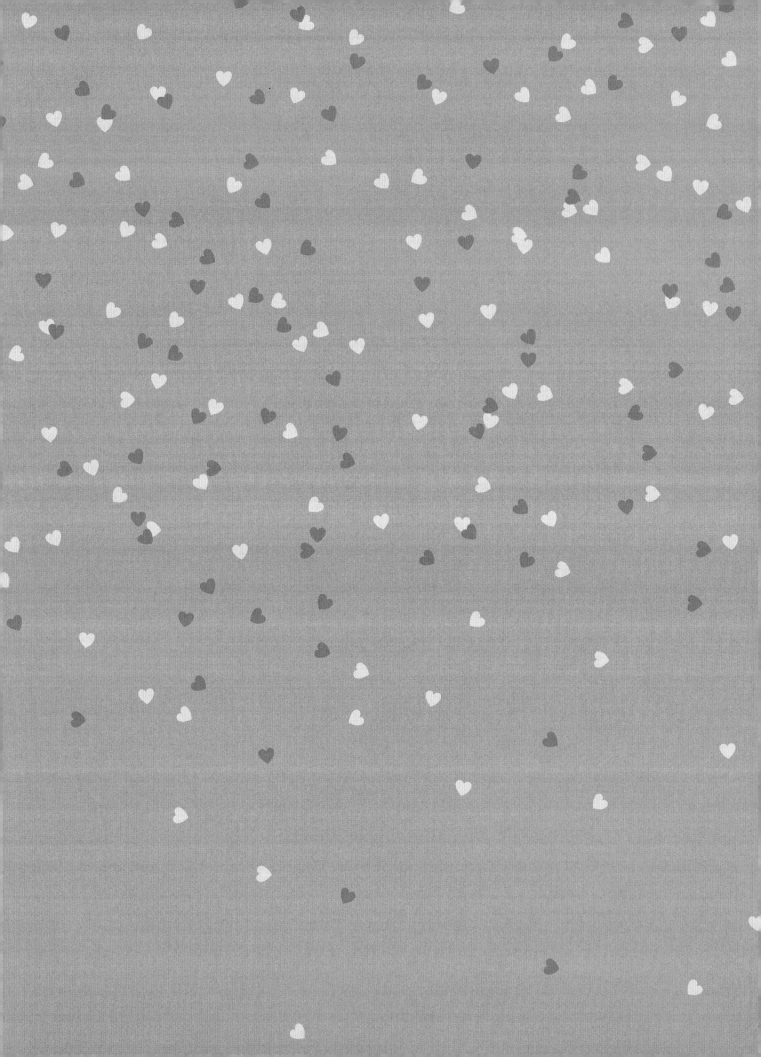

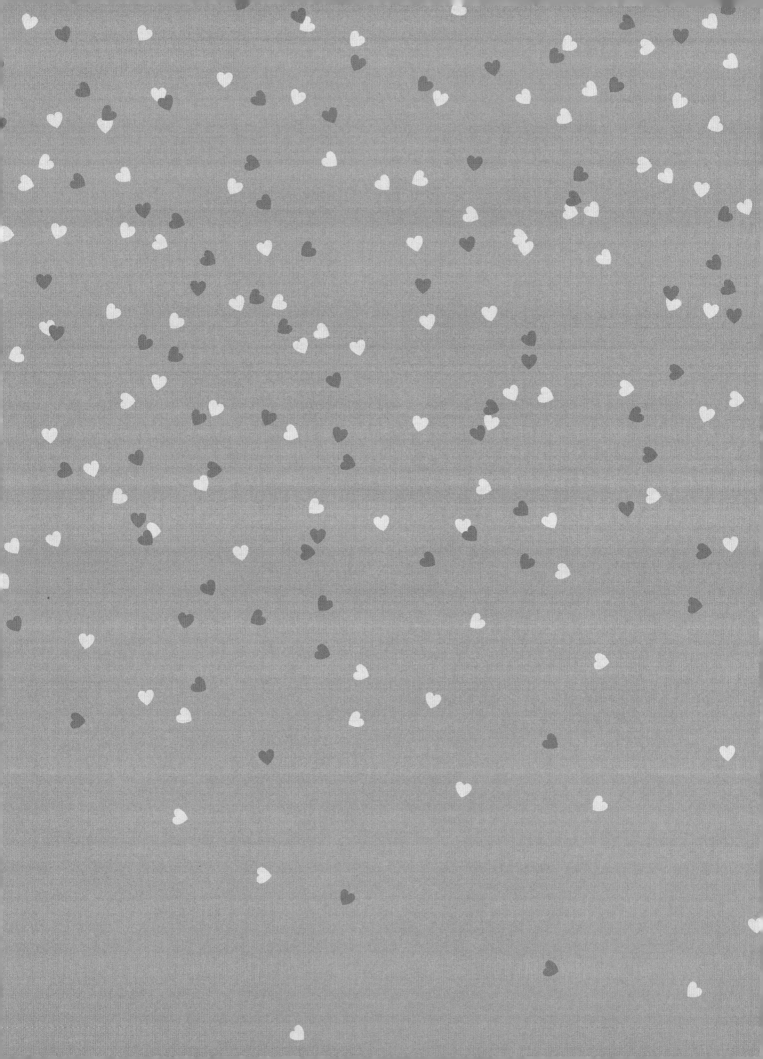

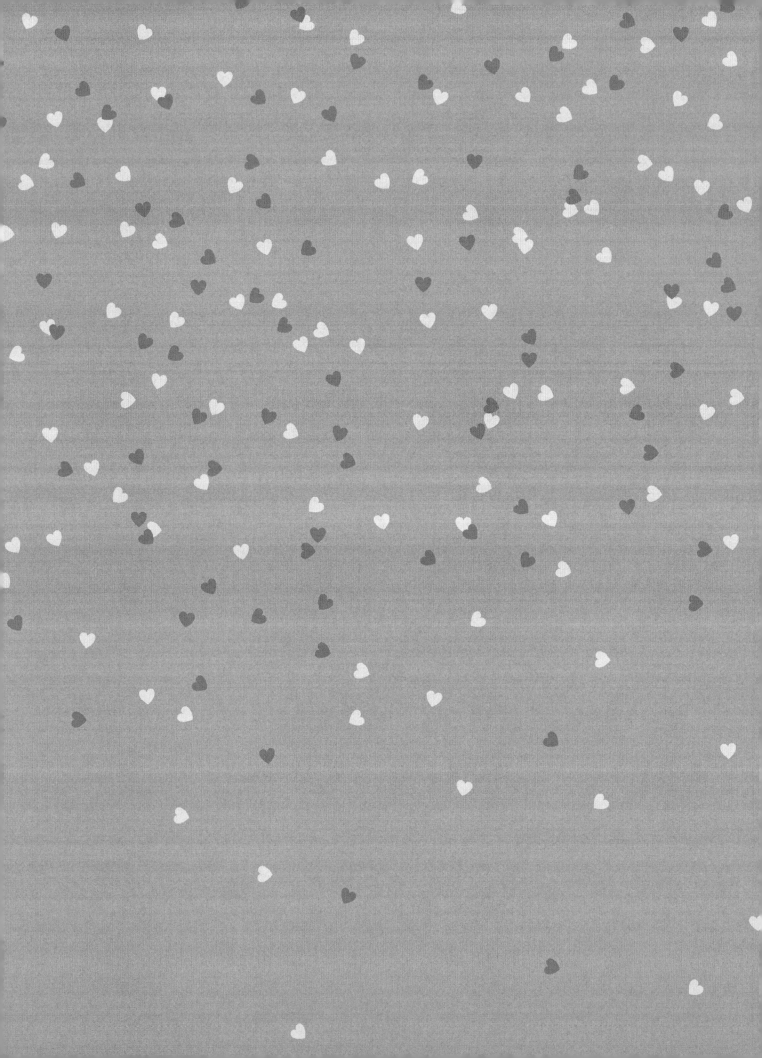

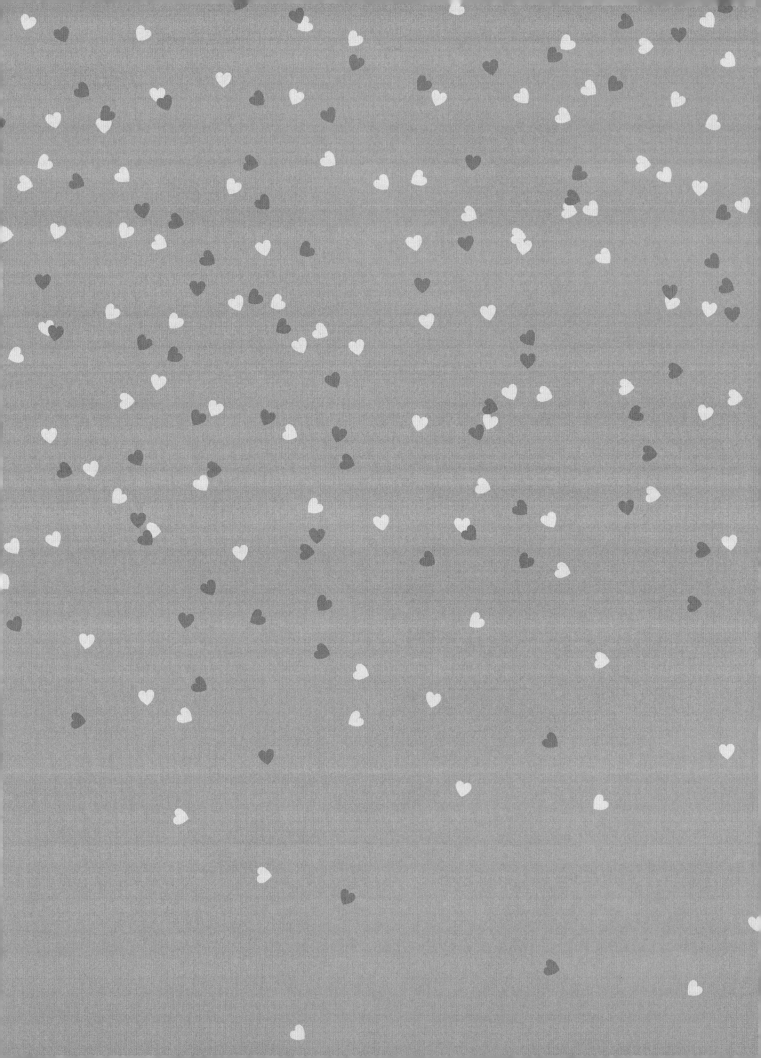

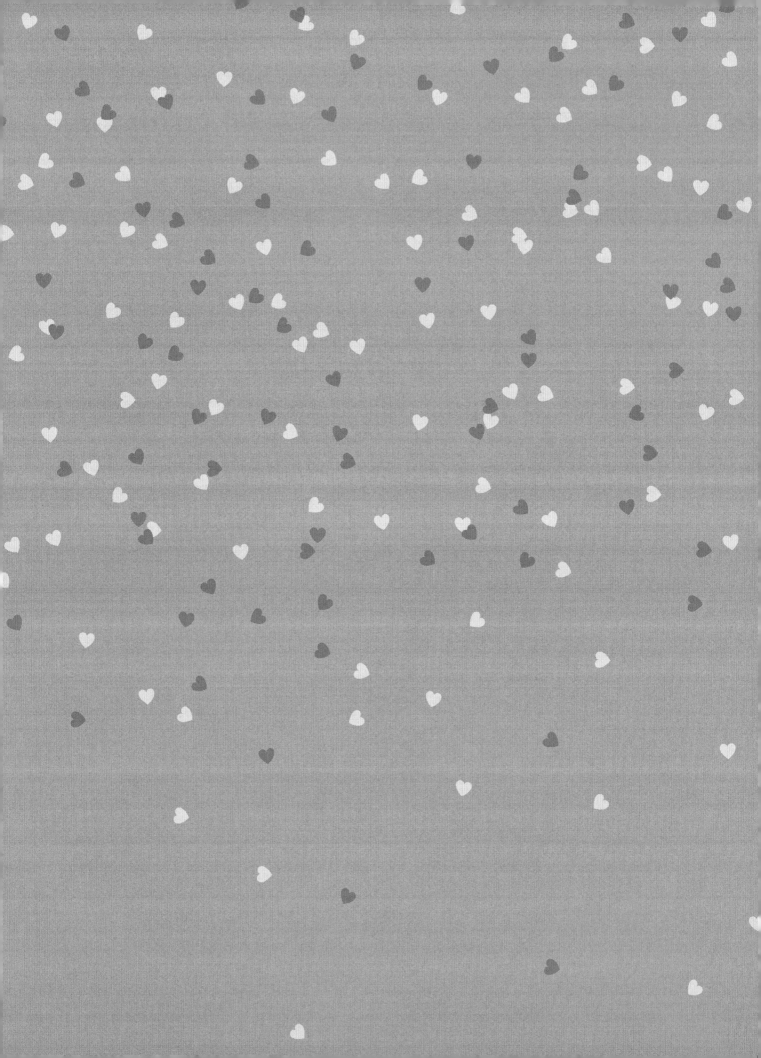

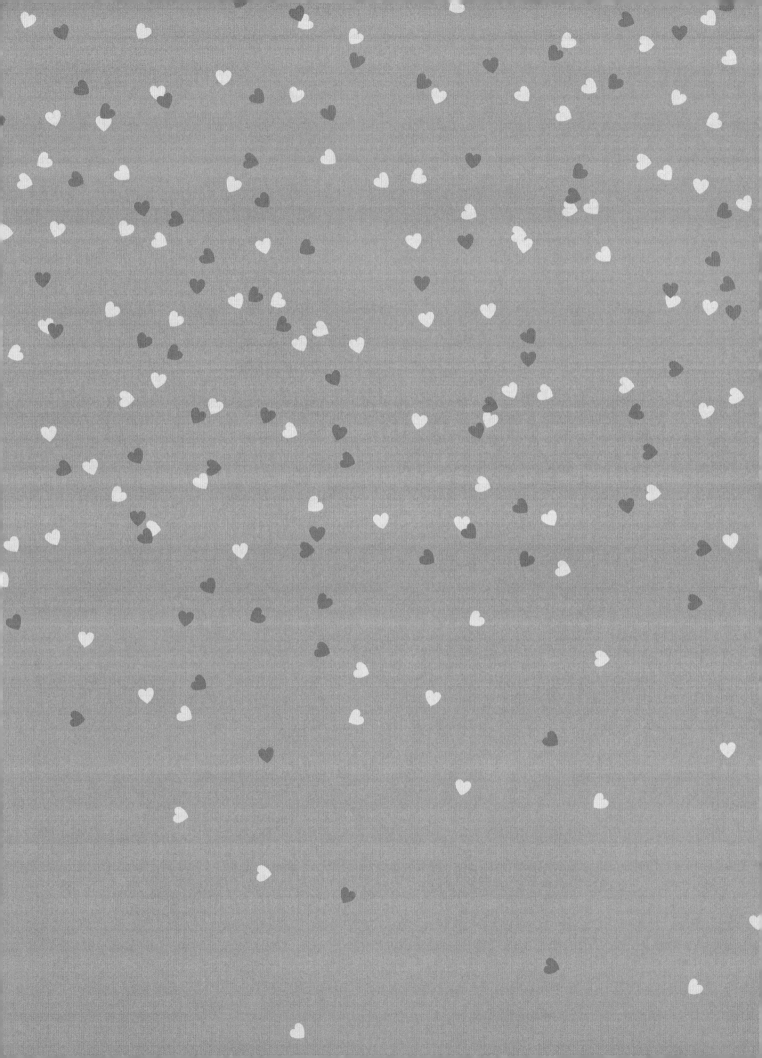

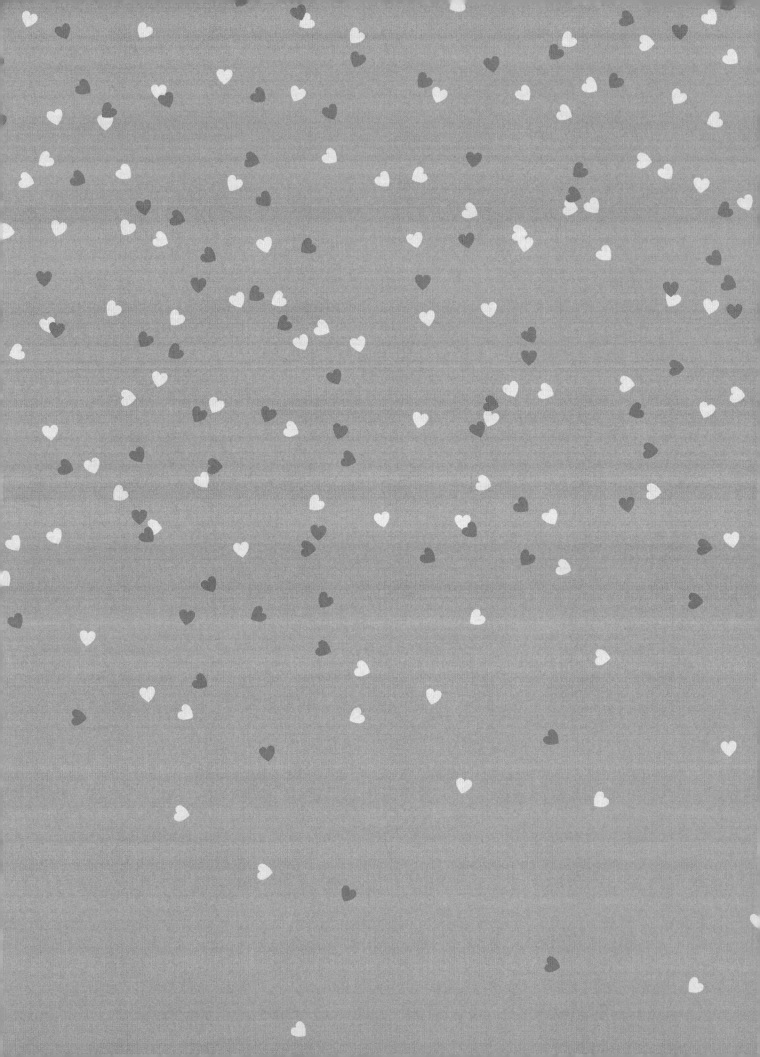

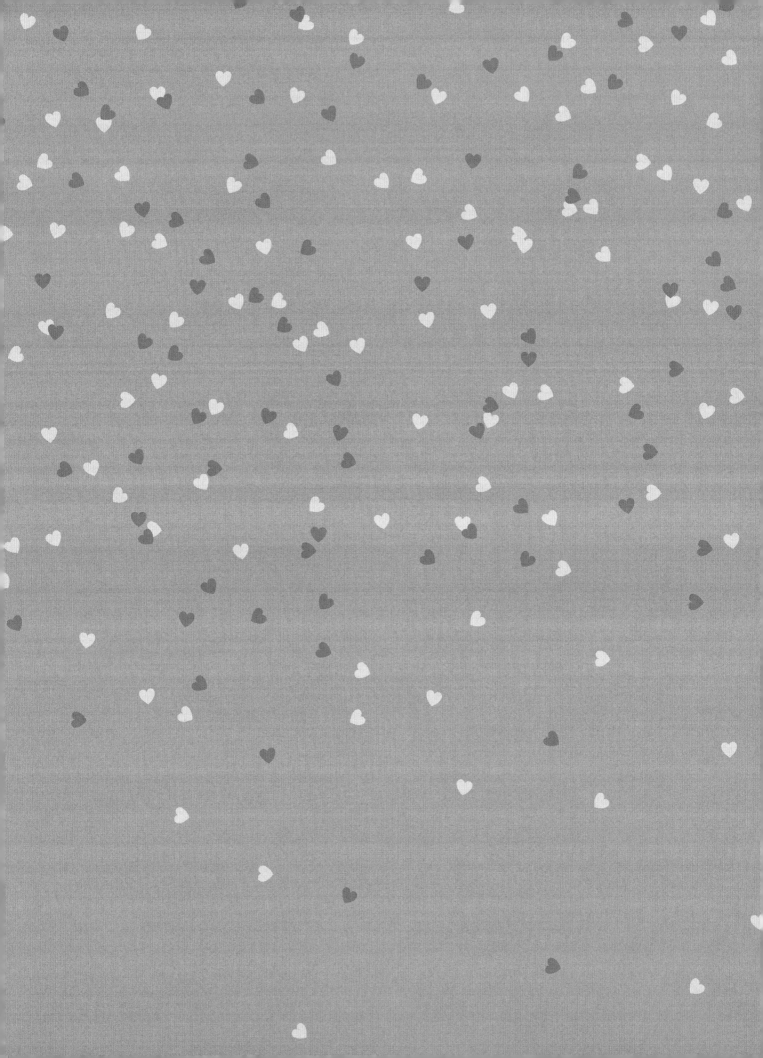

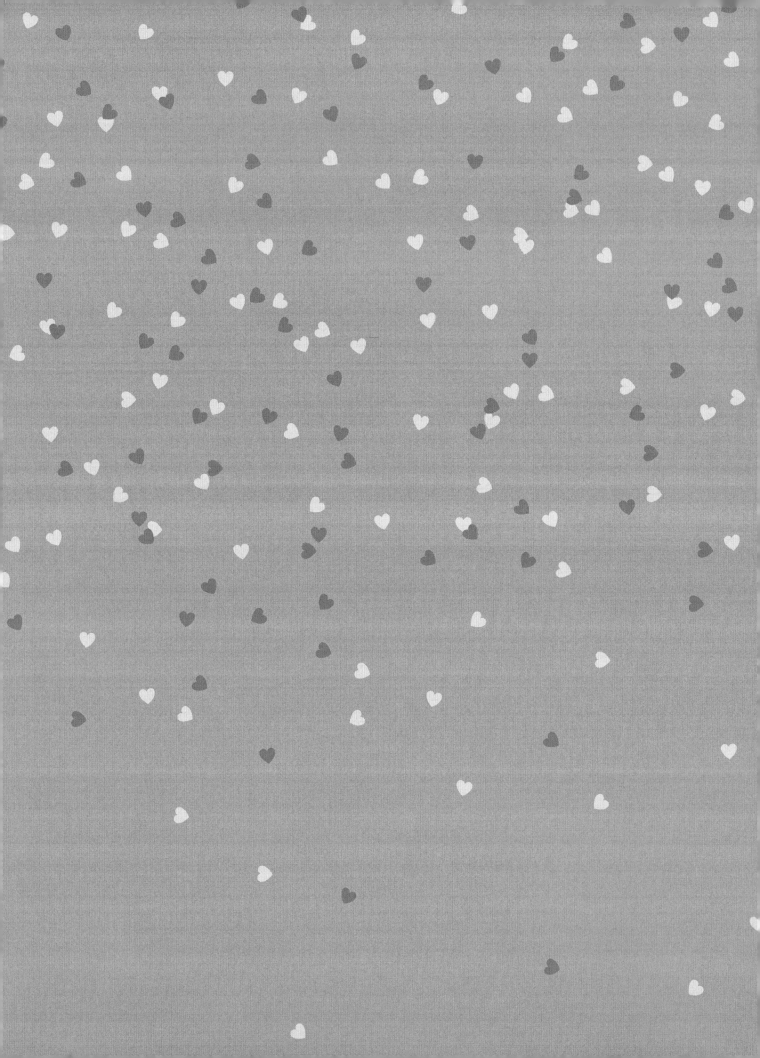

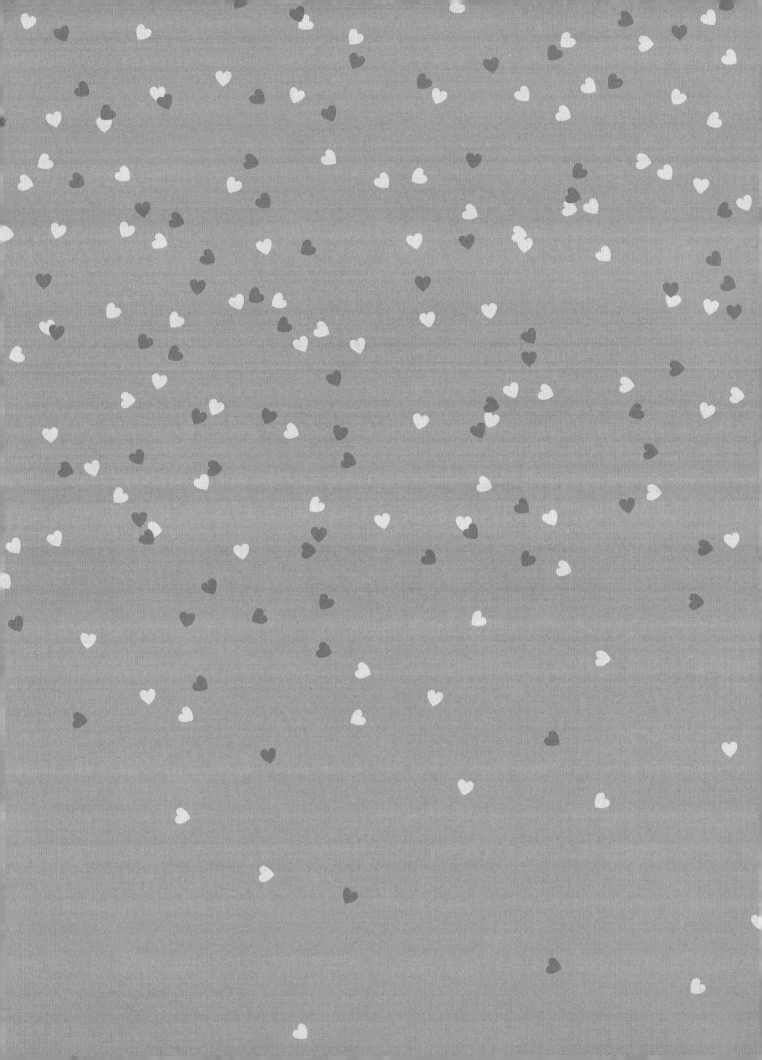

Made in the USA
Middletown, DE
05 March 2023

26250943R00060